Globalizing University Research
Innovation, Collaboration, and Competition

Previous Titles in the Global Education Research Reports Series

Asia: The Next Higher Education Superpower?

Women in the Global Economy: Leading Social Change

Latin America's New Knowledge Economy: Higher Education, Government, and International Collaboration

Developing Strategic International Partnerships: Models for Initiating and Sustaining Innovative Institutional Linkages

Who Goes Where and Why?: An Overview and Analysis of Global Educational Mobility

Innovation through Education: Building the Knowledge Economy in the Middle East

International India: A Turning Point in Educational Exchange with the U.S.

Higher Education on the Move: New Developments in Global Mobility

U.S.-China Educational Exchange: Perspectives on a Growing Partnership

Globalizing University Research
Innovation, Collaboration, and Competition

10th in the series of Global Education Research Reports,
supported by IIE and AIFS Foundation

By Karen Holbrook and Kiki Caruson

New York

IIE publications can be purchased at: www.iiebooks.org

The Institute of International Education
809 United Nations Plaza, New York, New York 10017

© 2017 by the Institute of International Education
All rights reserved. Published 2017
Printed in the United States of America
ISBN: 9780872063853

The views expressed in these chapters are solely those of the authors. They do not necessarily represent the official positions of the Institute of International Education or the AIFS Foundation.

Series Editor: Daniel Obst
Managing Editor: Courtney Lind
Copy Editors: Teresa Barensfeld
Cover Design and Layout: Pat Scully Design

Table of Contents

Foreword
ALLAN E. GOODMAN, PRESIDENT AND CEO, INSTITUTE OF INTERNATIONAL EDUCATION
WILLIAM L. GERTZ, PRESIDENT AND CEO, AMERICAN INSTITUTE FOR FOREIGN STUDY

Introduction   i

Chapter One
Institutional Organization to Promote and Support International Research   1

Chapter Two
Equipping Faculty, Scholars, and Post-Docs for International Research   21

Chapter Three
Engaging Students in International Research   57

Chapter Four
International Research Cooperation, Collaboration, Partnerships, and Alliances   101

Chapter Five
International Research, Innovation, and Entrepreneurial Ecosystems   143

Chapter Six
Connecting University International Research Programs with the Community, Region, and State   187

Chapter Seven
Assessing Your Institution's Global Footprint   209

Chapter Eight
Grand Challenges Unite the World and Promote Research Across Borders   233

Conclusion   253

About the Contributors   261

IIE/AIFS Information and Resources   263

Foreword

BY WILLIAM L. GERTZ AND ALLAN E. GOODMAN

The Global Education Research Reports series has spanned nearly a decade, exploring topics pertinent to the field of international education and timely subjects in our ever-changing world. In this series our contributors have analyzed exchange trends between the U.S. and countries such as India and China, and asked the question "Who goes where, and why?" to gain insight into mobility trends and what to expect in the coming years. Through their contributions we have garnered new insight into the knowledge economies in the Middle East and Latin America, and explored the landscape of women's participation in the global economy and the ways in which this fuels growth to create stable societies. They have provided a resource for institutions that wish to build or expand linkages with institutions in other countries, and looked at the local and global trends driving higher education policies in Asia.

This tenth and final Global Education Research Report provides a roadmap for universities wishing to encourage research on a global scale, inspired by current trends in higher education and an increased focus on international partnerships. Distinguished educators Karen Holbrook and Kiki Caruson look closely at the diversity of ways in which universities can support international research that involves both students and scholars. They also examine strategic partnerships among universities and the community and recommend ways that institutions can expand their global footprint. We, like the authors, are strong believers that language and cultural differences need not be barriers to globalizing university research, but instead can enhance cross-cultural understanding and linkages, providing more in-depth and comprehensive research than we have seen in years past.

Inherent in the missions of the international educational exchange organizations we are privileged to serve is the commitment to provide and support opportunities that foster international collaboration, where ideas can transcend borders and people can work together to address the world's most pressing problems. We are therefore proud to partner for this final report in the series, and hope that it can both inspire and guide faculty and scholars across the world as they take their research to a global level.

William L. Gertz
President and CEO,
American Institute for Foreign Study (AIFS)
& Trustee, AIFS Foundation

Allan E. Goodman
President & CEO,
Institute of International Education

Introduction

The global benchmark that matters is research performance.[1]

Globalization has changed how nations and communities envision and support economic advancement in the world's competitive landscape; how businesses seek talent, services, and products across borders; how geopolitical power is redefined; and how knowledge is redistributed. It has changed how citizens perceive and expand their own opportunities and how universities refocus their efforts in all aspects of their missions, embrace competition and collaboration, and promote innovation in an ever-changing world. It is the task of universities to create programs and develop the potential of people to become innovators and entrepreneurs in whatever careers they choose, and it is their challenge to create an environment and access the resources needed to fuel the research and innovation that will underpin and advance human and technological development.

Cooperation among nations is also essential to resolve the economic crises and differences that produce conflict and threaten security, to develop shared values, and to improve the civil and environmental challenges that confront us all. Partnerships with other nations (bilateral and multilateral) are mutually beneficial and must not only occur among governments and *nations*, but also within civil societies. It is in this domain that our universities play a significant role.

Research universities build their futures by being doggedly competitive, but they are also committed to collaboration and cooperation, underscoring U.S. Secretary of Education Arne Duncan's assertion[2] that international competition in education does not need to produce winners and losers. Enhancing education and economic viability in the United States and overseas is a win-win situation that grows the total economic pie. All three of the "C" words—competition, collaboration, and cooperation—describe the innovation ecosystem of today's universities, as well as today's world, and are essential for advancing a global innovation agenda (see Chapter 4). In this context, universities and governments have similar goals: develop a flexible workforce and prepare scientists and engineers in sufficient numbers, cultivate an active entrepreneurial culture; connect with vibrant markets for capital, trade, and talent; create an environment conducive to innovation and strong intellectual property protection; and prioritize sustainable initiatives that contribute to the well-being of the university community as well as society as a whole.[3]

Universities must understand their national needs and the roles and responsibilities they have in leading, sustaining, and, in some cases, restoring national competitiveness. They do understand competition as they encounter significant competition in recruiting talent—students and faculty—and in competing for research funds and recognition in the global rankings. Universities the world over are competing to recruit the best thinkers and the best ideas to propel their "innovation agendas" forward. A U.S. strategy, emphasized by all recent federal administrations, is to recruit the best and brightest students, educate them, and retain them. Other nations also have the "attract and retain" strategy in their national plans.[4,5] No country has a franchise on talent:

> *At any given historical moment, the most valuable human capital the world has to offer —whether in the form of intelligence, physical strength, skill, knowledge, creativity networks, commercial innovation or technical intervention—is not to be found in any one locale or within any one ethnic or religious group.*[6]

International collaboration and scientific diplomacy are critical but can be complicated and contentious. Political barriers among neighboring countries in some parts of the world are nearly impenetrable and prevent progress in cooperative research. If one uses multinational research in the Red Sea as an example, the barriers to scientific collaboration are tenuous at best. Egypt, Sudan, Ethiopia, Israel, Jordan, Saudi Arabia, and Yemen all border the Red Sea. Scholars in each of these countries conduct research in the Red Sea with international collaborators outside of the Middle East, while some countries in the Middle East are still firing missiles across their borders and preventing scientists from making connections that could facilitate work on issues related to coral reef biology, natural product development, fisheries production, and the exploration of uncharted regions of the deep trench.

Communities of researchers have recognized for years the value of science in forging relationships. These relationships develop and survive because scientists and engineers share a common body of knowledge and a language specific to the discipline—no matter what language they speak in their private lives. Physical boundaries do not "sectorize" the Red Sea, nor do they constrain the scientific investigations that are being undertaken—political volatility does. Even the power of science cannot alter some of the most recalcitrant political barriers, but inroads might be made when one-to-one relationships are established with the ultimate goal of larger-scale cooperation as nations adopt policies more conducive to international collaboration and cooperation.

Research stimulates the call to internationalization by higher education institutions (HEIs) and their students, researchers, and staff. International research can be conducted in any number of ways: through engagement with international partners for the purpose of knowledge generation in any field, through the investigation of global issues that transcend geographic borders, though the exchange of students and faculty, and from a desire on the part of individual researchers and scientists to move beyond the idea of "researching on" a topic to adopting the approach of "researching with someone," in many cases with a colleague who brings a different worldview to the topic of interest.[7]

There is a long history of research engagement among international colleagues through conferences, societies, international journals, joint publications, and collaborations in a discipline or a problem-based area. International conferences have served as forums for both researchers and universities to expand their global reach and are valuable in promoting new collaborations and opportunities for research engagement. They also serve to expand the "brand" of an institution, stimulate recruitment of students, strengthen existing partnerships, create opportunities for new relationships, and re-engage alumni.

Venues, such as conferences and society meetings, for connecting with colleagues and peers from around the world are essential, but so too are the institutional efforts made by universities to foster and support international engagement. In 2014, researchers from the University of Wisconsin and the University of Bristol developed a seven-week, massive open online course hosted on the Coursera platform in Silicon Valley.[8,9] This course, Globalizing Higher Education and Research for the "Knowledge Economy," was designed to help participants better understand the complex and dynamic changes associated with the internationalization of higher education and research. The goals for the course included developing an understanding of how and why universities are engaged in the globalization process through study abroad, programs and campuses developed overseas, international collaborative research, and international student recruitment, as well as what might be the implications of an international trajectory.

Course participants from across the world traded ideas about globalization, prompted by a list of keywords, some of them the cross-cutting themes we stress in this book—collaboration, competition, technology, entrepreneurship, inter- and multidisciplinarity, innovation, and innovation systems. Learning to communicate over distance and exchange ideas and information on a topic of such complexity require an open mind, creativity, trust, cultural sensitivity, and skill—exactly what is needed for successful international research collaboration.

The five themes of **collaboration, competition, innovation, integrated inquiry**, and **assessing value** appear in every chapter of this book in various interconnected ways. When any topic of research is considered, especially one of the sustainable development goals (SDGs; see Chapter 9) like food security, for example, it is immediately clear that countries compete for resources; rely upon technology, innovation, and entrepreneurship to improve production; demand education and the expertise of scientists, engineers, economists, biologists, environmentalists, social scientists, and humanists; and need a variety of resources, especially including financial resources. One can envision a network model with these features connected in a multitude of ways.

Research has always been international among colleagues and promoted aggressively by scholars, but the emergence of international research as a prominent university strategy is much more recent. In a recent survey of Canadian universities, 96 percent confirmed their desire for international research collaboration, but only a small percent of the universities reported that they have a specific strategy for international research collaboration[10] It may, however, be embedded in a more comprehensive research development strategy with goals to increase research and consulting income, improve technical capabilities, pool complementary competences and methodologies, increase fee-paying research-degree students, and help the university leapfrog from ordinary to world class.

Research in international settings and work toward global goals has become more visible in institutional and independent publications read by higher education professionals. Nearly all of the issues of *The Chronicle of Higher Education* feature full-page advertisements developed by universities to publicize their stellar international research programs, highlight their collaborations around the world, and market the work they do for society. Some ads even advertise for global collaborations, whereas others simply focus on issues that are important to the world. The ads describe initiatives that universities have developed to meet some of the global challenges, such as hunger, water quality and access, and health disparities. For example:

> *Seven billion people call this planet home. Including 347 million diabetics. Diabetes along with natural disasters, hunger, pollution and cancer are global issues, and that's why we're tackling them head on.*
>
> *Imagine the difference we could make if we combined our efforts with research institutions like yours.*

Let's do more than imagine. Let's collaborate. Bottom line. It's not about us. It's about the impact we make together. (The University of Florida advertisement in *The Chronicle of Higher Education,* February 13, 2016)

Chronicle advertisements also promote innovation, collaboration, entrepreneurship, and diversity—all features of dynamic and successful research programs and themes of this book.

Innovation is all about new perspectives, unexpected ways of approaching things that demand diversity. By bringing people together with different backgrounds, fresh thinking, and unique abilities, UCI is creating the new solutions and innovative ideas that are changing lives. In the classroom and in the world, it's not just about being different or evening respecting difference—it's about making a difference. (UC Irvine advertisement in *The Chronicle of Higher Education,* February 5. 2015)

Iowa State University features the crisis of hunger:

Hunger is a problem today and potentially a global disaster tomorrow. By 2050 the population of the globe will reach 9.6 billion. The speed of that growth is staggering. Iowa State's Destination 2050 initiative focuses on areas where it has global research prominence and impact. Iowa State's bioscience prowess has magnified the ability of crops and animals to provide the food sources the world needs. Destination 2050 also focuses on big data, critical materials, advanced manufacturing, and a student experience that will provide the scientists and leaders to solve generational challenges. (Iowa State University advertisement in *The Chronicle of Higher Education,* October 2, 2015)

University of California, San Diego's research is

keeping citizens of the world safe from cybersecurity, political violence, global conflict and environmental disasters requires innovation. Faculty in interdisciplinary research centers collaborate to find solutions to society's most serious issues." (University of California, San Diego advertisement in *The Chronicle of Higher Education,* April 24, 2015)

The University of Wisconsin-Madison's ad states "we are boundless." They emphasize fields that connect interdisciplinary partners and collaborative research "moving Wisconsin and the whole world forward." (*The Chronicle of Higher Education,*)

Mississippi State "imagine[s] a better world where we are" safe from cyber-attacks; food shortages are replaced with food abundance, "where [the] spark of an idea grows into a solution" and "inspiration gives birth to innovation." (*The Chronicle of Higher Education,*)

The University of Birmingham and other universities abroad (e.g., from Australia and the UK) have prepared advertising supplements to the *Chronicle* with articles about their collaborative research partnerships around the world, global research highlights, and international research fellowships.[11]

Global Research Universities are also placing advertisements in the *Chronicle* to attract students who have a "passion for research and a desire to shape minds." The Ashoka University in India, for example, has posted such an advertisement in collaboration with University of Pennsylvania, University of Michigan, University of California, Berkeley, and Carleton College in the United States; King's College, London; Sciences Po, France; and Yonsei University, Seoul, Korea, which advertises "the liberal arts for international minds" to recruit students to an all-English, four-year liberal arts college, instructed by an international faculty.[12]

Researchers at American universities, especially land-grant universities, have helped to establish universities abroad for well over 50 years through common research interests. Many of these relationships are still in place. In 1957, Atatürk University was established by law in Ezurum, Turkey, and in the same year, Atatürk signed a collaborative agreement with the University of Nebraska. In 2012, 55 years after the initial agreement, the University of Nebraska and Atatürk University reaffirmed the relationship with a new memorandum of understanding that strengthened the long-term partnership and expanded faculty collaborations and student exchanges in areas of food security and water management, education and human capital development, and public health and medicine. Both universities are well-positioned to leverage their shared resources and expertise for mutual benefit. Atatürk has put research into practice around the region and has contributed significantly to strong economic growth in Turkey.

The Ohio State University (OSU) was also a partner in the early development of Atatürk University, and in 2009 signed a university-level memorandum agreeing that the two universities would cooperate in the exchanges of theses, teaching materials, and other scientific and technological literature; research collaborations; the exchange of faculty, scholars, and students; teaching; and research. Since 2001, more than 50 Atatürk University faculty members from the fields of medicine, education, humanities, biology, and law have come to OSU, fully funded by their government, to work with OSU faculty members on collaborative research projects.

Through research strengths and unique capabilities, our universities are marketed to other institutions, governments, and the private sector abroad; it is through faculty research partners that the strongest relationships are forged, and that our research enterprise and long-lasting linkages with global partners are built by our students. Research credibility and output attract international graduate students, postdoctoral fellows and scholars, and new faculty. In addition, research can open doors into regions that are otherwise difficult to access. Research partnerships can account for a significant portion of a university's international collaborative activities; however, this may or may not be explicitly recognized.

The material in the subsequent chapters could be organized in many different ways because of the interconnectedness of the topics and the themes that define the discussion. All of the chapters provide information to enhance the productivity and prosperity of nations, as well as the opportunities available to universities and investigators, and they provide examples of the research they conduct to become best in class for themselves, their students, and their institutions, and at the same time, to engage in much desired partnership arrangements.

In this book, we introduce many ideas taken from real examples from the United States and abroad to help those who are interested in expanding global research at their institutions. The goal is to carefully choose examples that might serve as a springboard to stimulate the thinking of readers about what they might do in similar circumstances. The vast array of opportunities is impossible to capture, and we know many wonderful examples have been missed.

While globalization has brought enormous benefits, it has also intensified dangers. Wealth, income, and social power are dramatically unequal within and across international boundaries. Challenges such as access to health services, alternative energy sources, and sustainable development are common to all.[13] Our unequal world of "daunting complexity" demands cooperation and understanding. "As other nations challenge the United States technologically, scientifically, and economically, U.S. residents are becoming more aware that globalization will be beneficial only if we rise up to the challenges and the escalating competition."[14] Our universities recognize and embrace both the challenges and the competition, and they are at the forefront of innovation and knowledge generation.

NOTES

[1] Marginson, S. (2010, May 30). Point of View, The rise of the global university: 5 new tensions. *The Chronicle of Higher Education*, 56, 37:A76.

[2] Secretary of Education Arne Duncan speaking at the Council on Foreign Relations, October 19, 2010. Reported in Thomas L. Friedman, Michael Mandelbaum, *That Used to be Us: How America Fell Behind in the World it Invented and How we Came Back*. Farrar, Straus and Giroux, New York, 2001, p. 221.

3. Chad Evans, Council on Competitiveness, presentation at The Hague, Netherlands, 2005.
4. The Partnership for a New American Economy & The Partnership for New York City. (2012). *Not coming to America: Why the U.S. is falling behind in the global race for talent*. Retrieved from http://www.renewoureconomy.org/sites/all/themes/pnae/not-coming-to-america.pdf
5. UAE Vision 2021: United in ambition and determination (2010). United Arab Emirates Cabinet, 2010, http://www.Vision2021/ae/downloads/UAE-Vision2021-Brochure-English.pdf.
6. Amy Chua, Quoted in E. Alden (2010). Losing Ground in competitive immigration. World Politics Review, 27 July, http://www.worldpoliticsreview.com/articles/6142/u-s-losing-ground-in-competitive-immigration, p.1.
7. The idea of moving away from the perspective of "research on" a topic to "research with someone" has been articulate by the Volkswagen Foundation in Germany. The Volkswagen Foundation is an independent, nonprofit organization that has been funding research projects in all disciplines since 1962. https://www.volkswagenstiftung.de/en/funding/international-focus.html
8. See http://globalizinghigheredu.blogspot.com/p/1-universities.html.
9. Coursera is an education platform that partners with universities worldwide to offer courses online that are accessible to anyone.
10. Universities Canada. (2014). *Internationalization of Canadian universities. Quick Facts*. Retrieved from http://www.univcan.ca/media-room/publications/internationalization-at-canadian-universities/
11. Birmingham Global, a special advertising supplement to *The Chronicle of Higher Education* (Spring 2016).
12. Underwood international College. Yonsei University. (2016, February 12). *The Chronicle of higher Education,* p. A5.
13. Association of American Colleges and Universities (AAC&U). 2007. College Learning for the New Global Century: A Report from the National Leadership Council for Liberal Education and America's Promise. Washington, D.C., Part 2, p. 21.
14. Davies, G. K. (2006). *Setting a public agenda for higher education in the states: Lessons learned from the National Collaborative for Higher Education Policy.* The National Collaborative for Higher Education Policy: The Education Commission of the States**,** The National Center for Higher Education Management Systems, the National Center for Public Policy and Higher Education. http://www.highereducation.org/reports/public_agenda/public_agenda.pdf.

Chapter One
Institutional Organization to Promote and Support International Research

Introduction

Globalized universities are not new. By the late 20th century, many universities had added a global orientation to their existing missions of teaching, research, and community service.[1] The demands of the current "knowledge economy" include technology-driven innovation, a highly skilled workforce, and a global marketplace for ideas where innovation is not bound by geographic borders. Universities around the world have the potential to be at the forefront of their nation's knowledge generation and global competitiveness. Whereas opportunities for study abroad and cross-cultural learning have long been associated with the university enterprise, a clearly defined and resourced infrastructure for supporting international research engagement among students and faculty remains on the horizon for many institutions. Clearly, for international research endeavors to flourish, institutions must promote and support the activities that engender success.

Organizing and Optimizing International Research

Responsibility for the development and sustainability of a robust international research operation rests with a broad coalition of units. Clarity regarding the responsibilities of each of these stakeholders is important—as is the connectivity. Key stakeholders include university and college trustees and governing boards, the president or chancellor of the institution or university system, constituent organizations or campuses and their respective oversight boards and leaders, academic departments and faculties, individual researchers, scientists and staff, and students, as well as the broader university community, including industry. Stakeholder investment must come from across the institution and from the external community, locally and nationally.

The Chief Executive and Senior Administration

Optimizing the institution's organization for high-impact international research requires that the university's president or chancellor be a vocal and active champion. He or she will set the stage for the prioritization of international research with the support of the provost or senior vice president for academic affairs, the senior international officer (SIO), the vice president for research (VPR), and other key leadership officials (e.g., deans of health sciences, agriculture, engineering). A highly visible advocate(s) with the ability to influence the mission, vision, and/ or strategic goals of the university is essential for adoption and implementation of policies that will advance international research. A shared commitment to advancing global research between the institution's president/ or chancellor and its provost or chief academic officer is an absolute necessity. Several years ago,[2] the National Association of State Universities and Land-Grant Colleges (NASULGC) (now the Association of Public and Land-grant Universities, or APLU) Task Force on International Education published "A Call to Leadership: The Presidential Role in Internationalizing the University," which indicated that a university's leadership must lead and act to internationalize learning, discovery, and engagement. Today the APLU Michael P. Malone International Leadership Award, established in 2000, recognizes a president or senior-level leader for a career of outstanding contributions to further international education, specifically at state and land-grant institutions.

Building on its 50-year history of international engagement, Michigan State University (MSU) has one of the oldest and most established programs for international development and engagement. Under the leadership of its 20th president, Lou Anna K. Simon, MSU has made the global awareness and engagement of students, faculty, staff, and other constituencies an institutional priority. "Turning cutting-edge research into practical interventions for the betterment of society" continues to be a mission of the university, and MSU approaches its public land-grant status in a global context.[3]

New York University has positioned itself as a global university linked by global technology and faculty with brick-and-mortar campuses in Buenos Aires, Shanghai, Singapore, Tel Aviv, and Abu Dhabi, with more growth anticipated (see Chapter 4). This vast network was instituted as a strategy of its former president, John Sexton, and sustained by its current president, Andrew Hamilton, who is also a strong supporter of its globalized mission and international presence. "The world doesn't stand still," he has said. "In this 21st century, surely no one is suggesting that we educate fewer people familiar with the Arab language and culture. No one is suggesting that we should have fewer students who are familiar with the complexities of Chinese culture and political life.... N.Y.U.'s decision to open campuses in China and Abu Dhabi is so important. A presence such as N.Y.U.'s in these nations and societies brings more freedom of ideas, not less."[4]

As the chairman emeritus of Manipal Global Education Services and the president and chancellor of Manipal University, a deemed private institution in India, Ramdas M. Pai has pioneered India's first multidisciplinary and multicampus university into an internationally recognized education system known for high-quality medical education and research. He envisions Manipal Global as a "leading education services organization respected globally for academic, research, and business excellence providing affordable and flexible learning solutions powered by technology, innovation and passion." With six major campuses in five countries—India, Nepal, Malaysia, Dubai, and Antigua—Manipal University has expanded rapidly over the past 25 years in an effort to provide medical research and quality health care where it is most needed.

The "International Agenda" managed by the Presidential Committee of Humbolt University in Berlin "is based on the proposition that the dynamics of academic communication and collaboration are not restricted by geographical borders."[5] The university's strategic framework recognizes that excellence in research and teaching occurs in a global context and that only an international perspective and global engagement will allow the university to continue to maintain its reputation for excellence and innovation.

International engagement is important not only to large, research-oriented institutions with research-focused faculty and graduate students, but also to those universities that primarily serve undergraduate populations as well. In 2010, Daniel S. Papp, then president of Kennesaw State University (KSU)—a public undergraduate institution in the state of Georgia—established the President's Emerging Global Scholars (PEGS) program as a three-year program beginning in a student's freshman year. The program includes intercultural training, research, service learning, and international community engagement (see Chapter 3). The PEGS program includes a partnership with the Universidade Salvador (UNIFACS) in Salvador, Brazil, which provides an international, collaborative research experience for undergraduate students around one of seven global challenges. PEGS students begin their work with their Brazilian colleagues during a freshman-year trip to Salvador and continue the partnership when the Brazilian students travel to the United States for a reciprocal learning experience. Upon completion of the research project, students have the opportunity to present their research at KSU's Symposium of

Student Scholars, among other venues. According to KSU, the experience contributes directly to the competitiveness of its students for prestigious scholarships such as the Rhodes, Truman, and Goldwater.[6]

The Roles of the VPR and SIO

The SIO and the VPR must be senior-level positions with reporting lines to the president, chancellor, or chief academic officer. It is most beneficial when both the head of the research office and the senior international officer report directly to the institution's president or chancellor; however, this line of reporting is more common for VPRs than for SIOs. The international office is an essential partner for global research and therefore is deserving of a seat at the table where high-level decisions are discussed and decided. Strong leadership from the university's president or vice chancellor that incentivizes collaboration between the two offices will yield more substantial international research portfolios.

Both the SIO and the VPR (or their equivalents in roles and responsibilities) are in key positions to possess an awareness and appreciation for responsibilities and mission of the research enterprise and the importance of international engagement. Far too often, however, administrators from offices that either directly or indirectly support international research collaborate infrequently; rarely share personnel or physical space; have limited knowledge about each other's day-to-day activities; and may not speak the same "language" in terms of priorities, evaluation metrics, and business practices. There need to be more opportunities created for administrators in the research enterprise and those representing international initiatives to interact, form personal relationships, and identify ways for fostering greater cooperation between the two offices.

Nonetheless, there are many commonalities between the two offices. Both focus on the economic impact of university research and both research and international programs connect with the broader community. The talent recruited at universities should be international and engage in research. Both offices facilitate educational and career goals for students who are eager for international experiences through research, study abroad, internships, co-ops, service learning, and other activities. Both offices promote collaboration and interdisciplinarity; engage students; involve corporate sponsors; rely upon partnerships; and focus on innovation, creativity, and engagement.

Some universities have created leadership positions that connect the research and international offices. The University of Chicago, for example, employs a director of federal research development who reports to the university's office of federal relations in Washington, DC, but whose job directly supports the research office and indirectly the international office. The goal is to promote the university's research capabilities and accomplishments (at home and abroad) across funding agencies, science policy organizations, and professional societies. Developing and sustaining such relationships and strategic alliances is critical to the success of both large-scale, cross-cutting research initiatives and those that are faculty or discipline-specific. The leaders of university research and international offices may also work closely with advancement officers (there may be personnel directly assigned to enhance private funding for international activities), especially in the United States, where federal funding for research has been in decline or increasing only minimally; private donors and foundation funds are important sources of international research funding. The science and technology advisors stationed in embassies around the world are another resource for identifying areas of mutual interest and benefit and for finding collaborators (institutions and individuals) for international research efforts (see Chapter 6).

Mission, Vision, and Strategic Planning

International research and engagement deserves a defined role in an institution's mission and vision statements and in its strategic plan, and this is becoming increasingly common as a goal. A university or college's strategic plan should clearly identify how the institution plans to achieve the goals associated with its international profile. More specific goals should be articulated at the unit or division levels. The goals of internationalization should spread across units and not be pigeon-holed in the international office. Global research universities must integrate "international experiences and perspectives within teaching, discovery, and engagement missions of each academic unit within the university; successful internationalization requires [that] faculty, administrators and staff perceive internationalization as adding value to what they do and helping them reach their goals."[7]

According to the most recent American Council on Education report, *Mapping Internationalizing on U.S. Campuses, 2012* (same as footnote 8), 54 percent of doctoral degree–granting universities, 41 percent of master's degree–granting institutions, 42 percent of undergraduate institutions, and 22 percent of associate's degree–granting institutions responding to the survey indicated that their universities have mission statements that *specifically* refer to international or global education. Just over half (52 percent) of the institutions responding to the survey—which includes both public and private universities and colleges—have included international education as a key strategic priority. None of the 2012 survey questions directly address international research, although many of the respondents may have considered research to be a key component of a "global education."[8]

According to its vision statement, research and innovation at The Ohio State University is charged with "creat[ing] distinctive and internationally recognized contributions to the advancement of fundamental knowledge and scholarship and to solutions of the world's most pressing problems." Across both its mission and vision statements, Ohio State clearly identifies international research as a key component of its identity as a globally engaged university.

Beyond the borders of the United States, the Sokoine University of Agriculture at the University of Dar-es-Salaam, Tanzania, has articulated a vision of the university as "a centre of excellence and a valued member of the global academic community in agriculture and other related fields, with emphasis on impacting practical skills, entrepreneurship, research and integration of basic and applied knowledge in an environmentally friendly manner." The university's research motto encourages multidisciplinary research for sustainable development and the alleviation of poverty, thus also recognizing the need to attack a global challenge with the full input of a range of talents (see Chapter 9).

The Internationalization Strategic Plan for Appalachian State University in North Carolina builds upon both the university's mission and vision and provides a roadmap for developing, extending, and enhancing the range of international initiatives over a five-year period (2016–2020). The plan focuses on five strategic priorities including "increasing international research and faculty development activities."

The University of Glasgow's current strategic plan, Glasgow 2020: A Global Vision, emphasizes international research as the key avenue for extending the institution's global reach and reputation. A set of clearly defined metrics for success includes research income generated from outside the United Kingdom.

Other institutions are uniquely designed to promote and sustain international research collaboration. For example, the Oxford Martin School and its 30 institutes, founded in 2005, is a unique center for pioneering, interdisciplinary research. The school is a community of more than 200 scholars from the University of Oxford and across the world. It supports novel, high-risk, and multidisciplinary projects that may not fit within conventional funding channels, and it invests in research that cuts across disciplines to tackle society's most pressing challenges (see chapter 8).

As universities and their leaders adopt and refine internationalization plans and strategies for growing their global research portfolios, it is important to recognize that there are a multitude of recipes for internationalization. Each university must chart its own course, including organizational strategies that provide a foundation for institutional policies and programmatic strategies that establish the foundation for international activities and programs for the substantive functions of the university. Nonetheless, the following guidelines sourced from a speech given to the International Association of University Presidents at Bond University in Queensland, Australia, in October 2015 by the organization's secretary general, Alvaro Romo de la Rosa, are especially useful:

- Establish and communicate the university's international mission by reaching consensus among the faculty, staff, and students with regard to institutional policy on internationalization. Appoint a central coordinating body on internationalization at the institutional level, identify an office or offices responsible for international programs, and dedicate the necessary space and resources.

- Maintain financial and staff support at the level that is needed. Time and persistence are required to sustain international partnerships and initiatives.

- Establish clear coordination at the institutional level. This is no easy task, and the bigger the university is, the more difficult it will be to provide this level of coordination. Integrated planning is required, involving all departments, in order to minimize power conflicts or resistance to change by faculties or schools.

- Define decision-making roles and responsibilities. It should also be clear who decides the assignment of resources, who decides the priorities, and the level and types of collaboration expected between the vice presidents (or equivalent) for the international office, research, advancement, deans, and other key stakeholders.

- Make sure that periodic review is done of each program affecting the international mission of the institution.

- Examine the relationship between the university and the community, and leverage relationships wisely. This process includes examining relationships with consulates and embassies, with governments, with local businesses and industry, with national and international organizations, and with alumni.[9]

Research Expertise and Capability

Successful global research universities capitalize upon the talent and experience of faculty, staff, students, administrators, and supporters to create and maintain a high-impact international research enterprise. Signature areas of concentration for international research can only be established where depth and breadth of knowledge exist.

Established universities such as Iowa State have targeted the university's international research efforts by identifying five areas of research where the institution has global prominence and capacity. Under the presidential initiative Destination 2050, Iowa State has set research goals in biosciences, advanced manufacturing, critical materials, big data, and data security. For example, Iowa State's BioCentury

Research Farm is a first-in-the-nation research and demonstration facility dedicated to breakthroughs in biomass production and processing. The genomic work holds great promise in treating HIV/AIDS, Ebola, TB, and other diseases that could threaten a highly populated world.

Younger universities, such as the King Abdullah University of Science and Technology (KAUST), built from the ground up near Jeddah, Saudi Arabia, can design from inception the university's academic divisions and research centers to support the university's targeted research mission. KAUST's integrated and goal-oriented focus in the fields of biological, physical, mathematical, and environmental sciences and the engineering disciplines reflects national priorities. Scientists and engineers at KAUST seek to address topics germane to the future of the country as well as global challenges by focusing research efforts on topics related to water, food, energy, and the environment. By offering expertise in multiple research areas related to these broad topics, the university has created a collaborative and interdisciplinary problem-solving environment.

Individual researchers and research teams provide the research expertise and strength at universities. Among the researchers there is a deep reservoir of talent and knowledge that can be challenging to harness for the overall improvement of the international research enterprise. Universities should be creative in designing avenues for soliciting researcher participation in international programs, collaborations, partnerships, consortia and transnational projects (see Chapter 4).

Soliciting Feedback from Researchers

Individual colleges or faculties may wish to create a college or department officer and/or a global consultative committee for purpose of developing international initiatives and programs. One representative of such a committee could be invited to serve on an institution-wide committee. Discussion among one another as to college, faculty, or department activities, plans, and challenges benefits all and provides valuable general intelligence to the institution. The members of the group would be expected to share information with academic leaders and convey information back to their units with an emphasis on open, two-way communication. Such a group could meet on a monthly or quarterly basis or at least once a semester, with the agenda for each meeting developed collaboratively among the representatives from colleges or faculties and administration stakeholders. The group has a parallel in the associate deans for research organization present at many universities.

We have not chosen to dive deeper into college or faculty structure (e.g., departments) to make recommendations about additional responsibilities to support international research activities, but universities might consider ways of capitalizing on the knowledge housed in area study centers and institutes, as well as among faculty with deep knowledge of and familiarity with specific localities or regions. It is possible to identify a faculty member who is considered an "expert" or "ambassador" regarding specific countries or locations of opportunity. The individual would be expected to keep up-to-date about economic and political conditions, major strategic science and technology goals, and opportunities for engagement in the country/region. She or he would scan for new changes in policy or practices related to higher education programs, areas of research and development, and funding sources so that these opportunities could be brought to the attention of faculty and students. The leaders, experts, or ambassadors must have the tools to identify where there may be overlapping opportunities that would be of interest to interdisciplinary teams and international partnerships, and they should have an avenue for exchanging information (digital or face-to-face). To reward serious participation by in-house experts, these individuals would be rewarded with a small stipend, travel funds, and/or recognition for service.

Establishing and Sustaining an Ecosystem for International Research

Creating an environment, or ecosystem, for successful international research requires partnerships across university units and externally. Administrators and staff across organizational boundaries must value and understand one another's contribution to research engagement and identify ways of collaborating to advance internationally funded and focused research. Establishing a "community of practice" is one answer to the challenge of reaching a diverse set of stakeholders.

A Community of Practice for International Research

A community of practice is a group of people informally bound together by shared expertise and an interest in collaboration that is mutually beneficial. A community of practice brings together stakeholders from across the university and, if desired, from external partners, such as industry or community organizations. The motivations for forming a community of practice are many: to sustain connections with peers, respond to external changes, meet new challenges, respond to opportunities, and promote greater familiarity with international research activities and challenges among offices not naturally thinking about this topic. The community of practice for international research will build and improve the research support infrastructure by enlisting subject matter experts. A "community" or "network of support" is a creative model, strategically designed to help researchers, students, and administrators successfully balance compliance, legal, risk-management, and safety matters in activities that involve international engagement.

Objectives for a community of practice for international research include:

- Identify strategies for balancing the challenges and opportunities of international engagement.
- Compile a list of known issues and concerns related to international research collaborations and assessing the institution's ability to manage these issues.
- Identify gaps within the associated business processes and recommending solutions to address hurdles and streamline processes.
- Advance these streamlined processes as "best practices" supported by the community.
- Evaluate progress on a continuous basis via feedback, testimonials, or surveys from researchers and research administrators as well as through an evaluation of metrics established by the institution (e.g., percent increase in proposals submitted, percent increase in awards, and other key indicators with international components).

Communities of practice can drive strategy, generate innovation, solve problems, promote the spread of best practices, encourage cooperation and a shared sense of responsibility, and help organizations recruit and retain talent. Most importantly, communities of practice establish avenues of communication that encourage a vibrant exchange of ideas and knowledge.

A community of practice can exist entirely within a single academic unit or branch across division boundaries and include any number of individuals, but typically it has a core of participants who provide intellectual and social leadership and enthusiasm for the topic that energizes the group. Large communities are often subdivided in a meaningful manner in order to encourage people to take an active role.[10]

FIGURE 1.1. A COMMUNITY OF PRACTICE FOR INTERNATIONAL RESEARCH SHOULD INCLUDE REPRESENTATION FROM DIVISIONS AND UNITS THAT PLAY KEY ROLES IN INTERNATIONAL ACTIVITIES AND CAN PROVIDE THE NEEDED INTELLIGENCE FROM A VARIETY OF PERSPECTIVES.

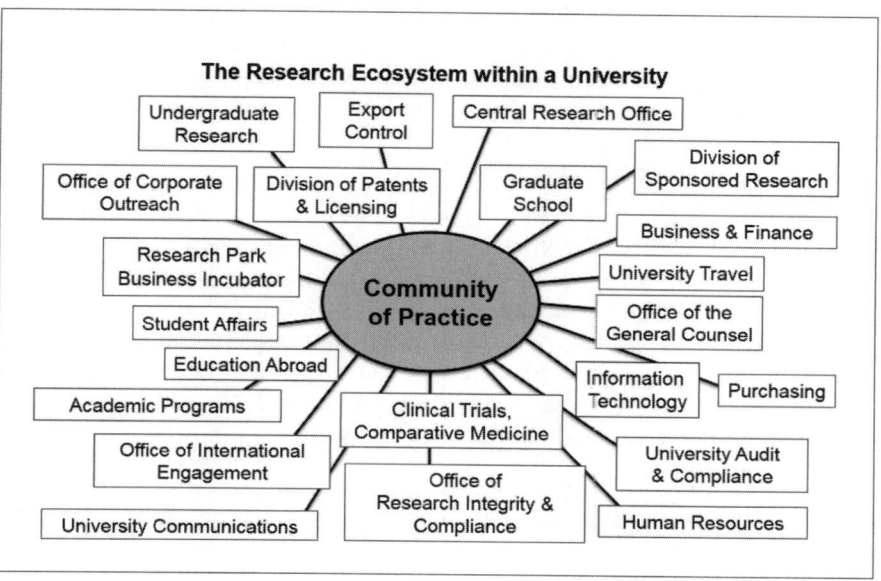

Dedicated Support Services for International Research

Universities may also establish dedicated offices to provide international research support. Such an office can be situated within the research area, the international unit, or a college, or it may be organized as a stand-alone unit that bridges the two primary offices (research and international) and has independent budget authority. There are several excellent examples of how universities have designed offices and programs to support globalized research endeavors that play to the disciplinary strengths of faculty and the strategic priorities of the institution.

Washington State University's International Programs Office houses staff who specialize in international research services including identifying and disseminating international funding opportunities, supporting internationally relevant proposals and strategic alliances, facilitating interdisciplinary partnerships, profiling the international interests of faculty and departments, and monitoring and evaluating the impact of the university's international research footprint. The International Programs Office works closely with other offices across the university, including the Office of Research and various colleges and schools, to promote research strengths in agriculture, clean technologies, and the health sciences.

The Ohio State University supports its Global Gateway offices in countries of cultural and economic importance, where faculty have established academic and research collaborations and Ohio companies have staked out a major presence. The goals of the offices relate to academic programming and students, alumni engagement or re-engagement, and the development of international corporate partnerships. With Gateway offices in Mumbai, Shanghai, São Paulo, Istanbul, Addis Ababa, Warsaw, and London, the university's Office of International Affairs offers seed-grant funding for faculty research projects and works with the Office of Research to support these international initiatives.

The Office of International Research Collaboration at Michigan State University (MSU) uses its knowledge of the faculty's international involvement to advance MSU's global research strengths, including agriculture and engineering, among other STEM areas of expertise. The office helps to assemble and support multi- and transdisciplinary research teams to address global problems and to connect the university's international research capacity with its network of partners throughout the world. Services include identifying collaborators within MSU and globally, providing guidance and strategies for proposal development and management, identifying funding sources, organizing training and workshops, and providing seed funding. MSU's Colleges of Engineering and of Agriculture and Natural Resources have partnered to administer an annual Academy for Global Engagement for early career, tenure-track faculty in both colleges. The Academy acts as an incubator for scholars with global aspirations, Participants are competitively selected, matched with mentors, supported as they refine their research ideas, and trained as effective advocates for their ideas during a visit to Washington, D.C. to meet with prospective funders. Given the university's emphasis on its global footprint, MSU researchers are encouraged to conduct innovative research and exercise leadership in the context oe global endeavors. They are supported by a highly skilled professional staff, internal funding opportunities, and a mandate from MSU's president to act as change agents and "disrupters" within the global community.[11] MSU is able to demonstrate that researchers who have participated in the Academy are more successful at attracting external funding and publishing and disseminating their globally-focused research than their peer equivalents who have not attended the Academy.

The 2017 Treasury Symposium hosted by the Treasury Institute for Higher Education identified "structuring global support and oversight functions" within universities as an important trend in university business practice.[12] The Treasury Institute promotes excellence in university financial management through educational programs and opportunities for sharing of best practices. A strategy for organizing global support systems presented at the Symposium by Western Union Business Solutions, the law firm of Hogan Lovells, and the University of Pennsylvania highlights a number of familiar challenges to the establishment of a dedicated unit or structure to support global research: an underdeveloped university-wide strategy for global operation, lack of issue ownership, decentralization that encourages a lack of coordination, and competing domestic priorities."[13] The support services infrastructure for global research at the University of Pennsylvania is housed squarely within the Division of Finance. but is also connected to the University's Office of Global Initiatives or Penn Global.[14] Situating its global support system within the Division of Finance was a deliberate structural decision made by the University in 2012. There are many options for how to organize global support services and where to locate them, but without a doubt financial issues such as payments to foreign nationals, labor and tax laws, banking, and purchasing of goods and services remain some of the more complicated and challenging aspects to international research projects. Involving your finance and legal teams in the effort to support global research is essential.

A number of universities have created comprehensive online resources for equipping researchers for the potential complexities of international research. The University of Washington's Global Operations Support website provides a comprehensive roadmap for international research endeavors. This easily accessible website offers guidance, tools, forms, checklists, and resources—including a comprehensive International Projects Start-Up Guide—for staff and faculty planning and administering research, projects or programs abroad. Dedicated support systems for managing issues relating to compliance, human resources, purchasing and payments, as well as legal matters recognize these areas as potential road blocks to successful international research.[15]

The University of Minnesota is another excellent example of a university that has dedicated considerable resources to sophisticated support services for international research. The Global Programs and Strategy Alliance, the central international office for the University of Minnesota system houses a Global Operations initiative that brings together university experts in the areas of tax, purchasing, legal, human resources, and compliance to assess issues, provide advice, and reduce internal barriers to successful international engagement. A dedicated network of subject matter experts from across the university provides customized guidance, options, and advice on projects of all sizes.[16]

Similar support services are available at the University of Arizona where staff within the Office of Global Initiatives link funding opportunities across researchers, international academic partners, and industry. Services include the identification of international funding opportunities, team and resource mobilization, proposal development, writing, budget management, submission and reporting to ensure successful grant submissions.[17]

The University of California System recently (2017) launched an online resource for global engagement known a UCGO. The comprehensive website includes modules for researchers, students, and program staff. In addition to proposal development and award management tools, templates and forms, the website offers training for ensuring compliance with federal regulations (e.g. export control, human subjects, and clinical trials) and access to a Global Research Forum where researchers from across the UC system can exchange ideas, seek answers to questions and collaboration to identify solutions to challenges.[18] UCGO is an example of a system response to the need for support services for international research across a vast constituency that includes ten campuses, five medical centers, three national laboratories, 238,000 students and more than 190,000 faculty and staff.

American universities are not alone in recognizing the benefits of coordinating the work of the international and research offices. The University of Oslo, Norway, supports an international research office that coordinates the university's research collaboration with universities and research institutes in Africa, Asia, and Latin America, and develops measures to implement global strategies. The office of International Research Promotion of Waseda University, Tokyo, is responsible for formulating guidelines to promote international research, establishing a database for international scholar exchange, supporting international research development, and hosting international research symposia.

International research offices are also well established among Canadian universities. The University of Saskatchewan's international research office supports research and training, manages international collaborations, liaises with international agencies, and oversees all contracts and grants related to international research. At the University of Ottawa, a similar office is the administrative center for promoting and coordinating the growth of international research and development and for establishing collaborative international research projects. Its responsibilities also include advocating for faculty and researchers with international interests, creating and administering international networks to facilitate collaboration and exchange programs, promoting the university's numerous institutional affiliations and linkages abroad, and managing relations with international organizations and donor agencies. The Office of International Research at McGill University in Montreal, advances international projects and outreach by supporting faculty across disciplines in all international activities, including fundamental research collaborations. The University of Waterloo reorganized its international unit, known as Waterloo International, by supplementing a traditional office of international programs with research and international activities, including proposal development and funding assistance, risk and safety services, outreach to agencies sponsoring international research, the management of international partnerships, and up-to-date information about university's current international activities. The University of Waterloo has a stated goal of becoming "one of the most internationalized universities in Canada," and Waterloo International is integral to that endeavor[19] (see Chapter 4).

Investing in Physical Spaces on Campus to International Research

Universities have dedicated spaces for students, faculty, and sometimes community members to test their innovative ideas and to engage in entrepreneurial endeavors (see Chapter 5), but rarely is there a physical space designed specifically for global research. Interdisciplinary and internationally connected research is more likely to thrive when interested parties and stakeholders share common space, laboratories, and equipment. Shared space encourages conversation, sustained interaction, and, ideally, fruitful collaboration. It is likely, however, that most research environments at research universities include international students and scholars as well as involve international collaborations. International research is not confined by disciplinary boundaries and is equally important to those in the sciences as it is to researchers in the humanities and arts fields. A dedicated space for sharing among internal (domestic) and external (international) colleagues is critical.

The University of Pennsylvania has created Perry World House to serve as the university's hub for international activities and as a vibrant state-of-the-art gathering place for students, faculty, and visitors. Through its Global Innovations Program, the Perry World House welcomes international fellows and professors from institutions around the world, provides opportunities for postdoctoral fellows and current students to engage in international research, and hosts international conferences on critical global issues. Founded in 2014, Perry World House functions as the intellectual center for the university's global engagement initiatives, including an on-campus think tank devoted to developing solutions to persistent and emerging international challenges.

Indiana University's Global and International Studies Building, completed in 2015, is designed to play a vital role in new international programs and foster greater interdisciplinary research collaboration between academic units previously physically separated and spread across the university's Bloomington campus. A signature feature of the building is the "Stones of the World" wall, which includes stone from 10 countries on six continents, as well as segments of Indiana limestone. The wall is emblematic of the university's long history of global engagement.

Creating an Oversight and Advisory Community

Internal Advisory Board

An internal advisory board consisting of a group of senior-level administrative and faculty leaders who are charged with providing guidance regarding budget, policies, and initiatives is especially helpful within an institution and across a university system. The group should include the chief academic officer; the SIO; and senior leadership representation from research, advancement, business and finance, information technology, student affairs (representatives from the community of practice), selected deans and faculty, and a member of the Board of Trustees who is especially interested in international activities. Their role is to aid strategic planning, provide oversight and insight, and advise the university about activities that are relevant to the success of international engagement (e.g., development, community and industry connections, and mobility opportunities). The group should meet at least twice a year and be kept informed of ongoing activities, new initiatives, and measures of goal attainment (success) in the interim. Such reporting requires collaboration across units responsible for promoting and sustaining international endeavors—research in particular. An executive group and subcommittees of the advisory board can be formed and called upon as needed.

External Advisory Board

In addition to the traditional institutional oversight provided by the Board of Trustees, an external advisory board of experts and peers is another avenue to improve and strengthen an institution's global activities and profile. A specific charge should be developed according to the mission and goals of the university and its global stakeholder groups, with the objective being to improve performance. The external advisory board can be small in number and each member can be expected to serve a renewable term of two to three years, with the opportunity to extend the time for an additional term if desired by both parties. Representatives to this group could include (for example) a president of a university that has globalization as a primary thrust, a member or former member of the Department of State, or a former Ambassador. Members should be knowledgeable about global research opportunities and challenges. The university should pay for the travel and lodging of the members and an appropriate honorarium for an annual meeting.

Governing Boards

The international research activities of an institution can benefit from input from the members of governing boards such as trustees (the University of Missouri system uses the terminology Board of Curators, and the University of Virginia has a Board of Visitors), especially in the areas of public–private partnerships and community linkages. Many members of these boards possess significant international experience and connections. International engagement should receive separate attention through board committees or workgroups to allow for a productive exchange of ideas and information. As internationalization and global research becomes a growing priority among universities and colleges, it must also be recognized by institutional and statewide governing boards as a distinct activity worthy of specific attention. The Association of Governing Boards developed a series of questions for trustees to ponder about global education that relate to risk, cost, economic impact, potential for fundraising and institutional reputation.

State and System Organizations and Initiatives

Each institution within a university system may have its own emphases regarding its global research portfolios, but all of them will have an international component to their academic programs, student activities, and faculty projects.

U.S. states now recognize the importance of internationalizing education and adopting statewide policies to motivate state governments, system offices, and coordinating boards to engage in internationalization efforts. There have been gubernatorial proclamations, legislative resolutions, foreign-student recruitment programs, internationalization goals in strategic and master plans, and increased funding for student exchanges. Universities attract international trade and foreign direct investment as a result of their international engagement, and the fiscal advantages of international students to a region and state are well documented. As of 2011, 23 states in the United States had passed a resolution in support of international higher education in at least one chamber of state government. State economic development offices and higher education offices in 47 percent of states have begun to coordinate on internationalization activities. California and Kentucky passed resolutions in support of international higher education in 2002, apparently the first. Very few states, however, have an individual appointed at the system level to oversee and develop international research and education.[20]

A survey of state education leaders, including governors and organizations in education, revealed the levels of support for internationalizing education. Those most supportive of international education efforts were state higher education committee members, university chief academic officers, university presidents, and members of the higher education systems, in that order; whereas all the leaders and education organizations were 62 percent (legislative education committees) to 89 percent (state higher education executive offices) in favor of preparing the state for a global economy.[21] Only 21 percent of legislative education committee members supported international education initiatives. It is surprising that the two goals (preparing for a global economy and international education) were not connected for many of the respondents.

Nearly 20 years ago, the University System of Georgia (USG) recognized that universities should be deeply engaged in globalization. Through the USG Regents' International Policy Directive of March 1995, established principles, goals, and implementation plans were formally articulated for developing strategic alliances and other collaborative initiatives to link the USG with other parts of the world. Cooperative agreements were established with institutions of higher education in Argentina and China, with plans for additional agreements in the United Kingdom, South Africa, the Pacific Rim, and throughout Latin America to promote collaborative research and service initiatives and for student and faculty exchange. The Regents of the USG directed the chancellor to create a statewide council for internationalization representing the system universities, industry, government, and other relevant agencies to carry out eight specific initiatives to internationalize the system and its institutions.

The State Council of Higher Education for Virginia distributed a survey in 2009 to determine the extent of internationalization and globalization of public and private higher education programs in Virginia. The response revealed detailed and extensive information about how internationalization figured into institutional mission statements, the curriculum, student experiences, research agendas, relationships with foreign universities, funding for international programs and activities, and economic development at home and abroad. It was clear that respondent institutions were deeply involved with institutions abroad—even many years ago when the survey was instituted.[22]

Global Washington was founded in 2006 by a small group of stakeholders from the University of Washington, the Seattle International Foundation, and Washington State University to identify resources to strengthen global development across the state. The goal was to create a statewide organization and build a political constituency in support of globalization of business, health, education, and the economy. In 2007, Global Washington was formally organized, adding business and foundation partners,[23] and evolved into a membership organization in 2008. The goals for the state were to (1) achieve a strong and unified advocacy voice for global development, (2) recognize the state as a model for collaboration, (3) increase efficiency and effectiveness across Washington's global development organizations, and (4) build a political constituency for global development. Today, the Global Washington consortium includes more than 12 academic institutions within Washington State and functions as a hub for resources and partnerships, and provides opportunities for researchers to disseminate their work to groups outside of academia, including industry and nonprofit organizations.

NOTES

[1] Austin, I., & Jones, G. A. (2016). *Governance of higher education: Perspectives theories and practices.* New York, NY: Routledge.

[2] Force on International Education. (2004, October). *A call to leadership: The presidential role in internationalizing the university.* Retrieved from http://www.aplu.org/library/a-call-to-leadership-the-presidential-role-in-internationalizing-the-university/file.

[3] Retrieved from https://msu.edu/about/thisismsu/executive/president.html.

[4] Lyall, S. (2016, March 4). Big man on a global campus. *The New York Times.* Retrieved from http://www.nytimes.com/2016/03/06/nyregion/andrew-hamilton-new-york-university-president.html?_r=0

[5] Humboldt-Universität zu Berlin (2015) Presidential Committee International Agenda. Retrieved from https://www.international.hu-berlin.de/de/internationales-profil/internationale-agenda/internationale-agenda

[6] For more information on KSU's PEGS program, go to https://web.kennesaw.edu/news/stories/cream-crop.

[7] Brustein, W. (2009). It takes an entire institution: A blueprint for the global university. University of Illinois at Urbana-Champaign, p. 3 (retrieved from https://oia.osu.edu/pdf/GlobalUniversityBlueprint.pdf), and as Chapter 15 (2009), in R. Lewin (Ed.), *The handbook of practice and research in study abroad: Higher education and the quest for global citizenship.* New York, NY: Routledge.

[8] American Council on Education. (2012). *Mapping internationalization on U.S. campuses. 2016 edition.* Washington, DC: Center for Internationalization and Global Engagement. Retrieved from https://www.acenet.edu/news-room/Documents/Mapping-Internationalizationon-US-Campuses-2012-full.pdf. The 2016 Mapping Internationalization on U.S. Campuses survey was sent to chief academic officers/provosts at accredited, degree-granting colleges and universities nationwide during the month of February 2016.

[9] Reprinted in Romo, A. (2015). Strategic international partnerships: The leader's role. *University World News, 393.* See also Banks, C., Siebe-Herbig, B., & Norton, K (Eds.). (2016). Strategic international partnerships: The university leadership point of view. In Banks, C., Siebe-Herbig, B., & Norton, K. (Eds.). (2016). *Global perspectives on strategic international partnerships: A guide to building sustainable academic linkages.* Washington, DC: Institute for International Education.

[10] Wenger, E. C., & Snyder, W. M. (2000, January/February). Communities of practice: The organizational frontier. *Harvard Business Review.* Retrieved from https://hbr.org/2000/01/communities-of-practice-the-organizational-frontier. For more information regarding communities of practice, see Wenger, E. C. (1998). *Communities of practice: Learning, meaning, and identifying.* Cambridge University Press; Wenger, E. C., McDermott, R., & Snyder, W. M. (2002). *Cultivating communities of practice.* Harvard Business Review Press.

[11] Retrieved from https://www.egr.msu.edu/global/global/academy.

[12] Retrieved from http://www.treasuryinstitute.org/

[13] Smith, Scott, Ferreira, William, and Koch, Artemis, "Establishing University Global Support Functions," presented at the 2017 Treasury Symposium, New Orleans, LA, January 29 – February 1, 2017. See: https://www.hoganlovells.com/en/events/establishing-university-global-support-functions and http://www.treasuryinstitute.org/symp2017

[14] Global Support Services at the University of Pennsylvania: https://global.upenn.edu/gss

15. Accessible at https://f2.washington.edu/fm/globalsupport/home
16. Accessible at See: http://global.umn.edu/operations
17. Accessible at See: https://global.arizona.edu/global-knowledge-network/grants-global
18. Accessible at http://ucghiresearchhub.ucsf.edu/
19. Retrieved from https://uwaterloo.ca/international/about.
20. The Nelson A. Rockefeller Institute of Government. (2014). *States go global: State government engagement in higher education internationalization.* Albany, NY: The State University of New York, p. 13. Retrieved from http://www.rockinst.org/pdf/education/2014-05-28-States_Go_Global.pdf.
21. Ibid., pp. 11–12.
22. State Council of Higher Education for Virginia, (2009, June). *Survey on International Programs at Virginia's Institutions.* Retrieved from http://www.schev.edu/AdminFaculty/global/InternationalProgramsFINAL.pdf.
23. Global Washington includes members of the leadership of Boeing, Microsoft, the Gates Foundation, Laird Norton Company, the Trade Development Alliance, the World Affairs Council, Starbucks, Pacific Northwest National Laboratory, Philanthropy Northwest, and PATH (a global health organization).

Chapter Two
Equipping Faculty, Scholars, and Post-Docs for International Research

Introduction

The ability to successfully recruit and retain talented researchers is critical to higher education institutions: for student learning, for research productivity, for enhanced global recognition, and for every university's core mission of knowledge generation. Today's global research universities seek talent from across the globe, not just within national or regional borders. As competition increases across borders for high-caliber scholars, the diversity of faculty in terms of nationality will only grow. The United States has been a beneficiary of intellectual migration. Scientists and engineers working in the United States are increasingly likely to be foreign born, primarily because the United States continues to attract large numbers of international students, scholars, and skilled workers from abroad despite immigration challenges that emerged following the events of 9/11.

International scholars working at colleges and universities in the United States—as researchers and instructors—numbered 134,034 in 2016, as reported by the Institute of International Education.[1] These visiting scholars fill faculty positions and offer students and colleagues a diversity of perspective in classrooms, laboratories, and the workplace. International scholars are also present in leadership positions within universities. In 2011, the Association of American Universities reported a significant increase in the number of foreign-born university leaders (presidents and chancellors): 11 of its 61 American member institutions as compared to five previously.[2] Not only is the profile of scholars or faculty and administrative leaders increasingly international, but the research questions they are addressing are more likely to be global in scope and theme (see Chapter 9). International engagement and mobility are essential for faculty to fulfill their role as facilitators of student learning and to advance their impact on the academy and society as a whole.[3] Equipping faculty for success in the international arena and incentivizing their global engagement encourages a robust exchange of ideas across national boundaries and establishes an institutional culture that recognizes and rewards international endeavors.

Researcher Incentives and Development Opportunities

Leadership and commitment to international engagement at all levels of university administration set the stage for faculty and student research activity in a global environment, but faculty are the key drivers of international research. For those faculty already involved in international collaboration, the advantages are very clear to them in the context of their research agenda(s) and academic programs, but their contributions must also be valued by the institution. International engagement must matter when researchers are hired, evaluated, promoted and tenured, and rewarded. Opportunities for faculty to become engaged in global work must be facilitated and resourced (for time, funding, and support services), and the work itself must be evaluated and recognized in a clear and tangible way.

Career Advancement: Tenure and Promotion

Faculty recognition according to clearly designed career advancement metrics is at the center of any institutional mechanism to encourage international research engagement. Working internationally and successfully can be time consuming and labor intensive. Researchers who have invested in international collaboration should, at the time of career advancement, be recognized for their efforts and rewarded for their accomplishments. It is common for universities and colleges to include activities that contribute to the academic reputation of a faculty member at the national and international levels, but fewer institutions define international engagement as a separate category for evaluation.

A 2015 report by the American Council on Education (ACE), *Internationalizing the Tenure Code*, examined 91 publicly available tenure and promotion policies at the institution, school or college, and departmental levels, from 61 U.S. colleges and universities that indicated that "international work or experience was a consideration" for faculty advancement.[4] Of the 91 policies reviewed, a majority mentioned international research activity as a criterion (51) for academic advancement and the importance of scholarly reputation within the international community (47).

The value placed on "depth" of a faculty member's international engagement, however, is open to interpretation. For example, the most commonly cited international activity within research is a presentation at an international conference—which may or may not take place outside the researcher's country of residence. References to international scholarly reputation often rely on language that refers to both the national and international arenas. The ACE Report concludes: "At the end of the day, the 'international' piece is usually, in effect, optional, which raises questions about the extent to which adding such language to the tenure code is likely to actually move the needle on faculty engagement in internationalization." But, the inclusion of internationally focused criteria in tenure and promotion policies remains important because such a policy identifies "international" as a valuable endeavor.

The University of Minnesota modified its tenure code in 2007 to include work related to faculty international engagement. The official tenure and promotion policy statement reads as follows: "International activities and initiatives by the candidate should be considered." Other universities have also adopted language that allows faculty to receive credit and recognition for international activities specifically. Rutgers University requires faculty to document international teaching (on and off campus), international student advising, funding received from international sources, and service contributions made to the international community. Likewise, Oregon State University requires faculty to document international engagement in teaching and service. Michigan State University evaluates global work within the framework of "service to the broader community," including a candidate's contributions to international studies and programs such as international instruction, international community service, international student advising, and efforts to build international competence among students.[5] It is worth noting, however, that language referencing international activities is far more common than language that specifically identifies globalized research as a criterion for career advancement. Policies will remain unique to each institution, but "formally incentivizing and rewarding internationally-focused activities in the tenure process gives junior faculty license to bring this work to the top of the list of competing priorities and sets the foundation for international engagement throughout their careers."[6]

In lieu of a formal reference to the value of international engagement in tenure and promotion criteria, guidelines for promotion should be aligned with the university's strategic priorities or goals. Notably, a significant percentage of higher education institutions (HEIs) around the world today define themselves as global research universities. It is important, then, that such a thrust match the expectations and rewards with the responsibilities that faculty undertake, and to encourage—not mandate—efforts in these areas through guidelines that provide direction to complement standards and values that already define excellence at a global research institution. Including international activities among the ways a faculty member can be recognized in tenure and promotion within the traditional standards of teaching, research, and service does not add a new category but rather a new measure of achievement within any one of the existing categories.

In addition to carving out space for international research within guidelines and requirements for career advancement, universities must invest resources into programs for all types of faculty (junior, senior, tenure- and nontenure-track, and post-docs) that support international research engagement (see below).

Recruitment and Hiring of Personnel

While international research activity can be incentivized and rewarded through the tenure and promotion process, it can be equally effective to consider international experience as a priority for new hires. Some universities have found that it is even more desirable to include an international dimension to advantage one job candidate over another at the time of recruitment than it is to use international activity as a mechanism for career advancement via tenure and promotion. Identifying international experience as a preferred quality for hiring can occur at the department, college, or university level. Senior administration might add a salary increment to hires, in which departments choose candidates with an international portfolio or could reward the department directly with travel funds or funds for research support. In other cases, the university might develop financial incentives, such as an annual bonus or salary adjustment, to those researchers who demonstrate tangible evidence of impactful and internationally engaged scholarly output.

Universities that have prioritized global engagement in their missions and strategic plans may establish dedicated funds for "international" faculty lines that can be used to establish depth of expertise—a cluster of hires with knowledge of Brazil or China. Or they can look for breadth of global expertise across disciplines—engineers, anthropologists, biologists—with experience in Africa or Asia, or consider a core group associated with a major international thrust that can attract significant funding (see big science, described in Chapter 4). Mechanisms for ensuring sustained collaboration across unit boundaries is essential once such cluster hires are made to avoid the isolation or "siloing" of faculty after they are situated across different departments or schools. Funds might also be used for faculty lines and startup packages, and as rewards for departments or units that hire in concert with the strategic goals of the university.

Another avenue for energizing internationally focused hiring is to create a competition across colleges, schools, institutes, and departments for faculty lines that have an international perspective. Such a program can be overseen by the university's senior international officer (SIO) or ideally between international and research offices, inasmuch as a goal is to recruit faculty who engage in international research. The SIO, however, is "responsible to make sure that the overall international needs as dictated by the teaching, discovery, and engagement missions of the university are addressed. Tenure would be held within the colleges and schools, but when such a line becomes vacant, it reverts back to the senior international officer who can choose to continue the line in the same college or re-open the competition."[7] A more bottom-up approach is to allow international hires to occur locally at the department or school level, guided by the university's discipline strengths or the regional or country interests, but still overseen by the academic units.

Time and Money

For international research to flourish, faculty members need resources in the form of time, funding, and support services. Opportunities for leave time or sabbaticals that extend over two semesters are especially useful for international mobility. Leave time must be accompanied by the continuation of full salary or at least 75 percent of salary for two semesters, and/or supplemental funding to assist with the cost of travel and accommodations. Given that most U.S. universities offer reduced salary for sabbaticals longer than one semester (roughly 16 weeks), researchers may need to find additional funds supplemental income, travel support, and living expenses for an international sabbatical. A handful of universities and colleges in the United States continue to provide full salary and benefits (e.g., health insurance, retirement contributions) to faculty recipients of Fulbright Awards. Thus, faculty on leave for Fulbright work may use their award stipend to cover the cost of travel and overseas accommodations with the added support of their regular university salary. Such a policy makes it easier for faculty to juggle financial responsibilities at home and afford participation in Fulbright Award programs where stipends are less generous and/or the cost of living abroad is comparatively higher.

Release time from university responsibilities allows faculty to work overseas for longer periods of time, which allows for greater engagement and collaboration. For this to occur, dedicated internal funds or faculty-generated external funds are essential both to offset the cost of a replacement instructor and for international travel and living expenses overseas.

Internal Funding for International Research

If an institutional priority is to engage in international work, then the support should be commensurate, but few higher education institutions have a dedicated budget for the international research conducted by their faculty, students, and staff, or for collaborative activities between their investigators and others at universities and research institutions outside of the country.

Financial resources provided by the institution for international work typically fund the personnel and some of the activities of an international office, international student services, tuition waivers, study abroad, and fellowships or scholarships.

Funds are also needed to allow faculty, staff, and students to travel internationally; initiate international collaborative research; provide required matching to obtain grants to conduct research abroad; recruit international scholars and post-docs; organize and conduct programs, conferences, and workshops; provide courtesy gifts to international visitors when they visit us and when we travel abroad; and allow the institution to undertake special opportunities such as the Institute of International Education (IIE) International Academic Partnership Program (IAPP)[8] and the IIE Scholar Rescue program (see later in this chapter). Individual schools or colleges may also provide specific funding for international activities germane to their mission and goals.

There are various sources of internal funding depending upon the institution. Public institutions can invest some of their education and general funds for international programs, activities, and the leadership and supporting staff for an international office, and a portion of returned facilities and administrative costs can be allocated for seed grants and international travel. In some universities, a percentage of the tuition from international students is used to promote international activities of the university, including research (e.g., Rutgers University's GAIA Centers, described below). Universities also may include international research programs among their priorities for university advancement and assign a development officer to this responsibility (described below).

Many universities have created seed-grant programs within an office of research and/or international office so that students and faculty can conduct pilot studies and establish international relationships that set the stage for external funds from agencies and/or private sources to obtain more substantial awards. Faculty senate research committees may also have a pool of funds under their discretion to award to colleagues for international presentations and travel.

The University of Texas San Antonio provides International Initiatives Grants to faculty who are working on new, sustainable global initiatives. North Carolina State University has a pool of $35,000 that is awarded in $5,000 seed grants to assist faculty members' international projects. The Ohio State University has set aside $2.3 million for faculty and students to engage in international research, study abroad, faculty development, and support for K–12 education. International Opportunities Grants at the University of San Diego are awarded from a $240,000 pool set aside for faculty to travel, experience new cultures, and promote research and scholarship. Grant recipients present the work they accomplish during International Education Week.

Indiana University (IU) Bloomington offers Mellon Short Term Faculty Fellowships to foster international, area studies, and global studies research that is conducted abroad for at least eight weeks in countries and regions of the scholar's choice. Faculty and graduate students may work together, and collaboration with local institutions is encouraged. Faculty are eligible for a stipend of up to $10,000, as well as travel and related expenses of research up to $10,000. The fellowships are part of the Mellon Innovating International Research, Teaching and Collaboration (MIIRT) Program, funded through a $750,000 award from the Andrew W. Mellon Foundation. The provost or executive vice president of the IU Bloomington campus serves as principal investigator on the Mellon grant. In her words: "We are grateful to the Mellon Foundation for its appreciation of the importance of scholars being able to do work in the country they are studying. This program directly enhances the careers of our graduate students and faculty members by giving them the precious opportunity to conduct meaningful international research. It also furthers the goals of our Bicentennial Strategic Plan, which emphasizes research and creative activity that links cultures and communities."[9]

The Global Advancement and International Affairs Centers (GAIA Centers) at Rutgers University have a remarkable range of funding programs to connect the university globally through international collaboration, deepen the global perspective of coursework on campus, plan and organize international research conferences, and showcase innovative programming on campus that highlights global issues and international affairs. International Collaborative Research Grants are available to tenure-track faculty and tenured faculty to support international research projects and programs initiated by faculty partnering with scholars at foreign institutions. About 10 grants of up to $8,000 each are made annually. A $100,000 fund is also available for grants to support service learning. The GAIA Centers, in partnership with the office of the senior vice president for academic affairs and offices of the Chancellors at the Camden, Newark, and New Brunswick campuses, as well as the Biomedical and Health Science campus, offer or facilitate funding opportunities for international research and teaching, and there are also grants to internationalize the curriculum and for interdisciplinary working groups who are rethinking regional and area studies. Biennial theme grants focus on a topic for the specific year (e.g., Global Urbanism in 2016–17), and seed grants are awarded competitively to support new or existing collaborative work or scholarship with colleagues in Tanzania.

Oregon State University's Faculty Internationalization Grant program allows 45 faculty to engage in collaborative research, professional development, teaching, and outreach abroad. Its Graduate International Grant program also supports international travel for graduate students doing research abroad. The University of South Florida (USF) has funded small cohorts of faculty from Ghanaian universities to come to USF to complete their PhD work and dissertations then return home where they are awarded their degrees from their own universities.

Large, transnational grants make internationalized research even more likely. For example, the Humboldt University of Berlin–Princeton University Strategic Partnership supports faculty, departments, programs, and centers seeking resources to sustain ongoing transnational research and teaching collaborations. Bilateral collaborative research ventures must include a balanced representation of scholars from both institutions and are eligible for funding up to $300,000 to support one to two years of collaborative activity.

The purposes and priorities for internal awards cited above are wide ranging and summarized here (with a few additions):

- Support for signature programs and research conducted abroad in collaboration with a recognized international partner, such as the Humboldt–Princeton partnership.
- Funding to enhance the depth and breadth of existing collaborations and relationships—especially if these projects also have a source of external funds.
- Expanded support for research programs in identified geographic areas or locations of emphasis and opportunity.
- Funding to partner universities—especially in developing countries—to support their faculty to complete terminal degrees with time at the partner institution (e.g., USF's Ghana Scholar Program).
- Facilitation of new multidisciplinary, collaborative proposals for international research.
- Development of joint institutes, centers, or laboratories with international partners by providing funding for travel mobility and other activities. This may be with a specific country, such as the Partnership University Fund, which supports collaborative research and student and faculty mobility between French and U.S. universities.
- Awards that support participation in global conferences.
- International research sabbaticals.
- Funds, such as the North Carolina State Faculty Excellence Program, for new hires and office or lab space in cluster areas that include global challenge research initiatives.
- Naming internal funding awards after strategic partnerships or for an individuals who are (or have been) supportive of international work gives such funding mechanisms visibility and prestige within the institution.

External Funding for International Research

Governmental sources and nonprofit organizations provide the majority of the more significant levels of funding for international research. In the United States, these agencies include the National Institutes of Health (NIH), the National Science Foundation (NSF), the U.S. Agency for International Development (USAID), the U.S. Department of State, the World Bank, the Bill and Melinda Gates Foundation, the Ford Foundation, and others. A multitude of organizations, associations, agencies, and nongovernmental organizations (NGOs) foster as many aspects of internationalization as the audiences they serve. Support is available to those just beginning to shape their international projects as well as those who are already seasoned professionals. These organizations target university leadership, students and faculty, decision makers and policymakers, in general, and specific individuals and groups such as engineering students, underserved students, research park leaders, countries recovering from disasters and/or working to escape from poverty and engage in democratic reform, and community leaders and their partners. A range of services to promote international connections and cooperation can also be accessed through these organizations. They provide the following:

- A forum for shared global dialogue and cooperation among university partners and universities with other partners such as cities and businesses

- Aid to incorporate a global dimension into learning and discovery

- Opportunities for training to improve professionalism in international affairs

- Benchmarking and consultancy to measure achievement in internationalization

- Economic and humanitarian assistance

- Opportunities for students to obtain international experiences in education, research and work

These services are delivered through activities and tools such as networking and partnerships; forums for collaborators; opportunities for mobility; exchanges, workshops, symposia, seminars, panels, and instruction; surveys; and opportunities to obtain financial support to underpin them. Their efforts are publicized through print and online publications such as magazines, newsletters, blogs, databases, and social media.

In the United States, several key government funding mechanisms support international research: The Fogarty International Center at the NIH, the Partnerships for International Research and Education (PIRE) program at the NSF, and the NSF International Postdoctoral Research Fellowships. Agencies, such as the

Chinese National Natural Science Foundation, award additional money to Chinese scholars with active NSF funding (through partnerships with U.S. colleagues) to catalyze greater international cooperation. The U.S. Departments of State, Energy, and Defense also support international research efforts and language acquisition. USAID supports a wide variety of capacity-building projects, and in-country USAID missions have their own budgets and funding priorities (see Chapter 8).

National Institutes of Health (NIH)

The Fogarty International Center at the NIH seeks to build partnerships between health research organizations in the United States and abroad. The center coordinates biomedical and behavioral sciences to reduce the burden of disease, promote health, and extend longevity for all people through basic, clinical, and applied research and training in developing countries. More than 5,000 scientists worldwide have received training during the last 40 years. Funded research generates data that guide national and international global health policies, including those related to social, ethical, and economic issues.

The Fogarty International Center has four divisions. The Training Division funds research grants, training grants, and fellowship programs in more than 100 sites. Some of the grants are made directly to universities in developing countries, while others go to U.S. researchers who are collaborating with colleagues abroad. The Division of International Science Policy, Planning, and Evaluation advises on international science policy issues, tracks international funding agencies and research trends in global health, and manages the Disease Control Priorities Project. The Division of International Relations facilitates opportunities for collaboration with foreign science funding agencies, the U.S. Department of State, U.S. technical agencies, and international organizations. The Division on International Epidemiology and Population Studies consists of U.S. scientists and foreign colleagues who conduct research on the epidemiology and mathematical modeling of infectious diseases, including guiding the development of countermeasures for potential bioterror agents and public health measures to control the spread of infectious disease.

National Science Foundation (NSF)

The NSF sponsors an annual program, Partnerships for International Research and Education (PIRE), that supports partnerships designed to strengthen the capacity of institutions, multi-institutional consortia, and networks to engage in international research and education collaborations in the science and engineering community. The goals are to generate new knowledge and discovery, to develop a diverse and globally engaged scientific and engineering workforce, and to facilitate greater student preparation for international research collaboration. The Partnerships for Enhanced Engagement in Research program is a collaboration between USAID and NSF for scientists from developing countries to apply for funds to work with U.S. collaboration partners on projects of interest to USAID (discussed in the next section). The Office of International Science and Engineering co-funds awards and supplements in cooperation with the NSF Directorates and maintains overseas offices in Paris, Tokyo, and Beijing to promote collaboration among U.S. and foreign scientists and engineers and their students, and it reports on developments in the international science and engineering community. International work can be added to new proposals or supplements to existing proposals after consultation with the disciplinary program manager.

U.S. Agency for International Development (USAID)

USAID is an independent agency of the federal government created in 1961 by executive order when the Foreign Assistance Act was signed into law. The history of the agency dates to the Marshall Plan reconstruction of Europe after World War II and the Truman Administration's Point Four Program. USAID receives overall foreign policy guidance from the Secretary of State and furthers America's foreign policy interests in expanding democracy and free markets while improving the lives of the citizens of the developing world. USAID has been the principal U.S. agency to extend assistance to countries recovering from disaster, working to escape poverty, and engaging in democratic reforms. USAID's strength is in its missions and field offices around the world, where work is done in close partnership with volunteer organizations, indigenous organizations, universities, industry, international agencies, foreign governments, and other U.S. government agencies. Each of the USAID missions has its own funding priorities, typically in the areas of food security, public health, education, technology, and the environment and sustainability. USAID's Broad Agency Announcements outline the priorities for the agency and set the stage for subsequent funding opportunities from the agency itself or its missions.

In November 2012, USAID announced the creation of the Higher Education Solutions Network, a multidisciplinary research and development effort led by seven "founding" universities working to evaluate and strengthen innovations currently in development.[10] In addition, USAID's more recent Global Development Lab represents an effort to create networks of people and organizations that have the ability to solve global development challenges on a large scale. The lab's focus is twofold: to produce breakthrough development innovations by sourcing, testing, and scaling proven solutions to reach hundreds of millions of people, and to accelerate the transformation of the development enterprise through collaboration achieved through the Development Innovation Accelerator. The USAID Sustainable Higher Education Research Alliances in Indonesia, a five-year, university partnership program funded by USAID and implemented by the Institute for International Education in collaboration with the Indonesian Ministry of Higher Education and Research, will establish Centers for Collaborative Research to foster linkages between Indonesian higher education institutions and U.S.-based universities and across diverse Indonesian universities.[11]

United States Department of State

The U.S. Fulbright Program, sponsored by the U.S. Department of State, Bureau of Educational and Cultural Affairs, awards approximately 8,000 grants annually to researchers, scientists, teachers, and practitioners from around the world. More than 1,200 long- and short-term grants are available for university faculty, administrators, and professionals to engage in teaching, research, and professional development abroad. Awards that facilitate research mobility are also available to non-U.S. scholars and students. Operating in more than 160 countries worldwide, the Fulbright Program is the flagship international educational exchange program of the U.S. government and is one of the largest and most successful programs of scholarly exchange of its kind.

Since its launch in 1946, the Fulbright Program has provided more than 360,000 participants—chosen for their academic merit and leadership potential—with the opportunity to exchange ideas and contribute to finding solutions to shared international concerns. More than 1,800 U.S. students, artists, and early career professionals in more than 100 different fields of study are offered Fulbright U.S. Student Program grants to study, teach English, and conduct research overseas, and more than 800 U.S. scholars and established artists teach or conduct research overseas through the Fulbright U.S. Scholar Program annually.[12]

In 2013, the U.S. Department of State, together with counterparts in the UK government, supported the Global Innovation Initiative (GII) to promote multilateral research partnerships between U.S., UK, and third countries (India, Indonesia, Brazil, China) on topics of global significance, such as food and security, climate change, public health, and urban development. To date, 37 partnerships have been funded by GII by the U.S. and UK governments.[13]

Select UK Programs

The United Kingdom supports several programs to attract foreign scientists for collaborative research activities. The Engineering and Physical Sciences Research Council offers a Visiting Researcher Program, in which a UK institution may invite a researcher from another UK institution or abroad to carry out research collaboration within its campus for up to one year. The program provides salary, living and travel expenses, and research supplies and equipment for the joint research project.

The council also offers a workshop program for faculty development that encourages collaborators from the UK to interact with researchers from abroad. This program also funds travel expenses for the UK researchers and local meeting expenses if the joint workshop is held within the UK.

The Royal Academy of Engineering has several international research support programs (also called schemes) to facilitate collaboration between UK researchers and non-UK researchers. The Distinguished Visiting Fellowship Scheme allows distinguished visitors from outside the UK to visit a UK institution for up to a month, and it provides travel support and living expenses. Global Research Awards allow UK engineers to travel abroad to conduct research for 3–12 months or in modules over three years. International Travel Grants from the Royal Academy allow graduate students, researchers, and faculty to receive partial funding for travel for up to two months for research activities abroad with both universities and industry.

Launched in 2014 and classified as official development assistance, the Newton Fund promotes economic development activities through partnerships between the UK and OECD countries such as Brazil, Chile, China, Colombia, Egypt, India, Indonesia, Kazakhstan, Kenya, Malaysia, Mexico, Philippines, South Africa, Thailand, Turkey, and Vietnam. The Newton Fund aims to strengthen science and innovation capacity through strong, sustainable, and systemic relationships. The fund's activities reflect three themes: capacity building among researchers and scientists, research collaborations in development topics, and collaborative solutions to development challenges through innovation.[14]

Additional Opportunities for Mobility: International Sabbaticals and Post-Doctoral Activities

Emerging nations frequently send researchers and post-docs abroad for access to laboratories, equipment, and technical skills; and international post-docs, teachers, and scientists are routinely hired in the United States across all disciplines. International mobility is also an important priority for scholars from the United States and Europe. As discussed previously in this chapter, time and money are absolutely essential to promoting international research activity. Although not an exhaustive list, the information below is intended to provide a sense of the scope of opportunities available for research sabbaticals for faculty and we also briefly address international programs to support post-docs.

- *Alexander von Humboldt Foundation Research Fellowships* support highly qualified scholars who are under 40 years of age of all nationalities and disciplines for long-term research projects in Germany.

- *American Australian Association* supports well-defined research projects in Australia in one of the following fields: life sciences, engineering, medicine, and mining.
- *American Council of Learned Societies* offers several fellowships which help scholars devote 6–12 continuous months to full-time research and writing. Awards are available to assistant, associate, and full professors with a PhD.
- *East European Studies Program* supports research that will contribute to a better understanding of the region and related policymaking.
- *New Perspectives on Chinese Culture & Society* supports projects in the humanities and social sciences that bridge disciplinary or geographic boundaries, engage new sources, develop fresh approaches to traditional materials and issues, or otherwise bring innovative perspectives to the study of Chinese culture and society.
- *American Research Institute in Turkey* provides fellowships in fields of the humanities and social sciences to engage in research projects in Turkey.
- *American-Scandinavian Foundation Fellowships* support scholarly research in Denmark, Finland, Iceland, Norway, and Sweden.
- *Camargo Foundation* offers fellowships for scholars to pursue projects in the humanities and social sciences related to French and francophone cultures. The foundation also sponsors the projects of writers, visual artists, photographers, video artists, filmmakers, media artists, and composers.
- *Charles Wallace Pakistan Trust* sponsors one scholar or a practitioner from Pakistan as a visitor to the Department of Politics and International Relations for one Oxford University term in each academic year, to advance the understanding of contemporary problems and issues facing Pakistan across a broad range of themes.
- *Chiang Ching-kuo Foundation for International Scholarly Exchange* provides fellowships, research awards, and travel grants for scholars conducting research in the humanities and social sciences related to Chinese studies or to Taiwan.
- *Council of American Overseas Research Centers* provides support to scholars who wish to conduct research in more than one country, at least one of which hosts a participating American overseas research

center. Fields of interest include the humanities, social sciences, and allied natural sciences.

- *German Academic Exchange Service* offers fellowships for short- or long-term research projects in Germany.
- *Guggenheim Memorial Foundation* offers fellowships to citizens from Canada and the United States to further the development of scholars and artists in all fields of inquiry and creative endeavors by assisting them to engage in research and knowledge acquisition.
- *Hugh le May Fellowship–Rhodes University* supports three- to four-month residential fellowships at Rhodes University in South Africa for senior scientists with a well-established research record, to work on research in philosophy; classics; ancient, medieval, or modern history; classical, biblical, medieval, or modern languages; political theory; or law.
- *International Research and Exchanges Board* offers several programs for U.S. scholars and professionals to conduct research in Europe and Eurasia.
- *Japan Society for the Promotion of Science* offers short- and long-term programs for researchers in fields of the natural and social sciences and the humanities. The society administers of a wide spectrum of Japan's scientific and academic programs including promoting international scientific cooperation.
- *Remarque Institute* supports research on political, regional, ethnic, religious, linguistic, cultural, and economic encounters and conflicts in contemporary Europe and between Europe and North America.
- *Social Science Research Council* provides fellowships to scholars from the social sciences, humanities, and the natural sciences through various international fellowship programs.
- *University of Edinburgh Institute for Advanced Studies in the Humanities Fellowships* offer support for scholars to undertake advanced study in Edinburgh focusing on the humanities and on specific research themes provided by the Institute.

There are many programs to support doctoral research and post-doctoral activities internationally—too many to list in this book. Here are a few: In the United States, the Fulbright-Hays Program administers funding for doctoral and post-doctoral research conducted outside the United States and supports a variety of overseas programs designed to foster training, research, and curriculum development in non-Western foreign languages and area studies. The NSF's International Research Fellowship Program provides awards for scientists and engineers in the early stages of their careers, including postdocs, to conduct research abroad. The Fogarty International Center at the NIH sponsors the Global Health Program for Fellows and Scholars, which provides supportive mentorship, research opportunities, and a collaborative research environment for early stage investigators (doctoral and post-doctoral scholars) from the United States and low- and middle-income countries, as defined by the World Bank, to enhance their global health research expertise and their careers.

The Ministry of Science and Technology of China has sponsored a post-doctoral program of one to two years for African researchers through the China-Africa Science and Technology Partnership Program. The program is designed to further enhance cooperation and exchange in science and technology between China and Africa and to build the scientific capacity among African nations.

The Oxford-Princeton Global Leaders Fellowship Program includes post-doctoral fellowships in world politics and political economy for individuals from emerging countries. Fellowships are awarded for a year's study at Oxford University, followed by a year at Princeton University.

Advancement and Fundraising

The Office of University Advancement and Alumni Relations is an important partner in generating funds for international research. Some universities provide development officers to work specifically with the international affairs offices, while others may focus on a single, major international program.

It is essential that development officers convey the importance of international research to the university's mission and why the university plays an important role in today's global agenda. They need to explain how international research contributes to the career opportunities of students, offers professional opportunities and development for faculty, and enhances the reputation of the university. These officers must also be able to describe how international research aids economic development of the community and local businesses—not to mention improving societal conditions across the globe. And, they must have firsthand knowledge of the university's current international programs, research connections abroad, and new opportunities for greater international connections.

University advancement personnel are encouraged to work with administrators and faculty to determine what opportunities are available within the local, regional, and international communities to support global research engagement (see diaspora communities in Chapter 6), and they may also wish to seek guidance from key stakeholders about how best to articulate the value of global engagement to potential donors, to convince them of the importance of including international programs and activities in their philanthropic gifts and to encourage them to become investors in the futures of students and partners with gifts that would enable both students and faculty to work and learn in international settings. A gift can "mean the world" to the professional development of a student or faculty member.

Information sharing can occur through presentation(s) to, or discussions with, the university's philanthropic organizations (e.g., a foundation board or office of advancement) that explain the centrality of international research to student success and the university's mission, as well as to discovering new and innovative solutions to universal problems such as energy, food security and sustainability, public health, and/or economic development. Development offices need to know where the university's subject-matter expertise connects with the interests of donors. It is equally important that development officers who are building a donor base that includes international donors have a working knowledge of customs, traditions, and norms for giving that are characteristic of the donors' countries of origin.

Certain international research programs at universities are highly attractive to corporate and/or foundation donors (e.g., Engineers Without Borders), and international initiatives announced from the president's or chancellor's office can be highly successful in raising money. The Chancellor's Global Education Fund at the University of North Carolina (UNC) Chapel Hill has raised more than $788,000 in unrestricted private gifts, cumulative over five fiscal cycles, from alumni, parents, students, and friends to support the university's strategic global priorities that serve the state of North Carolina, the nation, and the world. Investments are made in international student internships and fellowships (undergraduate and graduate), faculty research, course development grants, student and faculty global exchanges, and grants to strengthen and expand global partnerships, preferable with UNC strategic or emerging partners.[15] Awards are made to UNC faculty to travel abroad for joint research or course development, conferences, and symposia on topics of global significance, and to serve on student committees or other collaborative activities. Funds are also provided each year for one interdisciplinary student team to work together on a research or service project outside the United States.

The advancement officers will have the best understanding of the private sources for funding and the activities most likely to be supported, but they will need to rely upon administrators and faculty to help define their goals explicitly. The following are a few examples of advancement or fundraising initiatives:

- *Endowed research professorships* (named) connected to a specific geographic area of the world or work with a global perspective (e.g., alternative energy, infectious disease, or international diplomacy). The University of Georgia, for example, has an endowed professorship in global health matched with an endowed stipend for a graduate student so that research by both faculty mentor and student can be conducted simultaneously.

- *Visiting scholars.* Columbus State University has three endowed programs to invite scholars in Latin American studies and Asian students.
- A named *university lecture series* that focuses on the impact and outcomes of international research and engagement on a specific topic.
- Named *annual conferences or workshops* that support international research on a specific theme.
- *Facilities.* Development dollars were raised to pay for apartments for visiting scholars and to purchase the Spencer House at Oxford University (Columbus State University, Columbus, Georgia).
- *Funding for area or discipline centers, institutes, and activities*; for example an interdisciplinary center for sustainability, a center for the study of Latin American and the Caribbean, or an institute for the study of global security (food, water, human, cyber).
- *Funding for specific international collections* in the library.
- *Endowed study-abroad scholarships* for study or research experiences (e.g., the Wolfe Scholarship Program at The Ohio State University provides $2,000 to 25 students each year to study abroad. These funds are provided as an annual gift).
- *Special scholarships and exchange programs* that develop endowments for interactions with countries where the university has had long-standing and/or newer, but meaningful, relationships.
- *Funding for professional development* opportunities or programs for faculty interested in international research.[16]
- *Endowment for a fellows program* like the Foundation Fellows at the University of Georgia, the Franklin Fellows at North Carolina, or the Jefferson Fellows at the University of Virginia. Such fellowship programs typically offer one or more international research experiences to students over a summer and/or during shorter breaks in the academic calendar.

- *Development of promotional materials* in support of globally engaged research. Market international research engagement and its impact on billboards, public transportation, airport concourses, and other public venues. Include "call-outs" to international research in university brochures, marketing materials, and information associated with athletic programs. University research magazines invariably include articles about international collaborations and should be distributed strategically. The University of Florida, for example, places the summer edition of its research magazine as an insert into *Florida Trend*,[17] and thus the work of university investigators can be seen by 65,000 readers of the magazine, at least once a year.

Strategies for Tapping Sources of Support

Many universities organize mini-campaigns for special interest activities and programs (such as international programs and the graduate school) that do not have a disciplinary base (e.g., engineering, medicine, journalism, and communications) but cut across almost all programs in the university. No one earns a degree from these programs, but they support and enhance the work individuals accomplish within their disciplines and degree programs. Cornell University, for example, organized a $15 million international fundraising effort. Contributions from faculty and staff during annual giving campaigns can also be encouraged, especially if international programs are highlighted as a university priority. Other strategies can be adopted as well:

- Develop a method (in person or online) for collecting small donations at university or community events for the benefit of students' international research activities. This has been especially successful in "crisis" situations where funds are raised with rapid turn-around to support victims of natural disasters in other countries.

- Consider thematic fundraising events for specific diaspora groups. Individuals of international origin may wish to support the education costs of students from their countries to engage in a research project or experience that connects with others in their home countries.

- Disseminate research findings relevant to local community groups and acknowledge the importance of local-international research with members of diaspora communities—not all international research takes place outside the institution's borders.

- Promote partnerships with international universities that extend the resources available for research abroad, or establish graduate research programs with partner universities outside the country.

- Approach transnational or multinational corporations and businesses about their interest in supporting international research activities that align with their company's goals. These projects may include students and faculty (e.g., financial institutions, manufacturing, or technology).[18]
- Develop relationships with foundations and nonprofits that support international activities. These connections may open doors to grant activities (e.g., America India Foundation, Asia Society, and Asia Foundation).

International Alumni

The international alumni of the university make up an important group to look to for monetary gifts and other types of support. Maintaining meaningful connections with them while they remain in country or after they return to their home countries is essential and can be accomplished through faculty mentors, departmental offices, and college offices, as well as the university's development and alumni offices. Connections with international alumni can be made at various levels and by a number of offices across the university. Depending on the culture of the institution, such efforts might be centralized in the office of advancement or development, within an alumni or outreach office, within the international office, or by individual departments or colleges. At best, all of these units coordinate in this effort. At the university level, an International Alumni Council can serve as a vehicle for connecting with alumni from different countries, who remain in touch with the university and have a history of providing financial support or could be new donors.

Connecting with International Alumni at Home

International alumni living and working near to the university can be involved in specific dialogues regarding international research efforts with various university groups such as academic departments, researchers, graduate students, and administrators. They are a source of information about international events and opportunities, and they might also participate in thematic meetings or workshops on topics such as global business, global education, global health, global citizenship, and so forth. International alumni are key ambassadors for university outreach and fundraising especially among cultures where charitable giving to HEIs is uncommon. It is important to cultivate an awareness among international students, scholars, and alumni about their role in advancing the goals of the university—nowhere is this more critical than in the countries where government resources for public institutions are in decline.

Connecting with International Alumni Abroad

The Internet and social networks provide significant opportunities to stay connected with alumni residing abroad temporarily or having returned to their native countries upon degree completion. Databases created and maintained by a centralized alumni office or by individual alumni officers situated in particular colleges or units allow universities to stay connected with alumni who either received a degree from the institution or experienced the university as an exchange student or scholar and now live abroad. It must be clear that there are restrictions on how these data are used in order to protect the privacy of the individuals registered. A number of these alumni could help in their home countries in the recruitment of students, alumni networking, fundraising, and the identification of opportunities for research initiatives or collaborations for faculty and students. Alumni abroad can also help the university by hosting or assisting faculty and graduate students conducting research abroad or by connecting them with in-country funding opportunities or industry partnerships. Faculty traveling or living abroad while conducting research should make a special effort to connect with alumni in the geographical areas where they are working,

Many universities have established either formal or informal alumni clubs in locations around the world. The University of Wisconsin, for example, has organized more than 50 such clubs, often several in one country (e.g., India). Alumni groups abroad offer support to newly admitted students within their country before they depart, as well as welcoming graduates within the country when they return home. The Wisconsin Alumni Association assists the university in shaping its global agenda and identifying avenues for impactful engagement.

The International Alumni Chapter of the Alumni Association of the University of Nevada, Reno, is coordinated by alumni and staff in the Office of International Students and Scholars, rather than through the office of advancement or development. It was created in 2003 to assemble a global network of alumni who are international students and alumni living outside the United States, plus alumni and friends with international experiences and/or interests. Activities of the association include providing a forum that networks alumni who were international students or who have international interests for mutually beneficial activities, promoting cultural awareness in their communities; advocating for the importance of international education and intercultural experiences such as globalized research; and establishing an endowment for scholarships for international students, to support international programs and activities, and to capitalize on new opportunities.

Setting the Stage for Successful International Research Endeavors

Creating and maintaining a support ecosystem for international research will encourage sustained global activity and ensure knowledgeable assistance when problems or challenges arise. Universities almost without exception have resources and support available to advance and facilitate international research and global engagement by faculty, staff, and students who are already involved, as well as those who are interested in beginning international scholarly activities. Often, however, such services and personnel cross administrative units, rendering navigation of the support system for international research closer to mountain climbing than smooth sailing. A designated office or unit, as discussed in Chapter 1, for coordinating or bridging common, essential functions of the research and international offices or a "one-stop" for existing services and development of new services, as well as for identifying sources of funding to support international programs for research, is highly advantageous and is especially important for key tasks such as export control, risk management (travel and health), travel assistance, contract negotiation, intellectual property rights, and management of financial transactions and legal matters. The costs and benefits of these activities should be shared, optimally, among the research and international offices. Alternatively, a university may situate a research administrator in the international office or vice versa.

An example of a robust support system for researchers, as well as research administrators, is The Research Administration Information Network (TRAIN® at USF). The TRAIN team is part of the university's research support infrastructure to enhance the professional competencies of those who contribute to the research enterprise, through training and education, improving business processes and reporting, and enhancing communication within the university research community. TRAIN has provided a valuable support service to researchers by developing consistent practices and a network of highly competent, well-informed research administrators to support research across disciplinary, departmental, college, and campus boundaries. While the TRAIN enterprise is housed within the research office at USF, its members represent a community of practice composed of offices and units from across the university including the international offices at all three of its campuses.

Other ideas to expand a support ecosystem include the following:

1. Provide an online toolkit that includes quick links to guides and instructions, tools and forms, online training, and commonly used (or boilerplate) language, for each phase of the research administration life cycle. Include dedicated resources and guidance specific to international research.
2. Develop and keep an up-to-date funding opportunities database or catalogue that highlights sources for international research from national and

international agencies, foundations, NGOs, and other private or industry sources. Search engines such as PIVOT are excellent tools for identifying funding sources and potential collaborators. A digital newsletter with selected opportunities or the use of social media can inform scholars of new opportunities. Funding announcements to individuals according to discipline expertise, membership in interdisciplinary teams, past global activity, and other attributes increase the likelihood that emails and announcements will be read and acted upon. Information about international research opportunities gathered by the international and research offices (as well as with colleges or faculties) should be routinely made available within the university community in a coordinated fashion.

3. Assist researchers with networking and identifying collaborators within and outside the university by maintaining internal lists or a database of faculty who are interested in international collaborative research, sorting this information according to discipline or specialty and matching groups with funding announcements, and facilitating and supporting interdisciplinary team building, especially in the context of large, complex, interdisciplinary grant proposals.

4. Develop and maintain a searchable international engagement and activities database for faculty of the university (including all types of activities not just research) with information about researcher nationality, language capabilities, international awards, and other forms of international engagement including leadership in international organizations and consultant positions. Faculty can enter or modify their information as an entrée into a networked community. If this online tool is also outward facing, researchers external to the university will be able to use it to identify areas of expertise and collaborators as well.

5. Organize targeted workshops and training sessions for faculty, staff, and students about how to find funding for international research, how to navigate particular schemes such as Horizon 2020, the EU Framework Program for Research and Innovation, and to promote strategies for successful proposal writing and the responsible conduct of international research.

6. Assist faculty in navigating export control regulations and encourage compliance by advertising the point of contact for the management of export control policy and by assuring this individual(s) is readily accessible to faculty and students. Workshops on export controls, deemed exports, dual-use technology, and controlled equipment can be offered as face-to-face training and/or as online education, and certification of export controls familiarity can be provided to staff, administrators, faculty, and students who participate. A reference list of activities, labs, and

equipment that are restricted based on the nationality of a researcher should also be readily available.

7. Make the most of partnerships for student and faculty research collaborations and fieldwork experiences by creating an inventory or an accessible and searchable database that contains all the university's agreements with partner universities. This information can be housed separately or integrated into a larger international engagement database. Ideally, the database will contain information about the goals of the partnership; what activities have taken place or are currently ongoing; and outputs such as papers, conferences, and grants with each partner institution. If student exchange agreements are in place, include the extent of student involvement.

8. Regularly assess the productivity of international partnerships and their contributions to research activity—for both faculty and students. The University of Queensland in Australia has a sophisticated methodology for evaluating its international partnerships. The Partner Engagement Framework[19] measures engagement with international partner universities using 16 data-driven indicators related to various aspects of student learning, research, and staffing. The instrument allows the university to assess areas of strength and the potential for future engagement, as well as where further development of a partnership is needed. Data and results are presented on a sliding scale to demonstrate low, medium, and high engagement with international partners. Such data collection and evaluation are invaluable to measure the impact of international engagement and outcomes from partnerships (see also Chapter 4).

9. Design an interactive international engagement map that identifies where faculty and students are currently involved in research, training, or teaching. The information should be accessible beyond the university community. A mobile app can be created to access this type of information as well.

Until a university has comprehensively taken stock of its global footprint, it cannot hope to have a true picture of its depth and breadth of international engagement. This is especially true for international research by faculty who are independent and more internationally engaged than most of their employers are aware. Mapping the university's global footprint allows faculty and students to identify collaborators, mentors, or informed colleagues; it gives international students a sense of what the university is doing and where; it allows leaders to identify locations of strategic emphasis and opportunity—especially for research collaboration; and it assists with the design of metrics to evaluate and enhance the data supporting the university's ranking, reputation, and prestige.

Managing Risk and Ensuring Research Integrity

Risk and safety protocols associated with international research extend to technology, software, equipment, human health and safety, biosecurity (measures taken to stop the spread or introduction of harmful organisms to human, animal, and plant life), financial risk, legal risk (when operating outside domestic laws and jurisdiction), and the risk to the reputation of the university. Research norms and practices (in the field and in the laboratory), and rules and regulations regarding human and animal subjects vary across nations. Staff in both the research and international offices need to be aware of cultural and/or religious norms and sensitivities, and expectations regarding ethics. International research should be conducted according to the highest ethical standards, but applying one set of standards to all regions of the world is simply not possible. Sharing of best practices across borders is an excellent way to improve research conduct among all researchers.

Export control regimes are of particular importance to international research and universities that fail to adhere to their country's laws face stiff penalties. These regulations are designed for the purpose of protecting a country's economic and trade goals and for restricting the sharing of technology and goods that could contribute to the military potential of adversaries. Multilateral export control regimes allow nations to work collaboratively to combat the proliferation of chemical, biological, and nuclear weapons and weapons delivery systems.[20] Most of the information, technology, or software that a university shares with its colleagues and research partners is not export controlled or subject to trade sanctions. HEIs are designed to encourage knowledge sharing, but national laws (such as those in the United States) may require universities to monitor the transfer of certain items and information regulated for reasons of national security, trade sanctions policy, antiterrorism, or nonproliferation. Many countries maintain export controls similar to the United States that require federal "licenses" (or permission) for certain items that are personally shared with foreign nationals in country or abroad, shipped overseas, or delivered electronically abroad or to foreign nationals in country. The European Union has a classification system, and member nations may maintain their own protocols as well. Export controls officers who are knowledgeable not only about their national law but regulations from partner countries are critical for research-intensive institutions, globally expanding institutions, institutions with large numbers of foreign nationals, and institutions developing or using cutting-edge technology.[21]

Research and international offices must work together to manage the export controls operation within the university. To assist faculty and students, a single point person for export control management should be identified. Staff from both the research and international offices should be cross-trained about export controls laws and policies and how export control is managed at the university. Research and international offices (and other offices that serve students and visitors) should be aware of students, scholars, and researchers arriving from countries deemed "high risk" and where they will be working in university and medical laboratories. For example, U.S. export controls preclude the participation of foreign nationals in research that involves restricted technology without first obtaining a license or license exception from the appropriate government agency. Many universities use subscription software platforms for managing the export control screening process (eCustoms Visual Compliance, AEB's Compliance||Xpress, etc.).

While the management of export controls is well established in universities with successful records of international research engagement, far fewer universities employ one or more full-time dedicated risk and safety officer(s) whose role it is to provide (or coordinate) support services for students, faculty, and staff participating in university sponsored programs, activities, or other university affiliated travel outside of the country. Vital resources for researchers include country-specific information concerning in-country political, economic, social, and/or environmental risks; thorough risk and security assessments of travel destinations; advice concerning specific safety and security issues; risk mitigation strategies; and a dedicated 24/7 international assistance telephone number available to faculty, staff, and students traveling abroad.

Universities must maintain a reporting system for international travel by faculty and students and may choose to fund (or discount) the cost of travel insurance for faculty and students traveling out of the country. Accurate information about the location of travelers is vital to helping the university provide the highest quality of care (health, safety and welfare) for students, faculty, and staff while abroad. Risk and safety information can be sent electronically to those traveling abroad proactivity. A checklist of procedures for faculty and students to follow when conducting research and traveling abroad should be developed (possibly as an app) so that they are fully informed about financial issues, travel advisories, business practices, and export controls policies (each university will want to create its own list and method of delivery).

Intellectual Property

Researchers also need assistance navigating the labyrinth of rules and regulations regarding intellectual property (IP) assets and rights (patents, copyrights, and trademarks) and licensing agreements. Collaboration between the research and international offices is essential as IP becomes an increasingly important dimension of global research collaboration. It is essential to define and determine IP rights at the beginning of an international partnership; a pre-proposal or separate memorandum of understanding (MOU) may be necessary to clearly establish who (what entity) owns (or will own) what. Conduct due diligence *before* an IP or licensing issues arises, and be prepared for a variety of interpretation regarding ownership. Develop a cadre of contract managers with legal and global training who work collaboratively on international financial and IP issues. Know when to rely on in-house expertise and when the complexity of a project or partnership necessitates utilizing consultants and/or outside experts. Cultivating an approach to the management of international research requires adaptability and open-mindedness on the part of all parties involved (see Chapter 5.).

Recognition and Reward of International Activities within the University

Acknowledging the contributions and successes of researchers is just as important as incentivizing and supporting their international engagement. There are many ways in which a university might choose to recognize and reward global scholarship so that researchers view internationalization as a "value proposition" for their career development. Many of the examples included here are well-known but two characteristics are universally important: awards should be presented annually at events sponsored by the president, chancellor, or chief academic officer—in other words, the status of the awards should be commensurate with other prestigious university awards or activities; and the accomplishments of the recipients should be publicized inside and outside of the institution. In Chapter 9 we offer a discussion of how to support and reward innovation and entrepreneurship in the global community. Here we focus on examples of events and activities that recognize more traditional research endeavors:

A gala award event—either a breakfast, lunch, or dinner—is given for those who have contributed significant international research during an academic year and/or over his or her career. Specific criteria for awards can be determined to suit the profile of the institution.

Faculty research awards are given during International Education Week in November (United States) at a high-level event. International Education Week is a joint initiative of the U.S. Department of State and U.S. Department of Education that provides an opportunity to celebrate the benefits of international education and exchange worldwide. Other international events provide opportunities for synching international research awards in a broader context. For example, in 2015–16, the University of Pretoria in South Africa celebrated International Map Year. To celebrate International Women's Day in March of 2016, UNESCO organized, in cooperation with the Academy of Scientific Research and Technology in Egypt, a series of conferences to promote and recognize contributions to bioethics and the rights of women at Ain Shams University in Cairo. Global Entrepreneurship Week is also celebrated around the world each year (see Chapter 5).

The University of Texas at San Antonio awards the President's Distinguished Achievement Award for Advancing Globalization to recognize, encourage, and reward either an individual or a team of faculty who have significantly expanded the university's involvement in the global arena. The distinguished faculty will have made contributions in one or more of the following areas: the development and implementation of international components into the curriculum, study-abroad programs, and collaborations with foreign institutions. North Carolina State recognizes outstanding accomplishments in globally engaged teaching, research, extension, engagement, or economic development by its faculty and staff with the Outstanding Global Engagement Award. Successful recipients have made important international contributions in one or more of the following aspects of the university's mission: research and discovery, teaching and learning, engagement, extension and economic development, and impacts and accomplishments. Each September, on University Day, the Oregon State University Faculty Senate recognizes the extraordinary contributions of faculty and staff who enhance student, faculty, and staff awareness and participation in international education and research. The University of South Florida recognizes its Fulbright fellows every year during International Education Week and present medallions to those who have receive Fulbright Awards during the previous year.

In addition to individual awards, a team award for "Excellence in Global Engagement" could be given to one department or unit which has done exceptionally well supporting international research, implementing creative strategies to help faculty and/or students implement international research projects, or identifying best practices that facilitate international mobility.

Letters of recognition from the president, chancellor, chief academic officer, or other senior leadership are greatly appreciated, and they are further evidence of the university's prioritization of global engagement. The university might also choose to organize a Society of Global Fellows (or similarly named group) and hold regular receptions or events that connect the fellows with students and the broader community.

Faculty could be rewarded with a membership in the Phi Beta Delta Honor Society for International Scholars (or another professional group), in recognition of their international contributions. The Phi Beta Delta Honor Society has chapters across the United States and in Canada, Mexico, Italy, Switzerland, Ukraine, Bulgaria, and Uganda. The goal of the organization is to recognize the scholarly achievement of scholars and students and to provide a network on each university campus, and across institutions, of faculty, staff, and students involved in international endeavors.

The research and international offices could create a database of external international awards and identify faculty and student candidates who are eligible. Faculty may not be aware that they are eligible for an award or may feel as though they do not have the time to complete an application for an award or honor as compared to a grant application and thus could be assisted with the application process. While the Nobel Prize remains the penultimate recognition for international knowledge generation among scholars, there are many other opportunities for bestowing recognition for global scholarship. For example, the Ordre des Palmes Académiques (Order of Academic Palms) is a national order of France for distinguished academics and figures around the world who have made major contributions to French national education and culture. Universities that have invested in staff support for identifying qualified candidates and for application submission (collecting and organizing nomination materials) have seen their rates of success with awards increase dramatically.

Assisting Global Scholars at Risk

Across history and around the world, scholars have suffered harassment, torture, and persecution as a result of their work. In the worst cases, scholars pay with their lives for their dedication to freedom of thought. Scholar rescue programs are designed as a lifeline for threatened researchers who have a credible claim of being at risk in their home countries or as a refugee and those who are the victim of human rights abuses, censorship, intimidation and/or violence. The Spring 2015 issue of the IIE Networker is devoted to the topic of "Supporting Higher Education During Crisis and Recovery." Article from experts and practitioners provide advice for supporting students and scholars from troubled areas of the world.[22] These individuals are not only saved, but their work adds value to collaborative research around the world.

In response to the crisis in Syria, in late 2015, several UK universities announced scholarships and fellowships to professors and students fleeing the conflict. The Campaign for the Public University has called upon HEIs to provide refuge to scholars and students who will ideally be able to contribute to rebuilding their societies in the future. The University of East London, the University of York, and the University of Sussex have each designed programs for Syrian refugees. The program implemented by the University of York includes student scholarships, scholar rescue status for academics, and funding for public events to raise awareness about the refugee crises in Syria, North Africa, and the larger Middle East.[23]

Scholars at Risk Network

The Scholars at Risk (SAR) began in the Human Rights Program of the University of Chicago in 1999 and is currently housed at New York University. The network comprises many universities and has collectively helped hundreds of scholars from around the world. In 2001, SAR joined with other international education and human rights organizations to launch the Network for Education and Academic Rights (NEAR). NEAR is a clearing house of information about academic freedom and education rights and a coordinator of joint action on reports of academic rights violations. The NEAR offices are hosted by the Council for Assisting Refugee Academics (CARA).

Council for Assisting Refugee Academics (CARA)

CARA, an NGO headquartered in London, helps endangered scholars connect with colleagues within the wider academic and scientific communities, facilitating collaboration and ending isolation, so that when possible, they are equipped to rebuild their societies. CARA helps scholars build new lives and careers where they can use their talents and skills for the good of society. CARA also runs programs to help those trying to continue to work in their home countries. The support of more than 100 universities that make up the CARA SAR UK Universities Network is central to the effective delivery of CARA's work.

Together with CARA, the SAR Network helped to organize the CARA/SAR UK Universities Network, a partner network of universities in the United Kingdom working with CARA and SAR to help refugee scholars in the UK, as well as threatened scholars still in their home countries. SAR has also developed partner networks throughout Europe, the Middle East, and Africa, with the hope of building a truly global constituency pledged to promote academic freedom and defend threatened scholars and universities everywhere.

IIE Scholar Rescue Fund

The U.S.-based Institute of International Education (IIE), also a partner with SAR, established its endowed Scholar Rescue Fund (SRF) in 2002. The fund provides vital financial support to scholars facing grave threats so that they may escape dangerous conditions and continue their academic work in safety. The SRF fellowships have enabled over 625 scholars from more than 50 countries to escape from harm, find temporary refuge anywhere in the world, and continue to share their knowledge with students, colleagues, and the broader community. Candidates may undertake their fellowships at host colleges, universities, research centers, and other academic institutions in any safe country. Universities share the cost of the annual expenses for a scholar to live and work in their institution. The scholar's duties while on fellowship depend on the needs of the host partner and the scholar. Many SRF fellows teach courses, conduct independent research, participate in lecture series and conferences or seminars, and otherwise contribute to the university. The hope is that during the fellowship period, conditions in the scholars' home countries might improve to allow their safe return; if safe return is not possible, the goal is for scholar to use the period of the fellowship to identify a longer-term opportunity to continue their work.

IIE Iraq Scholar Rescue Project

In response to critical need, the SRF made a commitment in 2007 to protect Iraqi scholars who faced imminent threats to their lives and careers. The IIE SRF fellowship support allows Iraqi scholars to resume their research and teaching activities. Scholars receive funding to cover relocation costs from Iraq to the host institution as well as a living stipend and health insurance for a one-year period. Supplemental funding is given to scholars for participating in academic conferences in Iraq, in scholars' host countries, and internationally. SRF fellowship holders also receive funding for English language and professional skills training, distance education projects, and publishing costs. Fellowships may be renewed for a second year; renewals are determined by academic work carried out during the first year and by whether or not circumstances continue to prevent a safe return home.

IIE Artist Protection Fund

IIE developed the Artist Protection Fund, with support from the Mellon Foundation, to fill a critical unmet need to provide relief and safe haven to artists (from any field of artistic endeavor, such as visual arts, writing, music, dance, and theater) at host universities and arts centers in safe countries where they can continue their work on a large scale and for extended periods. While current emergency arts efforts in the United States and Europe advocate for artists and provide short-term assistance to get them out of immediate danger, a larger effort is needed to enable threatened artists to continue their work until conditions permit a safe return or resettlement in a more hospitable environment. Hosts are requested to provide matching support, which may include housing, studio space, and arts supplies.

The German Humboldt Foundation Philipp Schwartz Initiative–Germany

The Humboldt Foundation's Philipp Schwartz Initiative supports universities and research institutions in Germany that are able to offer a threatened scholar the opportunity of an extended research stay. The Humboldt Foundation imposes no restrictions with regard to country of origin or current location if the scholar is demonstrably threatened. Currently, 20 fellowships are available, which include fellowship subsidies of up to 3,500 euros per month for 24 months and a lump sum of 12,000 euros for the host institution.

APPENDIX

Organizations Supporting International Research Administration and Engagement

Associates in Cultural Exchange (A.C.E.) is a nonprofit, 501(c)3 corporation headquartered in Seattle, WA. Since 1973, A.C.E. has been working "to make the world your community" by helping people and organizations around the world establish relationships and build interpersonal networks across language and cultural divides. The organization has helped American businesses and universities create partnerships across the countries of the Arabian Gulf. A.C.E. core strategies involve language and intercultural education including English as a second language, a world language curriculum for children and young adults, cross-cultural orientations, academic and career preparation, tailored training programs, conference management, educational tours, and consulting services.

Association of Commonwealth Universities is the world's first and oldest international university network, established in 1913 in London. It is home to the Global Research Management Network and is a founding member of International Network of Research Management Societies (INORMS). The organization supports a number of capacity building initiatives in research management and research uptake across Africa.

Association of Research Managers and Administrators (UK) was organized in 1991, as the professional association for research managers and administrators in the UK. The majority of the 1,100 members are from the UK's 175 universities, but the association also includes members from hospitals, research institutes, and funders from the UK and other countries in Europe and Africa. Its mission is to facilitate excellence in research by identifying and establishing best practices in research management and administration, which it does by providing training for research managers and administrators; promoting networking activities for the exchange of best practice and for mutual support among members; and raising the profile of research management and administration as a profession.

The Australia Research Council supports international research collaboration, partnerships, developments, and policy in Australia.

Australasian Research Management Society was formed in 1999, for members working in universities, hospitals, medical centers, industry, government, and research institutes across Australia.

Canadian Association of Research Administrators was established in 1971 and represents 1,000 members of diverse backgrounds and is committed to advancing the profession of research administration through advocacy and opportunities for professional development and to improving the efficiency and effectiveness of research administration at post-secondary institutions, hospitals, and other research-intensive organizations. This organization collaborates with other organizations that are active in the research enterprise including the Network of Networks, Canada's alliance for excellence in clinical research.

CRDF Global is an independent, nonprofit organization authorized by the U.S. Congress and established by the NSF to promote international scientific and technical collaboration through grants, technical resources, and training. CRDF Global has worked in more than 40 countries in Eurasia, Asia, Africa, and the Middle East to manage programs and support emerging science and technology infrastructure, focusing specifically on programs of global threat reduction, global nonproliferation, biological, chemical and nuclear security, and public health security. CRDF Global advances international partnerships with colleagues around the world to strengthen the quality of research in all countries, generate new knowledge, and foster mutually beneficial relationships by providing grants and fellowships, conferences, proposal development workshops, and English language training. Funding is provided from several U.S. governmental agencies and regional science and research institutions in other countries.

Danish Association of Research Managers and Administrators was formed in 2006 and held its first formal annual meeting in June 2009. It has 130 members, with five large and five small universities. All universities in Denmark are represented, plus a few members from public and private sponsors and the private sector.

European Association of Research Managers and Administrators was formed in 1994 and has members in public and private research organizations from over 30 countries across Europe.

The Global Research Council is a virtual organization, composed of the heads of science and engineering funding agencies from around the world, dedicated to promoting the sharing of data and best practices for high-quality collaboration among funding agencies worldwide.

International Network of Research Management Societies (INORMS) was formed in 2001 to bring together research management societies and associations from across the globe to enable interactions, sharing of good practice, and joint activities between the member societies, to the benefit of their individual memberships. The nature of research management and administration is changing and becoming more professional. The economic and political imperatives and pressures are common across the globe. Each member society has its own distinct remit, constitution, membership, and geographical base, but each faces similar issues. The network enables the officers of the member societies to compare their national or regional issues and to learn from each other. Through INORMS, the partner organizations transfer training course structure, jointly develop training materials and content, and adopt comparable support mechanisms. The objectives of INORMS are to internationalize the body of knowledge on research management, exchange best practices, and develop international approaches to supporting the research enterprise. INORMS Congresses are held biennially, usually linked to one of the member societies' annual meetings. The first Congress took place in Brisbane in 2006, the second in Liverpool in 2008, and the third in Cape Town in 2010. The 2018 Congress will be in Edinburgh, Scotland. A journal, *Global Research*, is published by the organization.

International Research and Exchanges Board (IREX) is a U.S.-based nonprofit organization headquartered in Washington, DC, committed to international education in academic research, professional training, and technical assistance. IREX provides leadership and innovative programs to improve the quality of education, strengthen independent media, and foster pluralistic civil society development. Program activities include those focused on conflict resolution, technology for development, gender, and youth. Founded in 1968, IREX has an annual portfolio of over $60 million and a staff of 500 professionals worldwide. For over 20 years, IREX has received Title VIII funding from the U.S. Department of State, and with its partner IREX Europe, cross-cutting programs and consulting expertise are delivered in more than 100 countries.

Institute of International Education (IIE) is an independent nonprofit, founded in 1919, and is among the world's largest and most experienced international education and training organizations. IIE partners with governments, international development agencies, foundations, universities, and corporations, leveraging its international networks to collaborate on sustainable solutions for long-term development. The Council for International Exchange of Scholars joined IIE in 1997, and together, the two organizations continue to expand the Fulbright Program and its outstanding record of achievement. In 2010, IIE established the IIE Centers of Excellence to build higher education capacity, develop global academic partnerships, foster entrepreneurship and innovation, empower women through leadership, and conduct relevant research and policy analysis.

National Council of University Research Administrators (NCURA) was founded in 1959, and today the organization represents over 7,000 individuals with professional interests in the administration of sponsored programs at colleges, universities, teaching hospitals, and independent not-for-profit research institutes. NCURA's core mission is education, and it does this by providing over 40 programs each year with its training workshops, national conferences, television broadcasts, and online tutorials. NCURA has a robust website that includes virtual communities, designed by topic area, where colleagues may find the latest information and ask questions or provide information to each other. NCURA has an International Community, which is open to the world with the hope of sharing information and to promote understanding of research management practices throughout the profession. NCURA publishes a news magazine five times per year and has an online professional journal, *Research Management Review*. NCURA is also the publisher of numerous books on sponsored programs management. Each November, NCURA hosts its Annual Meeting in Washington, DC, where members gather for three days of more than 100 training sessions and workshops. NCURA maintains a national office in Washington, DC.

PraxisUnico was formed in 2010, by merging the Praxis and Unico organizations to become the UK's leading technology and knowledge transfer organization. PraxisUnico is an educational not-for-profit organization set up to support innovation and commercialization of public sector and charity research for social and economic impact. It encourages innovation and acts as a voice for the research commercialization profession, facilitating the interaction between the public sector research base, business, and government. PraxisUnico provides a forum for best practice exchange, underpinned by first-class training and development programs.

Research Councils UK represents the strategic partnership of the UK's seven Research Councils. It coordinates the country's global research strategy, supports key partnerships and funding opportunities, documents international activities, and sponsors teams located in China, India, the United States, and Europe.

Society of Research Administrators International (SRA) is a nonprofit association, founded in 1967, dedicated to the education and professional development of research administrators, as well as the enhancement of public understanding of the importance of research and its administration. SRA's mission reflects the following purposes: (1) the education of research administrators, professionals in related fields, and the public through the exchange of information, individual contacts, professional presentations, formal and informal meetings, and publications; and (2) the improvement of communications among researchers, host institutions and organizations, the sponsors of research administrators, and the general public. SRA continuously seeks to broaden and diversify its membership base of more than 3,500 individuals worldwide. SRA's mission and objectives reflect the demands of a growing profession. SRA's membership is drawn from universities, corporate businesses, health care facilities, governmental agencies, and nonprofit organizations.

Southern African Research and Innovation Management Association was formed in 2002 and has members across Southern Africa, including South Africa, Botswana, Namibia, Zimbabwe, and Lesotho.

The World Bank Research Alliance for Development is an informal, action-oriented, multidisciplinary network of researchers and academics that provides a platform for dialogue and exchange of ideas on international development. It currently comprises more than 700 representatives (individual members) from 450 academic institutions and research centers, as well as research units in NGOs, bilateral agencies, the private sector, and trade unions, from all over the world.

West African Research and Innovation Management Association was formed in 2007 and has members from across West Africa, including, Cameroon, Ghana, Nigeria, and Sierra Leone.

NOTES

[1] Institute of International Education. (2016). International Scholar Totals by Place of Origin, 2014/15–2015/16. In *Open Doors Report on International Educational Exchange*. Retrieved from http://www.iie.org/opendoors.

[2] Foderaro, L. (2011, March 9). More foreign-born scholars lead U.S. universities. *The New York Times*, p. A24. Retrieved from http://www.nytimes.com/2011/03/10/education/10presidents.html?_r=0

[3] O'Hara, S. (2009). Internationalizing the academy: The impact of scholar mobility. In R. Bhandari & S. Laughlin. (Eds.), *Higher education on the move: New developments in global mobility*. Second in a series of global education research reports. New York, NY: Institute of International Education.

[4] Helms, R. M. (2015). *Internationalizing the tenure code: Policies to promote a globally focused faculty*. Washington, DC: American Council on Education. The 61 colleges and universities were respondents to ACE's 2011 "Mapping Internationalization on U.S. Campuses" survey and indicated in the survey that "international work or experience was a consideration" in the tenure and advancement process.

[5] Criteria for reappointment, promotion, and tenure can be found in the faculty handbooks of each university. University of Minnesota: http://www.academic.umn.edu/provost/faculty/index.html; Rutgers University: https://uhr.rutgers.edu/faculty; Oregon State University: http://oregonstate.edu/admin/aa/faculty-handbook-promotion-and-tenure-guidelines; Michigan State University: https://www.hr.msu.edu/documents/facacadhandbooks/facultyhandbook/.

[6] Helms, R. M. (2016, spring). Internationalizing the tenure code. *IIE Networker*, 26–27. Retrieved from http://www.nxtbook.com/naylor/IIEB/IIEB0116/index.php#/28

[7] Brustein, W. (2010). It takes an entire institution: A blueprint for the global university. In R. Lewin (Ed.), *The handbook of practice and research in study abroad: Higher education and the quest for global citizenship*. New York, NY: Taylor and Francis, p. 258.

[8] IAPP is an initiative of the IIE Center for International Partnerships in Higher Education to increase the number of international partnerships between higher education institutions in the United States and abroad. Each year programs target specific countries, such as Mexico, Cuba, and Australia (IAPP, 2016. http://www.iie.org/iapp). Institutions prepare for the experience by developing an inventory of their interactions with the country, crafting a strategic plan with guidance, and visiting the country for a week with the goal of developing a strategic partnership(s).

[9] IU Bloomington Newsroom. (2015). *Faculty, students at IU Bloomington receive international research, teaching grants*. Statement made by Provost and Executive Vice President Lauren Robel. Retrieved from http://news.indiana.edu/releases/iu/2015/03/mellon-innovation-awards.shtml

[10] The "founding" universities include The College of William & Mary; University of California, Berkeley; Duke University; Makerere University (Uganda); Massachusetts Institute of Technology; Michigan State University; and Texas A&M University.

[11] Additional information about the Sustainable Higher Education Research Alliances in Indonesia can be accessed at http://www.iie.org/en/Programs/SHERA/Overview#.WEX08LIrKpo

[12] Retrieved from https://eca.state.gov/fulbright.

[13] U.S. and U.K. governments announce GII winners: Global Innovation Initiative Grants awarded to twenty-three university partnerships, April 24, 2014. Retrieved from: http://www.iie.org/Programs/Global-Innovation-Initiative/GII-Grantees/2014-GII-Grantees.

[14] To learn more about the Newton Fund, visit http://www.newtonfund.ac.uk/

[15] King's College London, National University of Singapore, Peking University, Tsinghau University, University of San Francisco de Quito, Minister of Health, Malawi.

[16] CIEE offers a series of International Faculty Development Seminars around the world. The programs are not research focused but do offer faculty an opportunity to experience international travel and the possibility of identify and developing new partnerships in the host country. "CIEE International Faculty Development Seminars provide faculty and administrators with access to rich academics, diverse intercultural experiences, and innovative approaches to learning and problem-solving that enhance syllabi, internationalize curricula, and increase global understanding on campus." Retrieved from https://www.ciee.org/international-faculty-development-seminars/seminars/

[17] *Florida Trend* is a monthly magazine covering Florida business, industry, education, and leisure.

[18] About 600 multinational companies control 25 percent of the world's economy and 80 percent of the world's trade. Of the top 100 companies in the United States, 52 percent are multinational companies. See Adams, J. M., & Carfagna, A. (2006). *Coming of age in a globalized world: The next generation.* Sterling, VA: Kumarian Press.

[19] Retrieved from http://www.uq.edu.au/international/partner-engagement-framework.

[20] U.S. Department of Commerce, Bureau of Security and Industry. *Multilateral Export Control Regimes.* Retrieved from: https://www.bis.doc.gov/index.php/policy-guidance/multilateral-export-control-regimes

[21] Retrieved from the Association of University Export Control Officers http://aueco.org/index.html

[22] IIE Networker. (Spring 2015). Retrieved from http://www.nxtbook.com/naylor/IIEB/IIEB0115/index.php?startid=34#/6

[23] Mogul, P. (2015). British universities offer scholarships to refugees as academics urge others to follow suit. *International Business Times UK.* Retrieved from http://www.ibtimes.co.uk/british-universities-offer-scholarships-refugees-academics-urge-others-follow-suit-1521474

Chapter Three
Engaging Students in International Research

Research is a driver for international student mobility.
Students go abroad to determine their futures.

Introduction

International education has emphasized study abroad programs as well as student and faculty exchange. International research may be part of these experiences, which are often efforts to find solutions to the global challenges that—because of their universality, complexity, and need for collaboration and multidisciplinary research—unite individuals, institutions, and nations (see Chapter 8). Solutions demand "experts" prepared in science, mathematics, technology, global knowledge, competence, cultural sensitivity, and language skills, who are committed to civic engagement at home and abroad.[1] These experts are the students who are educated in our universities. It is "through the process of addressing the world's problems that higher education is transformed"[2] and that students' breadth of understanding is expanded.

The partnerships established through research initiatives across borders take students into new and diverse environments and cultures, where they and their international colleagues become both teachers and learners, and they experience the life-changing potential of the international setting. Research experiences in partnership with others promote learning.

The act of teaching and learning itself builds bridges among people.[3]

STEM Education of U.S. and International Students

STEM Programs Connect Education, Innovation, Competitiveness, and the Economy

STEM (science, technology, engineering, mathematics) programs are at the forefront of education in virtually every country as the link between innovation, productivity, and the economy. Nations compare themselves in terms of the numbers of graduates they produce in the STEM fields and strive to recruit students nationally and globally to their universities. They also strive to keep their graduates, as it is the STEM graduates who provide "the critical input that drives the innovation-based economy forward"[4] and underpin the nation's competitive advantage.

The STEM areas have led the United States to the most prosperous times in the nation's history. In 2010, one in 18 jobs in the United States was a STEM job (7.6 million individuals), and it is projected that there will be 2.8 million job openings for STEM workers in 2018. The U.S. Department of Education projected the following increases in STEM jobs between 2010 and 2020.[5]

Mathematics	16%
Computer systems analysts	22%
Systems software developers	32%
Medical scientists	36%
Biomedical engineers	62%

Although the number of BS, MS, and PhD degrees earned by students in the STEM fields increased between 2004 and 2014[6], there is still an inadequate number of Americans who can fill these positions.[7] The United States produces fewer STEM graduates compared with other developed countries.[8] Students in non-STEM fields outrank those in the STEM fields by a factor of 5,[9] and census data[10] reveal that 74 percent of STEM graduates work outside of the STEM fields.

International students help drive the university research agendas, and when prepared with U.S. degrees, they enter the U.S. workforce, hold leadership positions in the top venture-backed companies, and start some of the most successful and innovative companies.[11]

Statistics collected every two years on the stay rates of foreign students who received doctoral degrees in sciences and engineering[12] from U.S. universities show that 65 percent of the science or engineering PhDs[13] are still living here 10 years after completing their degrees.[14]

The stay rates were slightly higher for women than men and correlated with the country of origin[15] and the scientific discipline. The stay rates were highest in computer science and computer and electrical engineering and the lowest for the disciplines of agricultural sciences, economics, and social sciences.

The interpretation of these data needs to take into account major national and international events[16] that influence whether each year's cohort of graduates will stay or leave. In addition, countries, especially in Asia, offer significant incentives to new doctoral recipients and seasoned professionals from their countries working in the United States to return home to join the faculties of the universities in their countries (see Chapter 6).

The United States does not capture as much of the talent that we educate because it is difficult for many foreign graduates to obtain an employment visa to pursue their careers in the United States. The numbers of highly skilled immigrants has decreased from 18 percent in 1991 to 13 percent in 2011.

American immigration policy now unintentionally undermines growth and prosperity.[17]

Other countries (e.g., Canada and Germany) have resolved this issue by granting permanent residency (even while in graduate school) to those who can boost the national economy, giving them an advantage compared with the United States. Canada's retention rate was 18 percent in 1991 and a remarkable 67 percent in 2011.[18] They have also improved the efficiency of the immigration process, provided benefits such as language classes (Germany and Luxembourg) to immigrants who remain in their host countries, offered subsidies and/or equity free capital to start a company (Chile), and created special entrepreneurship visas (UK).

The United States limits the number of H-1B visas for new skilled immigrant workers to 65,000 a year plus 20,000 holders of U.S. degrees. If there had not been a barrier to obtaining H-1B visas or green cards in the years 2003–2007, an additional 182,000 STEM graduates would have remained in the United States and contributed $14 billion to the GDP in 2008, including $2.7–$3.6 billion in tax payments.[19] Strategies to advance U.S. immigration policies and practices and to update rules that date back to 1965 have not been enacted.[20] The Immigration Innovation Act of 2015 would increase H-1B visa holders to 195,000 and remove the cap on foreign nationals with degrees from U.S. universities. No action has been taken on the bill (as of 2016).

Promoting STEM education must begin in the primary and secondary grades. Seamless education is a popular concept, and is the right one if we are to keep students on track in the STEM fields. Too many students become disenchanted with science and technology early in their precollegiate education and do not complete a high school curriculum that provides adequate preparation for college and the

STEM fields in particular. Many students who select a STEM major upon entering college change their major after a few courses. The skills needed for college attainment, jobs of the future, and success in the world require 21st–century skills, an awareness of other cultures, and an understanding of the connection between education and national security.[21] Research captures the minds and hearts of students and keeps them engaged.

Global STEM

In spite of the focus on STEM disciplines, and on international/global activities, only recently has there been an effort to combine "global" and "STEM" in focused initiatives. We do it unconsciously as we send students abroad, recruit students to this country and develop joint research, education, and service programs overseas. We could be even more innovative and creative in stimulating students to enter STEM disciplines if we capitalized on developing programs with a research emphasis that also prepared students to be better international citizens, collaborators, and colleagues. And, we need to do it early. It has been suggested that problems with U.S. STEM education may begin as early as elementary school and continue throughout the succeeding years of education.[22]

The curricula for students who elect STEM majors must include opportunities to gain an international experience. The percentage of students, nationally, who study abroad in the STEM fields is small. In 2012, only 3.9 percent of students who studied abroad were engineering students,[23] and only 1.6 percent of study abroad students were enrolled in math or computer science programs. There has been a misperception that the engineering curriculum makes it difficult, if not impossible, to engage in an international experience. Special attention has been paid to this issue.[24,25,26] Engineering careers today often include large multinational projects and an engineer at some time in his/her career will likely work abroad.

Thirty institutions signed the Newport Declaration to Globalize U.S. Engineering Education and Research in 2008, and the Institute of International Education (IIE) Global Engineering Education Exchange program (Global E3) connects 40 U.S. universities and 60 foreign universities in an effort to provide an international study, research, or service semester. The Georgia Institute of Technology designed its International Plan for engineering students who wish to have an international competence designation on their diplomas. Students spend six months abroad, and they are still able to graduate in four years. Many other U.S. institutions have developed specific programs to encourage engineering students to obtain overseas experience.[27] The Henry Samueli School of Engineering at the University of California, Irvine (UCI) created an international engineering program in collaboration with the UCI School of Humanities, whereby a student can earn a degree in mechanical engineering and a bachelor's degree in a language in five years.

Engineering students provide a great deal of valuable expertise through their research, service, and volunteer activities, especially in developing countries.[28] The Open University in the UK has developed new methods of hands-on, problem-based learning that can be employed in laboratory settings or elsewhere,[29] International Peace Corps graduate programs engage engineering students, and Engineers without Borders is a very successful program for engineering students to gain research experience while solving engineering problems around the world.

International Education Is "Moving Down"

Every experience in education is "moving down," meaning that the research experience that students once had only as graduate students is becoming embedded in the undergraduate experience, beginning as early as the freshman year. For the most enthusiastic students, this can continue throughout college, either by pursuing the same project or by sampling research projects with a number of different professors, often in different fields. In some majors, research is either strongly recommended or required. Then, moving this experience down to another level, it is also evident that more and more high school students and even middle school students become involved in research projects, either through a program organized by a university and/or through personal contacts or professional organizations.

Precollegiate International Research Opportunities

Internationalization has become more prominent in secondary schools and, in limited situations, in primary education. High school students and those even younger can attend schools with a universal international curriculum (international baccalaureate) or an international emphasis. Organizations such as the International Studies Schools Association bring together educators, curriculum developers, and university faculty interested in promoting global education and international studies for magnet schools, charter schools, rural schools, parochial schools, and other independent schools across the United States and Mexico. The focus of these gatherings is often on developing intercultural understanding and global citizenship.[30] The research experience, as part of the international experience, is limited, however, at the precollegiate level.

The first order for enhancing internationalization at the K–12 level is to incorporate this perspective into the training of teachers. A number of colleges of education introduce student teachers to practices that will help them develop curricula and design plans that emphasize global issues. Summer workshops that promote a global perspective to teaching are available, and more than 1,000 teachers have committed to IIE's Generation Study Abroad program, thereby ensuring that they will add a global perspective to their teaching and recommend to their students that they study abroad during college (see p. 90). The International Research and Exchanges Board (IREX) program, Teachers for Global Classrooms, provides training for American teachers to help their students develop skills for global engagement and knowledge.

Noah Zeichner, a teacher at Chief Sealth High School in Seattle, WA, began a program to understand the challenge of clean water, which has become a schoolwide learning community for global engagement that engages hundreds of students and dozens of teachers. The global issues class has become a 10th-grade core requirement for the students, and World Water Week has become an interdisciplinary, schoolwide event. This work has led to Zeichner's leadership of global education professional development sessions.

AFS, a leader in international education, not only provides materials for teachers to instruct all aspects of global competency but also, through Project: Change, offers scholarships for high school students to conduct projects abroad that make an impact on students in other countries as well as their own lives and perspectives.

These initiatives are an important introduction to internationalization at early ages, but they do not necessarily include an international research experience. There are examples, however, where elementary children are provided with the resources to use their creativity and test their ideas in makerspaces (see Chap 5). The United Nations International School has a CoLaboratory, a space where kids create products through interdisciplinary work using tools, materials, and display space to learn to design and to problem solve—in some cases, on projects related to global issues.

Several state governments have identified the advantages (primarily economic) of internationalizing education and developing initiatives in partnership with universities, colleges, and schools.[31] Global Washington, for example, put forth a comprehensive plan and commitment to global education in grades P–12 and higher education. The *States Go Global* publication—a comprehensive approach to global education—mentions P–12 in each of its six recommendations, with the understanding that such programs are important in building a cadre of students who will perform better on international standardized tests (PISA Scores among OECD nations). Discussion of research was included in Pillar 4: Collaborative and Innovative Research Programs.

Elementary School

Camp Invention is a weeklong summer day camp organized by the National Inventors Hall of Fame for children in grades 1–6 to develop STEM skills and focus on creativity, innovation, real-world problem-solving, and the spirit of invention. Founded in 1990, more than 600,000 children, led by certified local school teachers in 49 states, benefit each year. Campers get to know patent holders and hear personal stories about innovation.

Club Invention is an afterschool program for elementary school children also using inquiry-based, immersive skill-building STEM concepts. Club Invention has reached more than 82,000 children.

The Invention Project, also of the National Inventors Hall of Fame, empowers 6th-, 7th-, and 8th-grade students to turn an idea into an invention. Students learn to generate a concept, build a prototype, and market a brand working within simulated business deals.

Secondary School

Summer Programs at U.S. Universities for U.S. and International Students

Universities offer summer day-only or residential programs for high school students, with a full spectrum of courses in virtually every academic field.[32] Boston University hosts research internships for high school students in science and engineering in university labs, and Tulane University organizes an Emerging Scholars Environmental Health Sciences Summer Research Academy for 11th- and 12th-grade students with hands-on opportunities to conduct research and learn about careers in the environmental health sciences and public health.

The University of South Florida Pre-College Summer Programs invite high school students from the United States and around the world to explore and experience opportunities that engage them in hands-on experience. Through a series of programs, they may become certified in Mental Health First Aid, work with biomedical engineering faculty, fabricate two of the leading types of solar cells, and test a variety of measurements used in solar cell research and manufacturing. They can learn hands-on techniques to defend infrastructure from attackers, create a film-making project, engage in hands-on inquiry and discovery, and carry out research across several disciplines in medicine and the health professions. They develop creative and critical abilities with language to become productive writers, insightful thinkers, and deep readers.

The National Inventors Hall of Fame High School Leadership Intern Program provides professional leadership training and introductory concepts in entrepreneurship and intellectual property for the future scientist or engineer. Interns work with younger students who participate in the Camp Invention and Invention Projects.

High school students in 35 of Florida's 67 counties can attend one of Embry-Riddle Aeronautical University's (ERAU) 64 Gaetz Aerospace Institute programs that prepare students for college and the workforce. Programs are offered to pre-collegiate students online through the ERAU Worldwide campus and thus are transported outside of the United States. Partnerships with the Farm Bureau support work on the development and use of UAVs for agriculture science, and with the U.S. Navy, on unmanned underwater systems. These programs provide training (8th-, 9th-, and 10th-grade aerospace course) and even enough college credit to allow the students to enter ERAU directly or to articulate with a state college then enter ERAU as a junior. Teachers participate in STEM workshops. More than 2,900 students have joined an Aerospace Institute. The Gaetz Academy has the goal of becoming recognized worldwide.

Numerous precollege enrichment programs engage students in hands-on experiences and internships on U.S. campuses and abroad that focus on international topics and issues. For example, the American University School of International Service, Community of Scholars Program Study offers several precollegiate programs on world affairs,[33] and the University of Pennsylvania organizes a four week Model United Nations summer program and topics related to international relations. Lehigh University organizes a global entrepreneurship program.[34] Many of these programs do not include an overseas experience associated with the academic work but are important to introduce students to issues in the world at large.

U.S. high school students go abroad, and high schoolers from other countries come to U.S. universities through international internships, service-learning, and volunteer programs organized by universities, religious organizations, nongovernmental organization (NGOs), and commercial enterprises.[35] The University of Vermont offers a combination of online and a two-week study abroad program for students after 10th, 11th, or 12th grade, and several other universities offer online programs in many different disciplines and fields. Language immersion programs are available in Spain, France, and Italy, among others,[36] and opportunities for research are available through commercial organizations.[37,38,39] Personal relationships, however, are often the best way to place students in university research laboratories or in a field experience at home or abroad.

International High School Students Conduct Research at U.S. Universities

High-achieving high school students from all over the world come to the University of California, Santa Barbara Summer Research Mentorship Program to conduct research under the supervision of a graduate student, post-doc, and/or faculty mentor. The students also participate in a lecture series presented by university researchers, experience other aspects of university life, and interact with their peers.

Notre Dame University hosts about 20 rising junior and senior high school students from all over the world for a two-week, International Summer Physics Institute where they join a collaborative international team that uses the world-class facilities in the Department of Physics, works with real data from the Large Hadron

Collider at CERN, and assembles and tests detectors to study cosmic rays alongside of faculty experts. The program prepares students to think like a scientist about problems and data, establish a network of colleagues and mentors in physics, and learn about college and research in U.S. universities.

The University of Pennsylvania also offers opportunities for international high school students to join one of four 3-week, summer research academies[40] that provide a blend of class work and hands-on research. They learn project design and laboratory techniques, and they gain familiarity with the primary literature through journal clubs.

Smith College Summer Science and Engineering programs for select high school students from the United States and abroad provide four-week opportunities in the life sciences, physical sciences, and engineering to participate in "hands-on, cooperative, investigative and challenging learning." The program has engaged nearly 1,800 high school students from 46 states and 53 countries since it began in 1990. Other precollegiate summer programs feature a writing workshop, women's history program, and field studies for a sustainable future.

The Dr. Bessie F. Lawrence International Summer Science Institute, sponsored by the Weitzmann Institute of Science and the Davidson Institute of Science Education, Rehovot, Israel,[41] engages around 80 high school students from around the world in a one-month experience in biochemistry, biology, chemistry, mathematical and computer sciences, or physics research, conducting intensive, cutting-edge laboratory research and using sophisticated equipment. Students attend lectures from senior Institute scientists and are encouraged to lead seminars themselves. They deliver written and oral presentations on their projects at the conclusion of the program. The program is conducted entirely in English.

There are also a few opportunities for high school students to participate in international internships and apprenticeships with a research thrust. For example, the "Passport to India" program of the U.S. Department of State promotes privately funded internships for American high school and college students in offices and factories in India to work on joint projects.

Students gain an understanding of the people, history, culture, and rapidly changing infrastructure of India and work with local partners to address shared global challenges.

International Research Programs for Undergraduate Students in the STEM Disciplines

Programs to promote undergraduate research have become commonplace in universities and are even included in the strategic plans of university systems. A goal of the Board of Governors of the State University System of Florida is to "increase undergraduate participation in research to strengthen the pipeline of researchers pursuing graduate degrees."

The message to undergraduate students should be: "There is no such thing as undergraduate research, there is only research." All investigators, including students, follow the same methods, procedures, and ethics of the discipline. Undergraduate students are exposed to state-of-the art instrumentation and facilities (e.g., the National Science Foundation [NSF] Research Experiences for Undergraduates [REU], described later in this chapter), learn about leadership and teamwork, how to analyze results, prepare and deliver oral and written presentations, and anticipate the future of the work they undertake. When one reviews the work they have accomplished, the level and quality confirm that they have performed in the research enterprise as young professionals.

Adding *international* to the research experience adds value to an undergraduate education: International Research Experiences for Undergraduates (IREU). Students may select projects with an international component because the topic of their interest is global; their mentor or adviser collaborates with international colleagues; the resources for the project (libraries, museums, archives, galleries and theaters, and historic sites, etc.) are out of the country; or simply because they have a personal interest and desire to prepare themselves to live and work in a global society with people who have different political, religious, and cultural backgrounds and speak a different language. The relationships and collaborations students establish may continue throughout their careers.

The international research experience also promotes the elements of global learning (self-awareness, perspective-taking, cultural diversity, and personal and social responsibility) and global citizenship. These are included in academic programs as standard practice of research universities—and are imperative for successful international research collaborations.

Offices of Undergraduate Research

Most universities and colleges—as well as community colleges—have offices that promote undergraduate research and support students to develop as researchers by introducing them to research fundamentals, connecting them with a faculty-led research project, and providing resources to fund the projects and travel. Most of these offices concentrate on placing students on campus, but some of them, such as the Undergraduate Research Institute for the College of Liberal Arts & Human Sciences at Virginia Tech, also promote research opportunities for undergraduate students abroad. WebGURU also helps undergraduate students find opportunities for research in a variety of academic settings as well as private industry, although with a few exceptions where a U.S. university has an established collaboration with a foreign university, the experiences presented are within the United States.

Undergraduate Research Programs Offered and Funded by U.S. Universities, Government Agencies, and Scientific Societies

NSF International Research Experiences for Undergraduates (IREU) Programs are built on the foundation of collaboration among U.S. universities and international universities, national and international laboratories and facilities, industry, and other organizations at home and abroad. The NSF IREUs are often sponsored in partnership with other federal agencies, and additional funding comes from the university itself, the private sector, and other sources. In some instances, students at the U.S. university offering the IREU are restricted from participating in the program, and in other cases, only specific universities are invited to send their students to the program. In 2015, IREUs were located in the United States, Europe, Asia, Africa, South America, and Central America.

Most REU programs are in the STEM disciplines and extend over a 7–12 week period during the summer, but this varies with the program. NSF-supported students must be U.S. citizens or permanent residents of the United States. International students attending an IREU must be funded from a nongovernment source. Students from underrepresented groups, minorities, and women are encouraged to participate, and some programs make a special effort to include students who have limited opportunities to conduct research on their own campuses.

A stipend is awarded, often with the proviso that the students pay for their living expenses and costs such as visas and overseas telephones. Students stay on campus, in campus-arranged facilities, homestays (e.g., USF in Costa Rica) or in a private sector facility (e.g., the Minera Boleo Mining Company provides housing for the University of Missouri–Kansas City IREU students). Students typically have access to the libraries and computing and recreational facilities on the university campus. Some programs provide travel and/or medical insurance.

Orientation sessions for IREU students are organized at home prior to departure or in the foreign country upon arrival. Skills workshops, seminars, and online modules provide information ranging from the basics of the scientific method and experimental design to intensive language preparation, intercultural working relationships, scientific ethics, presentation skills, and laboratory reporting. One overseas program organizes a three-day, midprogram meeting for students to address research or cultural issues that may have arisen, and to reflect on lab experiences and share tips for working internationally. Students working overseas are typically joined by university students from that country to help them become globally aware scientists and engineers and improve their language skills.[42] A typical IREU also provides opportunities for professional development related to the practice of science or engineering.

During the session, IREU students prepare brief, informal reports or blogs and develop electronic notebooks for other students and faculty members of the group. At the conclusion of the program, a capstone experience is expected, such as a formal report, poster, or oral presentation at a local or regional research symposium or a national conference. Some programs require more extensive reporting. For example, students who participated in the NanoJapan IREU based at Rice University must conduct a follow-up project to encourage other university students to undertake an international research project, or they must lead a project that introduces middle or high school students to educational opportunities in the STEM fields.

Features of IREUs Unique to the Specific Programs

1. *Variable number and types of international partnerships:*

   <u>A single U.S. university collaborates with a single international university:</u>

   The University of Central Oklahoma and Uludag University in Bursa, Turkey, oversee a multinational team of scientists from the United States, Turkey, Greece, and Bulgaria to support students in an IREU to probe the link between pollinator species of solitary bees and honey bees that are invasive to the United States but potentially advantageous to agriculture in both countries.

   The University of South Florida and the Monteverde Institute, Puntarenas, Costa Rica, provide hands-on experiences for undergraduate students in civil and environmental engineering, anthropology, public health, and pre-med to address community health issues in rural Costa Rica.

   A single U.S. university collaborates with multiple international universities: Undergraduate physics students at the University of Florida (UF) can apply to an IREU Program in Gravitational Physics and work in some of the best gravitational physics labs in Europe and Australasia, and UF's chemistry department hosts an IREU at three sites in France.

   Twelve undergraduate students at the University of Michigan Center for Ultrafast Optical Science participate in the Optics in the City of Light IREU partnership with five French universities.

Multiple U.S. universities collaborate with multiple international universities:

Eleven U.S. National Nanotechnology Infrastructure Network (NNIN) members partner with laboratories in Japan, Germany, The Netherlands, France, and Belgium in the NNIN IREU.

2. *U.S. universities collaborate with national labs and/or industry:*

The DIMACS (Discrete Mathematics and Theoretical Computer Science) international academic consortium and public-private partnership was established by Rutgers University, Princeton, AT&T Labs-Research, Bell Labs, NEC Laboratories America, and Telcordia Technologies, with additional partnerships at Georgia Tech, Rensselaer Polytechnic Institute, Stevens Institute of Technology, Avaya Labs, HP Labs, IBM Research, and Microsoft research. The first four of the original partners remain engaged and have been joined by Applied Communication Sciences and the affiliate laboratories of Columbia University and Yahoo Labs. DIMACS, via Rutgers University, sponsors four separate but associated REUs. A few of the students participate in a follow-on program in the Czech Republic (see below).

The University of Missouri–Kansas City; University of California, Santa Barbara; Universidad Autónoma de Baja California Sur; Universidad de Guanajuato, Mexico; and the Minera Boleo Mining Company combine digital field-mapping techniques with state-of-the-art laboratory analytical work on the tectonic evolution of the Santa Rosalía basin area.

3. *The size of the program depends upon the partners and facility accommodations:*

A typical program is in the range of 10–20 students. Six U.S. undergraduate physics or astronomy students attended an IREU at the Cerro Tololo Inter-American Observatory in La Serena, Chile, and eight undergraduate student researchers participated in the Bermuda Institute of Ocean Sciences IREU.

4. *The number of IREU students participating in the international component of the REU may be limited:*

Ten to fifteen of the NNIN REU students will participate in an advanced research experience at the end of the summer in Japan, Germany, the Netherlands, France, or Belgium.

Three to five students in the DIMACS and mathematics REUs interested in combinatorics may spend the last few weeks of their program at the Center for Discrete Mathematics and Theoretical Informatics and Applications at Charles University in the Czech Republic.

5. *The timing of the U.S. and/or international segments of the program may not conform to the summer schedule:*

The program at Cerro Tololo Inter-American Observatory IREU in Chile for U.S. students and the Prácticas de Investigación en Astronomía for Chilean students are run during the Chilean summer, January through March.

The University of Minnesota–Morris IREU requires a two-year commitment. The field collection phase of the Baja Basins program at the University of Missouri–Kansas City takes place in Mexico during the winter and the analytical phase occurs on the Kansas City campus during the summer.

The first-year component of the Princeton IREU in molecular biophysics takes place on the Princeton Campus with the international follow-on experience in the Czech Republic during the summer thereafter.

6. *Access to an extraordinary research environment in the United States or abroad: students have opportunities to:*

- Use state-of-the-art equipment for computation, synthesis, characterization at the atomic and molecular scales, work in nanofabrication centers, and clean rooms—NNIN IREU and the complex of astronomical telescopes and instruments at the Cerro Tololo Inter-American Observatory in La Serena, Chile.
- Engage in research at CERN, Switzerland, the world's largest center for research in particle physics—University of Michigan IREU.
- Conduct field-based research programs at the Gulf of California Rift Margin Basins and Baja California Sur in Mexico—University of Missouri IREU.
- Investigate the origin and history of surficial deposits from the late Paleozoic age in Brazil—University of Minnesota–Morris.
- Carry out independent projects in biology, chemistry, and physics of the open ocean and reef-building coral and reef ecosystems;

molecular biology of marine organisms, and the effects, and consequences of global environmental change—Bermuda BIOS IREU.

7. *Examples of special requirements for participation in an IREU:*
   - Applicants to the Princeton IREU in molecular biophysics are required to have up to three years of work in chemistry, computer science, engineering, mathematics, or physics majors, among others, and a strong GPS (especially in the major).
   - UF requires undergraduate students in the UF chemistry and physics IREUs to have previous research experience.
   - The USF-Monteverde Institute IREU in Costa Rica requires Spanish proficiency.
   - The University of Minnesota–Morris REU partnership with the Universidade de São Paulo (USP) serves Native American women who are junior level, geology majors.
   - High school teachers spend three weeks at CERN under the auspices of the University of Michigan IREU at CERN.

The University of Central Oklahoma IREU program in Turkey describes the international aspect of the program as a "disorienting dilemma"—a transformative learning situation for students to work in a different culture with individuals who speak a different language, consider their own core beliefs and values, reexamine and perhaps adjust their understandings and assumptions of the world, and "shape their self-concept in science." These aspects of the REU are enriching beyond the scientific experience. "Disorientation" can also be a feature of international service learning and global volunteerism.

University Managed Undergraduate International Research Programs

Several universities have established research collaborations with colleagues at universities abroad and as part of the relationship, they have created international experiences for undergraduate students. The funding may be from research grants, the university, various special initiatives, the private sector, and/or philanthropic donations.

Kennesaw State (GA) President's Emerging Global Scholars (PEGS) program PEGS with Brazil supports freshmen members of the program to work virtually over a year with their counterparts in Brazil on a research project related to a global challenge before meeting in person to discuss the work, analyze data, and finalize a presentation or publication. Their projects range from "the crisis of worldwide aging" to "foreign investments and cross-cultural attitudes toward the economy." Students praise the program as a "high impact practice" (see also Chapter 1).

Teams of undergraduate research students at Clemson University work for two to four semesters across disciplines in the "Creative Inquiry Experience" program funded by the Creative Inquiry and Innovation Endowment. In 2014, a team designed a cervical collar of woven grasses in Tanzania and, in another project, produced low cost test strips for diabetics using a standard ink jet printer and glucometer. The latter project won the 2014 Lemelson-MIT (Massachusetts Institute of Technology) National Collegiate "Cure it" undergraduate prize for technology inventions that improves health care.

The University of New Hampshire features the International Research Opportunities Program and Summer Undergraduate Research Fellowships programs to support undergraduate students in all majors to conduct a research, scholarly, or creative project over nine weeks in a country that is not familiar to them, within traditional or diverse settings such as galleries, archaeological, and historical sites and field stations. Students prepare a proposal describing the research and preparation for the study and their knowledge of the language and culture of the foreign site. They are required to document the experience via Blackboard and blogs, and present their work and experiences upon returning home.

Beginning in 2011, MIT, and Hong Kong University of Science and Technology (HKUST) began the MIT-HKUST International Research Opportunities Program Summer Research Exchange Program to provide opportunities and travel funds for students to participate in faculty-mentored research exchanges at the two universities.

The University of Pennsylvania International Summer Undergraduate Research in Engineering students spend 8–12 weeks during the summer on a research internship in one of Penn Engineering's partner institutions abroad. An internship at Ulsan National Institute of Science and Technology in Korea provides freshmen, sophomore, and junior engineering students the opportunity to engage in cutting-edge research in alternative energy and nanotechnology. The Ruhr University Bochum, Germany, supports five Penn engineering undergraduates to engage in an intensive research experience in a cross-cultural team through a summer Research Internship Exchange Program.

The Universitas 21(U21)[43] Global Ingenuity Challenge is a short-term collaborative research or problem-solving experience conducted by U.S. and international undergraduate students. Teams of five students from the U21 network are invited to propose solutions to a real-life problem. They have two weeks to develop their response which they present in a two-minute video or pitch to the judges. The team with the most ingenious solution wins a prize of $1,000 per student.

Undergraduate Research Programs Sponsored by Associations and Other Organizations

The American Chemical Society (ACS) funds a 10- to 12-week summer IREU and ACS International Research Experiences for Students programs in the chemical and materials science fields. ACS selects up to 17 U.S. students or permanent residents from U.S. universities to participate in bilateral exchanges with universities in Germany, Italy, Singapore, or the United Kingdom[44] where they conduct research under the guidance of faculty and graduate student mentors. Participants meet in Washington, DC, for orientation. They are compensated for airfare and housing, provided a stipend, language training, medical insurance, and an opportunity to participate in the ACS National Meeting.

Undergraduate Research Programs Offered and Funded by Foreign Institutions or Countries

EuroScholars scholarships are available for undergraduate students from U.S. and Canadian institutions to engage in high quality, one to two semester-long academic research opportunities in several fields[45] at one of nine European Research Universities.[46] The student and the faculty supervisor choose a research project from among approximately 175 projects catalogued in the EuroScholars database. Applicants need a minimum of 3.4 GPA, ample laboratory experience in a scientific field and interest in a research career. Students will learn about scientific reasoning, research methods, theoretical principles related to the research area, scholarly communication, and the language and culture of the host institution and country, and they may engage in coursework while on site. They will prepare the results of their research project in a paper of publishable quality.

The von Karman Institute (VKI) Short Training Program in Fluid Dynamics welcomes university students from European countries, Canada, the UK, and the United States[47] majoring in engineering, physics, or mathematics to spend three to six months in a guided research project in environmental and applied fluid dynamics, aeronautics and aerospace, and turbomachinery and propulsion. Students will experience first-rate experimental test facilities, engage in computational and laboratory techniques, and become familiar with research methodology and team work. They are supervised by a faculty professor and supported by a research engineer, post-doctoral researcher, PhD candidate, or other member of the research team. A technical adviser assists with the technical aspects of the research and the operation of the test facilities and instruments. The data must be in a format for others to access and build upon, and then presented to the library. The student will prepare a final report, similar to a thesis in design and content with an indication the research direction in the future. A working knowledge of English or French is required.

The Center for Genomic Regulation (CRG) Summer Internship, Barcelona, Spain provides an eight-week summer research internship for eight competitively selected undergraduate students of any nationality in their final two years of studies in the life sciences or related subjects (e.g., bioinformatics, biomedicine, biochemistry, pharmacology, and chemistry). The student is supervised by the leader or a senior member of the research group on a project related to his or her interests. Prior lab experience is highly recommended.

DAAD (German Academic Exchange Service) Research Internships in Science and Engineering provide an opportunity for undergraduate students in biology, chemistry, Earth sciences, engineering, and physics of any nationality in the final two years of their studies, an opportunity to spend a summer working on research projects at German universities and research institutions. Doctoral students help integrate undergraduates directly into the lab work and serve as personal and professional mentors. The program provides practical research experience and an introduction to advanced research work.

The Switzerland International Summer Research Program for Life Science Students at the École Polytechnique Fédérale de Lausanne (EPFL), School of Life Sciences provides two months of intensive research training for 25 undergraduate students from anywhere in the world, studying at any university, interested in a research career in the life sciences. Students gain hands-on lab experience under the supervision of an EPFL Faculty member from the Brain Mind Institute, Institute of Bioengineering, Global Health Institute, or Swiss Institute for Experimental Cancer Research. Students participate in Friday seminars, the closing student symposium, and social events.

The ThinkSwiss Research Scholarship program is managed by the Office of Science, Technology, and Higher Education at the Embassy of Switzerland in Washington, DC. The program is designed to provide research opportunities for American and Canadian undergraduate and graduate students to conduct research at a public Swiss university or research institute for two to three months and to foster the exchange between Swiss, the United States, and Canadian universities and research institutions.

The Undergraduate Research Opportunities Program at RWTH Aachen University, Germany, fosters 10-week, hands-on, research partnerships for up to 60 qualified undergraduate students from the United States and Canadian universities The program is conducted in English, but students join German language classes at the level of their expertise and participate in a workshop on intercultural learning. A

German "buddy" helps them acclimate to the new environment. Scholarships for at least half of the visiting students defray living and travel expenses. Students present their work at a poster colloquium at the end of the program.

The University of Toronto Mississauga (UTM) International Research Opportunity Program Offered by the International Education Centre and the Experiential Education Office at UTM jointly organize a three-month summer research experience for students from Lund University, the National University of Singapore, the Chinese University of Hong Kong, Cardiff University, and the University of Paris Diderot, who are interested in biology, chemistry, environment, Earth science, geography, physics, and psychology. Students live on campus, use other university facilities, and may participate in class work.

The two-month summer opportunity at the Vienna Biocenter Summer School, Vienna, Austria_is a collaboration among the Institute of Molecular Pathology, Institute of Molecular Biotechnology, Max F. Perutz Laboratories and the Gregor Mendel Institute. About 20 students from around the world are selected to conduct research in the life sciences with leading researchers.

One of the largest international scholarship education, research, and internship programs is the Brazil Scientific Mobility Program administered by IIE. It began in 2011 to promote scientific research, provide training abroad for Brazilian students in the STEM fields, invest in educational resources within Brazil and abroad, increase international cooperation in science and technology, and engage students in a global dialogue. The program has now ended. The overall objective was to enhance Brazilian innovation and competitiveness. Brazil[48] funded 75,000 students with an additional 26,000 supported from the private sector.

Scholarships support one year of academic study plus an internship in one or more of 30 countries. The academic work may be obtained in one country and the internship conducted in another. Most of the scholarships are awarded to undergraduate students, but there are also funded positions for visiting PhD students, degree-obtaining students, post-doctoral training, specialized training in industry and visiting researchers. At least 346 U.S. universities have become host universities and more than 1,000 corporate partners have provided internships. The vast majority of students are engaged in engineering programs. The Brazilian students are required to return to their own Brazilian university after their period of study abroad. The program is concluding in 2016.

Programs for Graduate Students to Conduct Research Abroad

There are many programs and funding opportunities for graduate students who wish to pursue their graduate studies abroad, and while research is a degree requirement, funding for graduate programs, per se, is often targeted to the graduate studies component and not the research. Moreover, U.S. graduate students who wish to conduct their research abroad, especially in the STEM fields, are frequently funded by the grants of their faculty sponsors and professional organizations. In the reverse, international students who obtain their research training in the United States, are often supported by their own governments and from U.S. institutions. A few major international initiatives for graduate students include the following:

Master's International Program of the Peace Corps

The Master's International Program of the Peace Corps has been a three- to four-year program that combines graduate studies with volunteer service abroad at one of more than 90 U.S. academic institutions, providing students with an advanced degree and international experience. There were at least 162 Master's International graduate programs at the 90 institutions in both STEM and non-STEM fields. The program ends September 30, 2016, however, a student in such a program may be classified as a Master's International participant and complete the program.

Many universities support a Peace Corps Recruiter on campus who speaks with students in the classroom, presents to student organizations, and interacts with others in the community to promote Peace Corps programs.

The Whitaker International Fellows and Scholars Program was created in 2006 when the Whitaker Foundation closed. Beginning in 1975, nearly $600 million was awarded to U.S. universities to support the development and enhancement of biomedical engineering in the United States. After closure, the remaining funds were transferred to the IIE to create the Whitaker International Fellows and Scholars Program for biomedical engineers in the United States[49] to collaborate with their counterparts abroad.

Whitaker International Fellows and Scholars conduct research in a university or laboratory, pursue coursework at an academic institution, or intern at a policy institute, industrial, or nonprofit organization anywhere outside the United States and Canada over one academic year. Scholars go abroad for one semester to 24 months.

The NSF Summer Institutes for Science and Engineering Graduate Students are partnership programs with selected foreign counterpart agencies sponsor seven East Asia and Pacific Summer Institutes[50] for graduate students in science, engineering, and education. All summer institutes operate similarly and the research visits to a particular location take place at the same time. Applicants propose a location, host scientist, research project and duration of the visit and gain (1) hands-on research experience; (2) an introduction to the science, science policy, and scientific infrastructure of the location; and (3) experience in the society, culture, and language of

The Whitaker Program

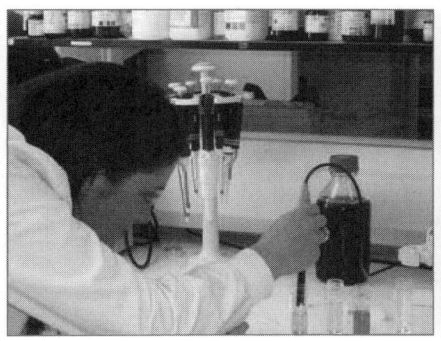

The Whitaker Program is a funding opportunity for emerging U.S. leaders in biomedical engineering to build collaborative ties with individuals and institutions overseas.

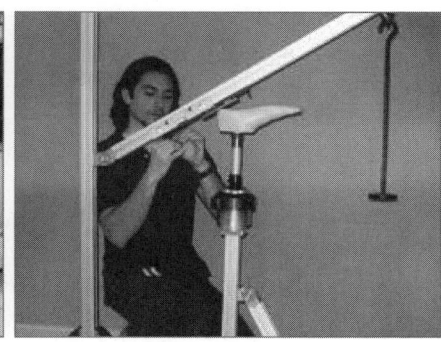

Whitaker Fellows Awards

Fellows are awarded grants for up to one year to take on a meaningful career-enhancing biomedical engineering project, including partial coverage of tuition.

Whitaker Fellows

Whitaker Fellows are recent BS recipients, graduate students, or professionals with less than a PhD degree, within three years of the degree.

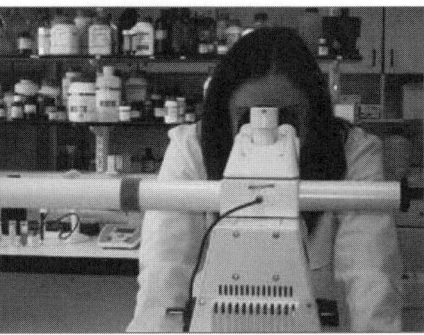

Whitaker Scholars

Whitaker Fellows are recent PhD recipients (post-docs) within three years of the degree.

the region. The program is designed to help students initiate professional relationships that will enable future collaboration.

International Dissertation Research Fellowships from the Social Science Research Council are available to social scientist graduate students in the humanities and humanistic social scientists to carry out research internationally on topics of complex social, cultural, economic, and political processes that advance knowledge of non-U.S. cultures and societies. The council strongly supports interdisciplinary work, the creation of international networks and projects along emergent lines of research, some of which have created new fields such as comparative politics and global security.

There are many specific programs that provide funding for students, post-docs, and faculty to carry out research with a specific country. For example, New York University (NYU) and French National Center for Scientific Research awards fellowships for research in France on three social science topics and the Japan-U.S. Friendship Commission provides a few fellowships to researchers in the social science disciplines for studies of modern Japanese society and political economics, Japan's international relationships, and U.S.-Japan relations.

University System and Country Partnership Graduate Programs

The Republic of Chile and the State of California have signed an memorandum of understanding (MOU), "A Collaboration for the 21st Century," which includes the Chile-California Program on Human Capital Development between the University of California System and Chile. The program funds Chilean students who wish to enter MS and PhD programs at any University of California institution and joint research projects between Chilean and U.S. scholars. The MOU also stipulates the goal of developing collaborations on issues of education, environmental protection, energy, agriculture, information, and communication technologies and trade. The MOUs opened the door to a series of bidirectional visits between the Governor of California, President of Chile, and various ministerial leaders. Efforts were further broadened to include agreements with California companies and trade agreements between Chile and California.

U.S. Graduate Programs Train Individuals from Developing Countries

The Thomas Jefferson National Accelerator Facility/Hampton University Graduate Studies Program offers a four-week international fellowship for graduate students from developing countries to meet with researchers and initiate or strengthen a research collaboration.

The Borlaug Higher Education Agricultural Research and Development (BHEARD) Fellowship Program began in 2014 to improve growth and productivity in agriculture in some of the "Feed the Future" developing countries by collaborating with researchers in the United States to train masters and doctoral agricultural researchers.[51] The program is managed by Michigan State University supported by USAID, APLU (National Association of State Universities and Land-Grant Colleges), and the International Maize and Wheat Improvement Center in Mexico.

International Research Conferences for College and University Students

Undergraduate and graduate researchers participate in local and regional research conferences or expositions—in the United States and abroad—as presenters and/or session moderators. Some of these conferences are generic and open to all students to showcase work ranging from the STEM disciplines to performances and displays of works of art. Even when students did not conduct their research outside of the country, there are many opportunities for them to present their work at international meetings and conferences. For example, since 2006, the students participating in the "Algorithmic Combinatorics on Words" REU at University of North Carolina–Greensboro have presented their work at conferences in Finland, Germany, France, UK, Italy, Spain, Portugal, Czech Republic, Slovakia; British Columbia and Ontario, Taiwan, India, and at home.

Some conferences are organized specifically to bring students from around the globe together to discuss contemporary, global issues. The biennial Education without Borders Conference sponsored by the Higher Colleges of Technology in the United Arab Emirates (UAE), was designed to provide a short-term, intercultural learning opportunity for students from six continents. The "mission is to engage students and experts from countries around the world in active dialogue about the globe's most pressing social challenges and empower them to create and implement solutions. Education without Borders uses education and technology to help create a world in which all people can lead free and dignified lives."[52]

The 2011 conference, entitled "Solutions to Global Challenges ... Diverse Perspectives; Unified Action," was attended by over 1,000 students representing 130 nationalities. The theme of the 2013 conference was "Bridging the Gap: Innovative Solutions to Global Educational Challenges." More than 3,500 students attended the 2015 conference in Dubai.

A few examples of other research conferences that include international participation include the following:

The Sigma Xi Annual Meeting & International Research Conference is an opportunity for undergraduates to present their research. Sigma Xi is an international, multidisciplinary research society with chapters at colleges and universities, industrial research centers, and government laboratories with members in more than 100 countries. The organization promotes the health of the scientific enterprise and honors scientific achievement.

The 2015 Walsh Exchange conference on International Relations Research is sponsored annually by Georgetown University to promote innovative undergraduate research in international relations by students around the world.

The Eastern Student Research Forum is a four-day, international symposium hosted by the University of Miami, School of Medicine, joined by 77 member institutions to showcase the research of graduate students, medical students, residents, and faculty in the biomedical and clinical sciences.

The American Institute of Aeronautics and Astronautics sponsors eight student paper conferences every year in the United States, Europe, and Australia.

The Office of the Dean of Undergraduate Studies at American University in Cairo, Egypt arranges an Annual Conference for Excellence in Undergraduate Research, Entrepreneurship and Creative Achievement.[53] Undergraduate students in all disciplines and universities may submit original work, including research papers/theses, scientific innovations, art and photography, musical compositions, film and documentaries, and literary and entrepreneurial works for presentation.

The Undergraduate Research Conference sponsored by Universitas 21 attracts students from diverse disciplines to organize seminars, student presentations and social activities, and tours that promote networking and stimulate discussion. The meeting is held in a different country each year.

Undergraduate students who attend the Forum on Education Abroad Undergraduate Research Award Annual Conference are nominated and selected competitively to present research that was conducted during an education abroad experience. "Research" is interpreted in the broadest sense, representing a wide range of academic fields and outcomes from international experiences that demonstrate the students' understanding of other cultures and societies. Award recipients present their research at a plenary luncheon.

The International Conference of Undergraduate Research is an annual forum and a virtual conference for undergraduate researchers around the world to interact with one another from their home institutions over a 24-hour period through state-of-the-art videoconferencing technology and social media. Students present their work in any discipline in joint sessions with peers across the globe. They gain skills in communication and leadership, obtain feedback on their research, and exchange ideas. The inaugural conference in 2013 was a grassroots initiative of students and staff from Monash University and the University of Warwick to be an environmentally-responsible, affordable, multidisciplinary program that would internationalize the student experience. In 2015, the conference was held concurrently in Australia, the UK, Singapore, Malaysia, Japan, South Africa, and the United States.

More than 1,000 student leaders, innovators, and entrepreneurs from around the world gather at the Clinton Global Initiative University (CGI U) Annual Meeting where they attend the plenary sessions, participate in working sessions, network with their peers, build skills and potential partnerships that focus on the five areas of emphasis: Education, environment and climate change, peace and human rights, poverty alleviation, and public health. They design a Commitment to Action project with the assistance of university representatives, topic experts, and celebrities attending the conference. On the final day, all attendees participate in a Day of Action in the local community. Over $900,000 in funding opportunities were available to CGI U 2015 students to help them turn their ideas into action.

The *Undergraduate Journals and Conferences Directory (UJCD)* encourages undergraduate scholarship by facilitating undergraduate publications and conferences. The UJCD lists journals—electronic and paper—and conferences, that will consider undergraduate student essays, research papers, poetry, short fiction, photography, cartoons, art, and so on, without regard to the undergraduate student's institutional affiliation. The directory is regularly updated.

Internships and Practicums

International Internships can be a differentiating factor for students in career searches and a competitive advantage for universities in recruitment. Approximately one million American students engaged in an internship during the summer of 2014, and 68 percent of students in an undergraduate program will have served at least one internship before graduating.[54] An internship can be an entrée to a career, an opportunity to "try out" one's presumed future employment, meet a future employer, gain practical experience in a domestic or global market, and when performed abroad, can be a transforming experience that fulfills all of these benefits while gaining communication skills in a socially and professionally different culture.

Internships benefit both the students and the host organization. Students are exposed to personnel and practices within a particular field in the private sector and increase their network of contacts, colleagues, and friends. They gain practical experience, explore potential careers, and learn skills that make them more competitive on the job market and when applying to advanced degree programs. In many cases, an intern is offered a position within the organization where he or she interned. Companies and organizations benefit from the talent of the intern and have the opportunity to assess the student for future employment. International internships increase a student's understanding and appreciation of the world and their place within it.

Universities, companies, government agencies and other organizations encourage students in a number of fields (most notably engineering, science, business, and education) to engage in internships as part of their undergraduate or graduate studies. Internships are also available for high school students. They may be full-time, part-time, long-term, or short-term. Many of them are unpaid but offer academic credit. Others are paid and still others require students to pay for participation. Payment for the work of an intern was legally challenged by the Black Swan Case in 2013 with a favorable result that supported payment, but was overturned in 2015.

In 2013, the Black Swan Case determined that the interns working for Fox Searchlight on the movie *Black Swan* should be paid. This decision opened the door for other unpaid interns who had worked for media companies to sue for back wages. The decision was overturned in 2015, ruling that interns did not need to be paid if the work they performed was more of a learning experience than a financial benefit to the employer. In reaching this conclusion, an open-ended list of considerations such as whether the training was similar to that of an academic program and could qualify for academic credit, and whether the work "complements, rather than displaces, the work of paid employees" was applied. The court also opined that each situation would be a separate case and thus it was unlikely that a class action suit could be initiated. The Department of Labor Fact Sheet #71[55] presents six criteria for determining whether an intern has entered into an employment relationship and should be paid. The legal issues surrounding employee versus volunteer status of the internship are presented in a publication by Intern Bridge.[56] Institutions today are also focusing on new issues such as insurance expectations and liability issues related to the placement of students in internships.

Universities, especially colleges of engineering, connect students with an internships abroad, often through alumni. NYU, for example, has created summer global internships and volunteer opportunities in locations where they have academic programs.[57] The internships may be characteristic for the region. For example, students engage in entrepreneurship and civil and human rights internships in Tel Aviv, environmental sustainability internships in Sydney, and corporate finance and accounting internships in London. Some of the NYU programs are in partnership with internship placement organizations (see below) and can be credit or noncredit earning. Those that provide academic credit typically involve coursework at the NYU institution within the city. There are various requirements for language proficiency. Students also learn about art culture, education, politics, and the economy of the city and country.

International internships and apprenticeships with nonprofit organizations and government labs can also be found on the web, via social media, and using hashtags such as #internabroad or the same hashtag plus the name of a country of interest. Not-for-profit and for-profit organizations such as Goinglobal, Cross Cultural Solutions, and InternshipDesk, for example, connect students with internships but, in contrast with many internships which provide some support to the student, the student pays the organization for the opportunity provided, travel, housing, and supervision. Cross Cultural Solutions has opportunities for students to sign on for one-of-a-kind internships in several fields of health, education and community development in 10 countries in Asia, Africa, and Central and South America, whereas InternshipDesk offers internships opportunities for American students in Shanghai, Delhi, and Tel Aviv and for international students in Chicago. Universities subscribe to some of these services.

International Internship Programs offered by American University Systems and Universities

The University of North Carolina Exchange Program (UNCEP) was formed in 1997 to foster exchange partnerships in teaching and research between the University System of North Carolina's 15 campuses and eight global regions.[58] International internships through UNCEP are arranged in conjunction with exchange study at partner universities and through affiliation with selected international internship providers in London, Dublin, Sydney, and Germany.

Medical students at Wilkes University can elect an internship or interprofessional clerkship in Tanzania and/or conduct global health research in Tanzania with multiple partners from Uganda. Partnership students from Tanzania and Uganda also come to Wilkes each year. This is only one example of the many such programs offered through U.S. medical schools.

Oregon State University established 10-week, full-time global internships and research experiences in 1996 under the title of IE3 (International Education, Experience, Employment) and since this time has placed more than 1,500 students in 82 countries. Students obtain academic credit.

Cornell University sponsors fellowships and internships in Chile, Argentina, Germany, and Switzerland. The U.S. Congress-Bundestag Youth Exchange for Young Professionals program in Germany is a yearlong, jointly funded fellowship that supports 75 American and 75 German young professionals to study and engage in internships in each other's countries, living with hosts in a cultural immersion program.

The University of Pennsylvania sponsors an International Internship Program in partnership with nonprofit organizations in developing countries in Asia and

Africa. Placements with nonprofits or NGOs may require office work or hands-on work at field sites, schools, or clinics. The University provides each intern with an award to offset expenses, including flight, visa expenses, housing, and food. The University of Pennsylvania website features recent experiences of students.

The MIT International Science and Initiatives program places 750 MIT students in engineering, architecture, science and management each year in paid internships that provide industrial and research opportunities in domestic and international companies, startups, university research institutes, and NGOs.

Graduate students working on a master's degree at the Patel College for Global Sustainability at the University of South Florida participate in an internship at sites on five continents to conduct research over the summer. Each student designs and executes a project in one of the four areas of emphasis of the college: water, energy, tourism, and entrepreneurship, in collaboration with a partner or organization (including local and national organizations, universities, governments, national parks, and private enterprise). A map at the college identifies each student, project, and partner.

The Global Training Initiative at North Carolina State provides directed study and internship opportunities for international students including a course on U.S. culture and higher education. It also provides professional training for local and global businesses and facilitates obtaining new grants and research for the campus.

Internships Overseas Sponsored by an Organization or the U.S. Government for American Students

The U.S. Department of State Pathways Internship programs offer unpaid internships for undergraduate and graduate students in U.S. embassies, consulates, and diplomatic missions throughout the world that provide an introduction to federal careers. The Internship Temporary Program and the Internship Experience Program begin in high school and extending through graduate and professional programs. Students engaged in the first program work during holidays and breaks whereas interns in the latter program are appointed to permanent, excepted positions without a termination-specific date. Students can learn in more than 265 sites influenced by foreign policy. Internships are also available at Consular Offices within cities in the United States and around the world[59] (see Chapter 6).

Internships Sponsored by Joint Agreements between the United States and Another Country

The Maine-France Partnership between the University of Maine System and eight universities in France provides opportunities for students from Maine to become involved in internships and research in France and for French students to study in Maine.

Internships Sponsored by Foreign Countries

*i*LEAD (innovative Local Enterprise Achievement Development) is a program for National University of Singapore graduates to gain firsthand experience in practical and theoretical entrepreneurship by working full-time over a seven-month period as an intern in a local startup or a high-growth company. They also engage in a "technopreneurship" (entrepreneurial marketing, technological innovation or new product development and new venture creation) or a discipline-based module then travel to Israel, Silicon Valley, U.S., Beijing, Shanghai, or Germany to obtain insight into foreign startup culture. Feedback from the companies has been uniformly outstanding, citing the advances and successes brought about by students, and praising the program for producing the next generation of successful entrepreneurs.

International Practicums

The University of Tampa College of Education sponsors a practicum that concludes with a four week (of 14 weeks) teaching internship in a Department of Defense school in Italy and Nursing has a practicum in the Dominican Republic that provides health screening and teaching about healthy lifestyles.

> Education students at Albion College developed an international practicum with middle school at Noisy-le-Roi to draw comparisons between French and American education.

Professional Organizations Arrange Internships

An Internship Directory presents over 27,000 opportunities abroad.

Internships: http://www.ceinternships.com, http://www.internexchange.com, http://www.princetonreview.com/cte/search/careersearch.asp. The Princeton Review also publishes two internship guides: "The Internship Bible" and "The Best 109 Internships."

International Service Learning

International service learning is a near universal practice that has become well established in the scholarly literature as an important research area. It is included in this chapter because there are many parallels between international service-learning, research, and volunteer activities.

> *Global service learning is a community-driven service experience that employs structured, critically reflective practice to better understand common human dignity; self; culture; positionality; socio-economic, political and environmental issues; power relations; and social responsibility, in all global contexts.*[60]

Service-learning experiences can be designed in virtually all academic disciplines and professions, but it is often more characteristic of the curricula in colleges of education, humanities and arts, international studies, and the social sciences than in the STEM fields. Kennesaw State University, for example, organized a songwriting workshop for a foundation in London and a children's festival in Russia.[61]

Several years ago, Robbin Crabtree published a useful discussion about international service learning. She emphasized the importance of connecting with grassroots organizations to assure the work proposed is in synch with local needs, has an appropriate budget, and provides a means for collaboration and indicated that the experience "transforms" his or her thinking to another level.[62]

Hartman and Kiely[63] have described five distinctive characteristics of global service learning: (1) commitment to development of student intercultural learning; (2) focus on structural analysis linked with consideration of power, privilege, and hegemonic assumptions; (3) position within a global marketization of volunteerism; (4) immersive; and (5) engaging global, civic, and moral imagination.

International service learning is an opportunity for students to translate their knowledge and skills from the classroom into practical applications, meaningful service, and reciprocal learning with individuals and a community.

> *Fundamental to ... [service learning] ... is the concept of multilateral reciprocity—that students, educators, educational institutions, communities and others benefit mutually from the process and results of international/intercultural service learning.*[64]

A service-learning experience may be out-of-country for a brief duration or extend over a semester. Credit may be given either for the preparatory work alone or the entire program.

A structured period of debriefing after the weeks abroad allows students to reflect on the experience. Students may be required to record their experiences in a journal, research paper and/or presentation as they do in an international research experience.

The edited book, *International Service Learning: Conceptual Frameworks and Research*,[65] discusses the topic from multiple perspectives.

University-based International Service-Learning Programs

Buck-I-serve at Ohio State is a weeklong, substance-free program planned through the Office of Student Life and held during university breaks to provide students direct experience through interdisciplinary service-learning courses and research projects to learn about social justice in diverse environments as they help community partners in different parts of the world.

Student athletes, an alumnus and an Oregon State University political science professor participated in a nine-day Beavers without Borders program to help with construction and renovation of Batey housing (sugar cane workers or company town) in Santo Domingo, Dominican Republic.

Students entering Northeastern University in the spring are required to undertake a service-learning program abroad in the fall in Australia, Britain, Costa Rica, Greece, or Ireland.[66]

The U21 Social Entrepreneur Corps at the University of Connecticut leads a program in Guatemala that builds upon a social entrepreneurship initiative to support and advise Guatemalan communities, focusing on women entrepreneurs. The program fosters international collaboration, engages new technologies, and provides a commitment to global citizenship. The students described the experience as an opportunity of a lifetime to *make a real difference*.

Engineers without Borders (EWB) was started on the University of Colorado-Boulder campus in 2002 and today is an international, nonprofit, humanitarian organization (EWB-USA) with the International Federation of National Engineers Without Borders/Ingeneiurs Sans Frontiers (EWB-I). Nearly 15,000 EWB members belong to and work in at least 47 countries on five continents. Chapters of EWB are organized on university campuses where students undertake research projects with community members abroad in the areas of water supply, sanitation, civil works, structures, energy, agriculture, and information systems. The projects provide practical, sustainable, equitable, and affordable solutions and build local capacity, particularly in developing countries.

Projects are designed in the context of the local, social, cultural, and geographic circumstances then implemented. The impact of the work is measured in the areas of planning, monitoring evaluation, and learning. EWB students describe themselves as "catalysts of change." Examples of some programs include the following:

- EWB students at the University of Arizona redesigned a fish hatchery in Guatemala increasing the production during breeding season.
- EWB Students from the University Maryland College Park worked with community members in Ethiopia to construct a recreation

center, plan and gain resources for a coffee shop and library, and participate in constructing a concrete bridge.

- The University of California, Los Angeles EWB chapter is constructing a schoolhouse for children in Nicaragua, rainwater catchment systems in the highlands of Guatemala, and refurbishing donated computers to local underfunded schools.

- EWB students from the University of South Florida have designed a means to bring clean water to the 500 residents of a community in the Dominican Republic that currently obtains its water from a polluted river.

EWB-USA raises funds from companies and multinational corporations, societies and professional organizations, foundations, university centers, institutes, and individuals—including the EWB students. The Alcoa Foundation, for example, has invested more than $600,000 in grants to EWB-I for basic infrastructure projects; EWB-Fort Lewis College raises all of the money for its programs (about $20,000 for each village), and the University of Florida has established an endowment fund with lead gifts from an individual and CH2M Hill.

EWB Brazil partnered with the Federal University of Vicosa and the Culture, Environment, Education and Social-Economic Development Agency of Vicosa to create training and professional development programs for students and professional engineers, and EWB-Canada recently launched the Global Engineering Leadership Certificate that is being implemented at universities across the country.

The University of Pennsylvania has three international service-learning programs, Engineers without Borders, the Global Biomedical Service Program (GBS) and the International Development Summer Institute, in which more than 800 engineering undergraduates have participated since the programs began in 1999.[67]

Undergraduate students in the GBS program joined students from Hong Kong Polytechnic University in a 16-day experience to construct orthotics for children with neuro-musculoskeletal disorders and prosthetics for amputees. In 2014, 12 U.S. students and their counterparts from HKUST worked in Huizhou, China, and in 2015 they worked in Guangdong Province, China to provide clinical services to individuals in underserved communities.

Around 20 U.S. and African undergraduate students from the University of Pennsylvania College of Engineering, *the Africa Centre, the* Technology Consultancy Centre of the College of Engineering at Kwame Nkrumah University of Science and Technology and several NGOs in Kumasi, Ghana collaborate in a four-week International Development Summer Institute to gain applied learning and intercultural experience in the fields of health, history education, micro-finance, and technology. The program begins with five weeks of pre-program preparation on campus.

Penn engineering students also participate with the Agnes Irwin School (Rosemont, PA) to design and implement a power solar system, upgrade a computer lab and deliver a "coding academy" with the Gashora Girls Academy in Science and Technology in Rwanda.

The Ohio State University students from the College of Engineering and the Knowlton School of Architecture City and Regional Planning program learn the concept of "humanitarian engineering" by collaborating with Ghanaian partners to develop sustainable technologies in housing, community planning, cultural planning, biogas and solar energy, health care, water, sanitation, agriculture, education, governance, and economic development. They assess the needs during fall semester, then research, design, develop, prototype, and plan engineering solutions to meet the needs identified by the local communities. They also evaluate the entrepreneurial opportunities that could be developed as a result of the projects.

Programs and outcomes from international service-learning experiences can be submitted to the *International Journal of Research on Service-Learning and Community Engagement,* a peer-reviewed online journal dedicated to the publication of high quality research focused on service-learning, campus-community engagement, and the promotion of active and effective citizenship through education.

International Service Learning at Foreign Universities

Project-based, course-based and/or community-based service-learning experiences are also incorporated into the curriculum at universities around the world[68,69] with the same goals as the U.S.-based programs.

The Office of Service-Learning was established at Lingnan University in 2006 with funds from the university and a private donor, to become the first stand-alone, service-learning office among the universities in Hong Kong. Lingnan has categorized four types of programs and the desired impact of the effort:

- **Direct Service-Learning.** Person-to-person service projects that directly impact individuals who receive the service.
- **Indirect Service-Learning.** Students work on broad issues, environmental projects, and community development projects that have clear benefits to the community or environment.
- **Research-Based Service-Learning.** Students gather and present information on areas of interest and need-based projects.

- **Advocacy Service-Learning.** Students educate others about topics of public interest to create awareness and action on relevant issues.

The Service-Learning Asia Network is a forum for colleges, universities, and institutions interested in service learning in the region. Service learning in China is called "social practice" and engages students in volunteer service for special events and/or within the community and rural areas. This activity is endorsed by the university as an extra activity for students but is not necessarily adopted within the curriculum.

NGOs Promote Service Learning and Internships

In 2014, the IIE established Generation Study Abroad with the goal of doubling the number of U.S. students studying abroad by the end of the decade (600,000). "Study abroad" in the broadest sense is any kind of activity that engages a student overseas for an educational experience, including research, internships, and service learning. As of May 2016, more than 650 universities (100 outside the United States), organizations, and education associations had joined. Importantly, more than 1,000 K–12 teachers pledged to encourage their students to develop a global perspective and to study abroad in college.

International Service Learning® is a 20-year-old NGO based in Corpus Christi, Texas, that focuses primarily on health care. Volunteers work in underserved communities in 12 countries under the direction and approval of the local health care ministry to assist and work under the guidance of health care professionals. They gain insight into global health issues and culture while providing aid to countless individuals.

Professional Organizations Partner with Universities

In the 1980s and 1990s, experiential learning and community engagement became important in preparing students to understand and appreciate their roles in contributing to civil society at home and abroad, and in accord, many professional organizations were started to connect high school and college students with internships, service learning, and volunteer opportunities. A significant number of such enterprises offer experiences and work camps around the world; many have a specific focus on topics such as health and health research, children, women's empowerment, technical assistance, wildlife conservation, and the environment (for example).

International Partnership for Service Learning™ (IPSL) was founded in 1982 as the first international, not-for-profit, educational organization to serve students, colleges, universities, service agencies, and related organizations around the world. More than 3,400 colleges and universities in the United States and in 25 other nations are involved. The programs are collaborative and short term or semester-long. Each site and experience are well described in brochures which also itemize the focus of the curriculum, local university partner, language of instruction, credits per semester (16–19; most at 18), housing accommodations, service opportunities, and academic excursions. IPSL also organizes conferences, research, and training activities for faculty and service-agency staff and has developed an accredited, master's degree program in International Development and Service.

Iowa State University Service Learning in Peru is an eight-week, summer service-learning program in Peru in partnership with ProWorld-Peru. The company consults with community leaders to assess the community assets and projects for the students. Participants live with a Peruvian host family.

Northwestern University Global Engagement Studies Institute offers service-learning programs in Bolivia, the Dominican Republic, India, Kenya, Nicaragua, South Africa, and Uganda for teams of students to collaborate with partner organizations such as the Foundation for Sustainable Development, Social Entrepreneur Corps, and ThinkImpact. They join nearly 400 students across the country to work for positive and sustainable change in the areas of health, education, environment, youth, women's empowerment, social enterprise development, and micro-finance

Assessing and Evaluating International Service Learning

Purdue University has prepared a list of tools to assess international, global and multicultural studies that have a service-learning component:

- Assessing and Evaluating International Service-Learning
- Civic-Minded Graduate Diversity & Oppression Scale
- Social Justice Advocacy Scale
- The Munroe Multicultural Attitude Scale
- The Multicultural Efficacy Scale
- Multicultural Competency Change Scale
- Global Cultural Knowledge and Awareness Aptitude Scale
- Cultural Awareness Profile
- Intercultural Sensitivity Scale
- Assessment of Intercultural Competence (AIC)
- Benefits, Events, and Values Inventory
- Counseling Inventory: A Self-Report Measure of Multicultural Competencies

Volunteering Abroad

International Voluntary Service dates back more than 85 years.[70] It has elements of both research and service learning and is another means of applying classroom knowledge. Many universities, centers and institutes, and student-led organizations create opportunities for students to volunteer abroad, typically during a winter interim session or spring break.

The International Alternate Spring Break (ASB) offers an opportunity for both service learning and volunteer programming and has become common practice at universities and colleges. It is arranged through various university offices and centers as well as professional organizations.

University Offices That Manage the ASB

- Service Learning
- Volunteer Services
- Student Affairs
- Office of Student Leadership and Service
- Global Learning
- Community Engagement and Service
- Center for Civic Engagement and Public Service
- Center for Civic Engagement and Learning
- Center for Experiential Services and Career Learning
- Center for Volunteerism and Social Action
- Student leadership and Civic Engagement
- Office of the Dean of Students
- Global Engagement Studies Institute

An ASB is an opportunity for undergraduate students (primarily) in all disciplines to obtain a meaningful and beneficial international experience working on a project and interacting with individuals who need assistance. The work that students accomplish in this brief (typically one week) international venture draws upon their creativity, activism, sense of inquiry, and leadership. One organization (IASTE) noted that "students who have successfully overcome the challenges brought on by international work experience stand out from the crowd at interview."

> *These experiences open the volunteers' minds and hearts to new realities and bring into sharp perspective what is truly essential.*[71]

Some of the programs are student run (Vanderbilt University) and others are led or facilitated by students who have had experience at a specific international site with the local community. A university center, or on-campus organization, may initiate an ASB that is specific to its academic focus and mission. For example, the Center for Nonviolence & Peace Studies at the University of Rhode Island in partnership with the Office of International Education offers a training and cultural experience in Nepal during spring break, and the Hillel Foundation at the University of Miami has organized trips to Argentina and Israel to connect with Jewish community organizations.

The programs are grounded in service related to social justice issues such as poverty; homelessness and inadequate housing; food insecurity; environmental sustainability; issues of women and children; and limited education, racism, domestic violence, and health illiteracy.

Like all of the international ventures described thus far, volunteer work begins with a period of preparation for students to learn about regional history, language, culture, and politics and to prepare for the project. Project discussions may also occur after the students are on the ground and connect with the grassroots groups and/or local not-for-profit organizations.

Numerous professional organizations and NGOs partner with universities or manage their programs independently (see below). Each organization designs, plans, and arranges programs in coordination with university calendars; some will customize an experience for a student who has a specific goal. The range of sites for volunteer activities arranged by these organizations can be broader than a university can arrange alone.

Alternate Spring Break (ASB) Programs at U.S. Universities

Iowa State University, El Salvador offers groups of 12 or more students who are accommodated in a volunteer house in San Salvador where they collaborate with the local citizens to rebuild homes and roads, tutor, and provide recreational activities for children. They feed malnourished babies and offer literacy and computer training. The student volunteers also participate in various historical, cultural, and recreational activities.

Social work students at the Florida State University ASB in Grenada collaborate with a local agency in Grenada to engage volunteers in projects in Mt. Parnassus, St. George's focused on strengthening healthy families, reducing domestic violence, and minimizing the risk of exposure to sexually transmitted infections. Planning sessions on campus introduce the students to the cultural and social dynamics in Grenada, and organize task groups to develop training materials and activities for adolescent mothers.

Students at James Madison University work with not-for-profit organizations and volunteers in Central American countries to build houses and restore communities, help in schools, engage in reforestation, and build stoves for Mayan families and playgrounds for children. They also assist with rehabilitation and empowerment services that help people assimilate back into society.

The San Jose State University program in Oaxaca, Mexico, is a partnership among Associated Students' Cesar E. Chavez Community Action Center, Student Involvement, and the Department of Health Science to create a sustainable economy through art, community education, and environmental stewardship.

Utah Valley University students serve a severely underfunded primary school at risk of closing in a community just outside of Managua, Nicaragua. The students work with children on educational activities, English classes, sports, after-school programming, site beautification, and other projects. Multiple universities throughout the United States collaborate on this project.

Groups of Eastern Michigan University students visit Haiti to focus on social justice issues, specifically, environmental sustainability, and reforestation projects.

University of Southern California, Thailand, Mexico, and Guatemala programs enlist students to volunteer at an orphanage in Thailand, work with a nonprofit to empower women, teach microfinancing in India, continue work with the effects of eco-tourism in Isla Mujeres, Mexico, and assist with an elementary school in Guatemala.

The Office of Service Learning at Eckerd College plans drug and alcohol free weeks for students to work on projects such as maintaining trails in a forest in Iceland, community development in Belize, and environmental sustainability with an organization in the jungle in Puerto Rico and at a mountainous preserve in Costa Rica. The have helped with rescued animals in wildlife sanctuaries in Puerto Rico, Nicaragua, and Guatemala; worked with an indigenous community in the rain forest in Ecuador; promoted economic development for a community in the Dominican Republic; provided health and medical care to local residents in the Yucatan, Mexico; and worked with orphan children in Panama.

Professional Organizations Support Alternative (Spring) Breaks

Many not-for-profit and for-profit professional organizations connect volunteers to opportunities and offer services such as on-site orientation and accommodations. Volunteers usually pay fees for these experiences. Universities provide information to students for such programs but do not guarantee them.

The organizations can direct students to immersion, experiential learning program opportunities in developing and developed countries, across all continents, to engage in a range of activities. Go Volunteer Abroad is a database of such opportunities.

Upholding Values in International Research Engaging Students

As U.S. universities expand into other cultures, there is a need to investigate before committing to a program overseas whether there could be a situation that compromises our values. Some of our partners in other countries may not be in a position to uphold the principles of academic freedom, research integrity, openness, and human rights and equality—all basic tenets of our academic institutions. The UAE's Vision 2021 points out the importance of "resisting the value-flattening effects of globalization."[72] The prospect of revenue generation cannot override some of these very important values we would never sacrifice through partnerships in our own country.

> *Maintaining our fundamental values while embracing cultural differences will be a challenge for all of us. It will not be conflict free.*[73]

As students—from any country—consider sites for research, internships, service learning, and volunteer activity, it is important to consider the nature of the environment, whether it is compatible with the standards and mores of their university and countries. Decisions may need to be made to go forward or to withdraw. Certainly, there are safety issues in many parts of the world and risk management offices at universities can advise on those locations, but there are also human rights issues that may come to the fore. Students from LaSalle College in Newton, MA, for example, were planning a service-learning trip to Uganda when they learned that the Ugandan government had passed a harsh antigay law making homosexuality punishable by imprisonment. After considerable deliberation, the trip was continued even though the laws of the country were unacceptable to the university and its constituents. Upon return, the students, faculty, and community took the opportunity for candid discussion facing a serious moral question, ultimately leading to the decision that the relationship would end.[74]

Before establishing the Duke-Kunshan partnership in China, the university developed an important document describing the criteria to be satisfied for this venture to proceed.[75] These criteria were codified in a set of core principles that can relate, in general, to student, faculty, and partnership engagements abroad being considered. They will be mentioned again in terms of developing physical and virtual partnerships with international colleagues, organizations, and governments. Paraphrased, they state that Duke's engagements will do the following:

- Ensure academic freedom as the foundation of academic quality.
- Preserve integrity and enhance reputation.
- Engage with partners who have clearly shared goals.
- Work in regions that maximize opportunities for students and faculty.
- Create and cultivate significant opportunities in research, teaching, and addressing global problems.
- Prioritize programs for financial sustainability.
- Become a good citizen of the region, develop connections, and build assets.
- Minimize encumbrances and risks, and maximize freedom within a cultural context.

Underlying all of these issues is the importance of intercultural education, a core skill gained from evolving relations among cultural groups that prepare individuals "for meaningful and ethical work in a multicultural, global society."[76] Understanding and tolerance are fostered by common experiences and result in respect and the realization of common values. As we develop global consciousness and global competence and become global citizens, global leaders, and global stewards, we must also understand that truth is grounded in personal understanding, for others will see "truth" from different backgrounds, experiences, and perspectives—and the two visions may not coincide. This has been described as "the concept of simultaneous truths."[77] These truths may be tested in international collaborations.

NOTES

[1] The Council of Graduate Schools. (2007). *Graduate education: The Backbone of American competitiveness and innovation*, p. 2.

[2] Bender, T. (2001). Then and now: The disciplines and civic engagement. *Liberal Education, 87*(1), 6–17.

[3] Yojana, S. (2010). Global: UN forges world partnerships with universities. *International Professors Project*, p. 148. http://www.universityworldnews.com/article.php?story=20101120090132925.

[4] Science progress. (2011). *U.S. scientific research and development*, Retrieved from www.scienceprogress.org

[5] U.S. Department of Education. Retrieved from www.ED.gov

[6] Bidwell, A. (2015). More students earning STEM degrees, report shows. *U.S. News and World Report*. http://www.usnews.com/news/articles/2015/01/27/more-students-earning-degrees-in-stem-fields-report-shows.

7. The Partnership for a New American Economy & The Partnership for New York City. (2012). *Not coming to America: Why the U.S. is falling behind in the global race for talent* (pp. 6–7). Retrieved from http://www.renewoureconomy.org/sites/all/themes/pnae/not-coming-to-america.pdf

8. Overall, the United States is outranked in STEM graduates by South Korea, Germany, Canada, and the UK, and the rate of growth of students majoring in the STEM fields is at the bottom of the academic disciplines. Only 4.4 percent of U.S. students are studying engineering, whereas 33.9 percent of students in Singapore, 10 percent of Israeli students, and 6.1 percent of students from the United States are preparing in engineering fields. Ibid., p. 30.

9. Ibid., p. 6.

10. United State Census (2014). *Majority of STEM college graduates do not work in STEM occupations.* Release No. CB14-130. Retrieved from http://www.census.gov/newsroom/press-releases/2014/cb14-130.html

11. The Partnership for a New American Economy & The Partnership for New York City. (2012, May). *Not coming to America: Why the U.S. is falling behind in the global race for talent.* Retrieved from http://www.renewoureconomy.org/sites/all/themes/pnae/not-coming-to-america.pdf

12. Finn, M. G. (2011). *Stay rates of foreign doctorate recipients from U.S. universities.* Prepared for the Division of Research Resources Statistics of the National Science Foundation by ORISE (1–19). This paper includes significant information on stay rates according to countries of origin of the students, "circulation (leave and return cycles) of graduates and other facts about the universities, countries, and disciplines with the highest stay rates." Retrieved from https://orise.orau.gov/files/sep/stay-rates-foreign-doctorate-recipients-2011.pdf

13. The fields evaluated include physical sciences, math, computer science, agricultural sciences, life sciences, computer/EE, other engineering, economics, and social sciences.

14. Finn, M. G. (2014). *Stay rates of foreign doctorate recipients from U.S. universities.* Prepared for the Division of Science Resources Statistics of the National Science Foundation by the Oak Ridge Institute for Science and Education (ORISE). Retrieved from https://orise.orau.gov/files/sep/stay-rates-foreign-doctorate-recipients-2011.pdf.

15. Highest for students from China and India—significantly above the others, then Iran, Romania, Bulgaria, and Yugoslavia; lowest for those students from Thailand, Jordan, Brazil, South Africa, Chile, New Zealand, and Indonesia.

16. For example, 9/11 and tightened security and restrictions, current global economic downturn and declining job market, period of postdoctoral study in the United States, difficulty in obtaining visas, etc.

17. The Partnership for a New American Economy & The Partnership for New York City. (2012). *Not coming to America: Why the U.S. is falling behind in the global race for talent* (p. 9). Retrieved from http://www.renewoureconomy.org/sites/all/themes/pnae/not-coming-to-america.pdf

18. Ibid., p. 15.

19. Furchtgott-Roth, D. (2013). The economic benefits of immigration. Issue Brief No. 18, Manhattan Institute for Policy Research. Retrieved from http://www.manhattan-institute.org/html/economic-benefits-immigration-5712.html

20. Ibid., pp. 21, 24, 25, 34–35.

21. Klein, J., Rice, C., & Levy, J. (2011). *U.S. education reform and national security* (Independent Task Force Report No. 68). Council on Foreign Relations (1–59). http://i.cfr.org/content/publications/attachments/TFR68_Education_National_Security.pdf.

22. U.S. Congress Joint Economic Committee. (2012). *STEM education: Preparing for the jobs of the future* (6, 8–9). Retrieved from http://iedse.org/temp/wpcontent/uploads/2015/02/www.iedse_.org_documents_STEM-Education-Preparing-for-the-Jobs-of-the-Future-.pdf

23. Institute of International Education. "Fields of Study of U.S. Study Abroad Students, 2002/03-2011/12." *Open Doors Report on International Educational Exchange*, p. 75.

²⁴ Lohmann, J. R., Rollins, H. A., & Hoey, J. J. (2006). Defining, developing and assessing global competence in engineers. *European Journal of Engineering Education, 31,* 119–131.

²⁵ Grindel, T., (Ed.). (2006). *Final report of the Global Engineering Initiative: Educating the next generation of engineers for the global marketplace.* Hanover, Germany: Continental AG, pp. 1–108.

²⁶ Due to the lockstep or highly sequenced curriculum.

²⁷ See examples of several programs in Leggett, K. (2011). Encouraging STEM students to study abroad. *International Educator* 20(4), p. 44.

²⁸ UNESCO. (2010). *Engineering: Issues, challenges and opportunities for developing states* (Report 29). Retrieved from http://unesdoc.unesco.org/images/0018/001897/189753e.pdf

²⁹ Interactive screen experiments; 3-D immersive environments; roving field technologies; robotic observatories; remote experiments and MegaLab experiments. Retrieved from www.open.ac.uk/esteem

³⁰ The Oxfam Global Citizenship Program for early learners through age 19 identifies the ability of a globally competent student to investigation the world beyond their immediate environment, recognize their own and others' perspectives, effectively communicate their ideas with diverse audiences, and translate ideas and findings into appropriate actions to improve conditions. Retrieved from http://www.oxfam.org.uk/education/global-citizenship

³¹ Lane, J. E., Owens, T. L., & Ziegler, P. (2014). *States go global: State government engagement in higher education internationalization.* Albany, NY: State University of New York, Nelson A. Rockefeller Institute of Government. Retrieved from http://www.rockinst.org/pdf/education/2014-05-28-States_Go_Global.pdf

³² Drexel University and Temple University, both located in Philadelphia, PA, offer summer courses for high school students through nearly every college.

³³ The programs include (1) Worlds Apart, World Together, Conflict, Culture and Cooperation, (2) Diplomacy and Dictators: U.S. Foreign Policy in an Uncertain World, and (3) Global Public health and Environmental Sustainability in the 21st Century. Retrieved from http://www.american.edu/sis/CommunityofScholars/About-the-Program.cfm

³⁴ *Explore foreign policy, international relations, and global politics.* Retrieved from http://www.upenn.edu/almanac/volumes/v62/n20/summercamps.html#academic

³⁵ Service Learning in Barcelona and Service Learning in Paris are programs of cultural immersion through community service and study sponsored by www.study-serve.org.

³⁶ Academic study associated pre-collegiate academic enrichment programs. These programs are frequently organized with universities. Retrieved from www.asaprograms.com

³⁷ The Summer Science Program offers rising high school seniors an opportunity to conduct research in celestial navigation at the New Mexico Institute of Technology, Socorro, New Mexico, or at the University of Colorado, Boulder. Retrieved from http://www.summerscience.org/

³⁸ The Institute for Broadening Participation, Pathways to Science: Science, Technology, Engineering and Mathematics website offers (2015) well over 200 formal opportunities primarily for U.S. high school students to engage in STEM learning and/or research opportunities. Retrieved from http://www.pathwaystoscience.org/

³⁹ Musiker Discovery Programs and Discovery Internships. Retrieved from http://www.summerdiscovery.com/

⁴⁰ Biomedical Research Academy, Chemistry Research Academy, Experimental Physics and Social Justice Research Academy at the University of Pennsylvania.

⁴¹ The program has been ongoing since 1969.

[42] Healy, N., & Rathburn, L. C. (2013). *Developing globally aware scientists and engineers in nanoscale science and engineering.* Paper Id# 6264 presented at the American Society for Engineering Education Annual Conference: Developing Globally Aware Engineers and Scientists in Nanotechnology, Atlanta, GA, June 23–26. Retrieved from http://www.asee.org/public/conferences/20/papers/6264/view

[43] Universitas 21 is the leading global network of research-intensive universities that work together to foster global citizenship and institutional innovation through research-inspired teaching and learning, student mobility. The 25 members collectively enroll over 1.3 million students and employ over 220,000 staff and faculty. Their collective budgets are greater than $25 billion, including an annual research grant income of more than $6.5 billion. Retrieved from http://www.universitas21.com/

[44] Germany (University of Jena, Ulm University, and the University of Hannover), Italy (University of Perugia), Singapore (National University of Singapore), and the United Kingdom (University of Strathclyde).

[45] Projects are available in arts and humanities, performing arts, biology, chemistry, engineering, mathematics, physics, astronomy, computer science, medicine, biomedical sciences, law, economics, management, politics, and social studies.

[46] KU Leuven University, Belgium; Leiden University, the Netherlands; Utrecht University, the Netherlands; University of Helsinki, Finland; Ruprecht-Karls University, Heidelberg, Germany; Ludwig-Maximilians University, Munich; University of Zurich, Switzerland; University of Geneva, Switzerland; Karolinska Institutet, Stockholm, Sweden; University of Helsinki, Finland; Ruprecht-Karls University, Heidelberg, Germany; Ludwig-Maximilians University, Munich; University of Zurich, Switzerland; University of Geneva, Switzerland; Karolinska Institutet, Stockholm, Sweden.

[47] Albania, Belgium, Bulgaria, Canada, Croatia, Czech Republic, Denmark, Estonia, France, Germany, Greece, Hungary, Iceland, Italy, Latvia, Lithuania, Luxembourg, the Netherlands, Norway, Poland, Portugal, Romania, Slovakia, Spain, Turkey, the United Kingdom, and the United States.

[48] The Brazilian Ministry of Science and Technology's Council for Scientific and Technological Development–CNPq and the Ministry of Education's federal Agency for the Support and Evaluation of Graduate Education (CAPES).

[49] Graduating seniors, graduate students, post-docs, or early-career professionals.

[50] Australia, China, Japan, Korea, New Zealand, Singapore, and Taiwan.

[51] As of 2016, students from Malawi, Uganda, Mozambique, Bangladesh, South Sudan, Cambodia, and Ghana are engaged in the BHEARD program. Retrieved from http://bheard.anr.msu.edu/about_borlaug_higher_education_for_agricultural_research_and_development

[52] Bozic, M. (2009). Education without borders. *International Journal of Young Leaders, 1,* 65–68. Retrieved from http://leadersjournal.org/index.php?option=com_content&view=article&id=75&Itemid=11

[53] The conference is now in its tenth year.

[54] The internship: Generation i. (2014, September 6). *The Economist.* Retrieved from http://www.economist.com/news/international/21615612-temporary-unregulated-and-often-unpaid-internship-has-become-route

[55] United States Department of Labor. (April 2010). *Internship programs under the Fair Labor Standards Act* (Fact Sheet #71). Wage and Hour Division.

[56] Brown, M. R., & Seltzer, J. (2014). Employment issues for internships, 1–8), *Intern Bridge.* Retrieved from www.InternBridge.com

[57] Accra, Berlin, Buenos Aires, Florence, London, Madrid, Paris, Prague, Shanghai, Sydney, Tel Aviv, and Washington, DC.

[58] Australia, Brazil, China, Finland, Germany, Mexico, Taiwan, and Uruguay.

[59] Zinggeler, M. V., & López-Gómez, C. L. (2010). Internships at consular offices: A gateway top international communication and careers. *Global Business Languages, Challenges and Critical Junctures, 15*(8),105–115.

[60] Hartman, E., & Kiely, R. (2014). Pushing boundaries: Introduction to the global service-learning special section. *Michigan Journal of Community Service Learning*, 21:55–63.

[61] Paracka, D. J., Buddie, A. M., & Dumas, D. S. (2015, February*). Global scholarship: From service learning to community engagement.* Retrieved from http://globalsl.org/global-scholarship-from-service-learning-to-community-engagement/

[62] Crabtree, R. D. (2007). Asking hard questions about the impact of international service learning. *Conversations on Jesuit Higher Education, 31,* 39–42.

[63] Ibid.

[64] Thomas Winston Morgan, President, IPSL Service Learning + Community Engagement, in a letter of support for a proposed certificate service learning and public engagement at Portland State University, 2009.

[65] Bringle, R. G., Hatcher, J. A., & Jones, S. G. (Eds.). (2011). *International Service Learning: Conceptual Frameworks and Research.* Sterling, VA: Stylus.

[66] Wilhelm, I. (2012). For a growing number of freshmen, packing for college requires a passport. The Chronicle of Higher Education, 140–148.

[67] Gutmann, A. (2014). Assessing undergraduate education at Penn. A selected topics self-study report prepared for the Middle States Commission on Higher Education, 42–57.

[68] Xing, J., & Ma, C. (Eds.). (2010). *Service-learning in Asia: Current models and practices.* Hong Kong University Press.

[69] Lin, P. L. (2011). *Service learning in higher education: National and international connections.* University of Indianapolis Press.

[70] Lee, H., & Imre, B. (Eds.). (2011). White Paper on International Voluntary Service: Global Strategies for Global Challenges. Coordinating Committee for International Voluntary Service. Paris, France: UNESCO House.

[71] A quote from the Iowa State University description of their ASB in El Salvador in accord with the Project FIAT International.

[72] UAE Vision 2021 (12). Retrieved from https://www.vision2021.ae/en

[73] Brodhead, R. H. (2011). Talent knows no borders. American campuses abroad. *The Chronicle Review.* December 9, 2011. Review B9-B10.

[74] November 19, 2014. Information communicated as an email.

[75] *Duke-Kunshan Planning Guide.* Prepared by the Office of the Provost, Office of Global Strategy and Programs. Updated March 15, 2011.

[76] United Nations Educational, Scientific and Cultural Organization (UNESCO).

[77] Adams, J. M., & Carfagna, A. (2006). *Coming of age in a globalized world: The next generation.* Bloomfield, CT: Kumarian Press.

Chapter Four
International Research Cooperation, Collaboration, Partnerships, and Alliances

Introduction

Never before has there been such an explosion of working globally, expanding our presence globally, and caring about global problems that can be approached—and ideally resolved—by university investigators and students in collaboration with other academics, governments, and the public and private sectors as research and funding partners. World-class research is inherently international and a significant thrust of a research university,[1] but universities often leave faculty to their own devices and personal relationships to establish research relationships with international colleagues. A few U.S. universities and universities abroad have offices specifically designed to promote international research (see Chapter 1). There are many ways and variations in purpose for establishing such relationships, but none are more compelling than the efforts of scientists and engineers along with colleagues in the social sciences and humanities to solve pressing health-related, social, and environmental problems, to name only a few, and to use these combined disciplines for diplomatic purposes. It has been suggested that "whole-brain engineers and scientifically inspired humanists foster more than just innovation," but "yields flexible individuals who adapt to unanticipated changes as the world evolved unpredictably."[2]

> *International research collaboration is basic and essential to research activity*[3]
>
> *...through science collaboration, we can build bridges of trust and cooperation for the benefit of all.*[4]

The University of Waterloo (Canada) suggested a series of initiatives to promote international research, and this occurred more than 15 years ago![5] Most of these are in play today and are a good reminder of potential strategies:

- Attract international conferences and events to the university then showcase the research.
- Advertise university strengths in major journals and research or scholarly publications (see *The Chronicle of Higher Education*).
- Establish seed funding to promote and support new international initiatives.
- Include international initiatives in fundraising efforts (see Chapters 2 and 3).
- Develop a reporting system that identifies and tracks international research projects (see Chapters 2 and 8).
- Ensure that policies and guidelines related to faculty performance reviews and promotion and tenure encourage participation in research and teaching that has an international focus (see Chapter 2).
- Establish a target in overhead funds generated from new international projects to help support international initiatives.
- Establish guidelines to distribute overhead funds from international projects and tuition income from international students to those who lead international initiatives.

Collaboration is a long-standing practice of scientists worldwide. Formal and informal interactions are relatively straightforward across academic units within institutions, across universities within the country, and with other partners such as government, industry, national labs and nongovernmental organizations (NGOs). Grant mechanisms promote these—typically interdisciplinary—interactions. Research collaboration among international partners has also been characteristic of scientific activity for scores of years, taking advantage of compatible expertise through both formal and informal partnerships, as well as other activities such as conferences, workshops, joint publications, consultations, site visits, exchange, and training.

Scientists have always belonged to a kind of international fellowship, based on collaborations grounded in common interests and values that cut across national lines.[6]

Such relationships rise to a significant level of complexity when investigators work across national borders in more formalized, long-term, open-ended, and strategic research relationships. True partnerships and alliances, joint projects, research consortia, and even brick-and-mortar collaborations for education, research, and capacity building are now the norm.[7] Difficulties in making them work need to be addressed and resolved.

Motivations, Benefits, and Challenges of International Research Collaboration[8]

Each university, government, and industry partner can outline the advantages of international collaborative research, but in reality, most of the motives are common to all of them: economic, scientific, and technological competitive advantage; greater opportunity; specialization and a multidisciplinary approach to finding "socially-responsible solutions to science and engineering problems"; access to the best talent worldwide and to new and emerging international markets; shared costs of research, technology, and other infrastructure; enhanced funding, scaling a project; increased speed to results; greater prestige for the institution; and potential for longer term projects.[9] Organizations and international governments, in particular, also recognize that international research interactions:[10,11,12,13,14]

- Promote economic development, exports, and FDI.
- Build capacity of civil society and elevate women and underrepresented groups.
- Become a vehicle for student and faculty recruitment.
- Open doors to build lasting relationships.
- Promote knowledge and research quality by combining perspectives. International research publications have a significantly higher citation impact than single-country authored papers.
- Provide experiences that promote professional development and cultural understanding.
- Provide access to unique sites and populations.
- Strengthen areas of weaknesses.
- Engender goodwill—a tool for science diplomacy and foreign policy.

This long list of benefits makes collaborative international research seem imperative for progress, productivity, and competitive advantage to the mutual benefit of collaborating parties. Governments see the advantage of scientific collaboration and international partnerships and often make such relationships part of their strategy to enhance their prestige and competitive advantage.

> *Governments have become drivers of internationalization of higher education, particularly because it relates to public diplomacy, national security and economic development.*[15]

Abu Dhabi, for example, cites international partnerships and collaboration as a strategy to upgrade higher education and to underpin a change from an oil-based economy to the development of semiconductor, aerospace, renewable energy, and health industries. This plan requires United Arab Emirates (UAE) universities to extend their research focus.[16]

Singapore began to invest in science and technology strategy in the 1980s by co-funding projects with the UK, China, and Japan (among others) and developing programs and research centers, with top international universities and industry on the Campus for Research Excellence and Technology Enterprise (CREATE) of the National University of Singapore. The priority areas for these interactions include energy, health, new materials, and sustainability. A position paper on internationalization of Australian science emphasizes the importance of collaboration:

> *The last major Australian invention that did not involve some international input was probably the stump-jump plough in 1876.*[17]

The Global Research Council is an "extreme partnership" among the heads of research councils and funding agencies of 60–70 countries. It was established in 2012 at the Global Merit Review Summit convened by then director of the National Science Foundation (NSF), Subra Suresh, to promote rigorous peer review and scientific integrity (that year's topic).[18] The meetings continued as a venue to discuss issues and develop principles to strengthen the global scientific enterprise. Regional meetings were convened to settle upon a few prospective themes for future annual meetings: Open access and scientific integrity, supporting the next gen researchers, and building education and research capacity. The group meets around the globe hosted by scientific agencies of two countries.

But there are also challenges to engaging in global research collaboration and partnerships. In 2014, young scientists were asked for their views on the biggest challenges to global collaboration.[19] Their insightful responses included: Inflexible cultural norms that drive ethical behaviors, attitudes and partial truths;[20] inefficiencies and time frames in research; limited funding for collaboration; managing technical "secrets"; regulatory mandates; fear of being "scooped"; language barriers;

safeguarding intellectual property and rewarding innovation and creation; overemphasis on competition and to focus on short-term gain versus long-term stabilization of a relationship; data-sharing responsibility; national security; and the need for policies for coordinated sharing of resources, funding equipment, data, and talent. They offered impressive suggestions and ideas to resolve some of these issues.

Other barriers that inhibit smooth international research collaborations include differences in the laws, regulations, and customs of a country; racial and gender biases that may evolve from historical imbalances of power;[21] inadequate human subjects protection in a partner country and political, economic, and social conditions that engender risk. The need for consistency in peer review of research proposals across countries based on expert assessment, transparency of the evaluation process, impartiality, appropriateness, confidentiality, and integrity and ethical consideration was emphasized at the Global Merit Review Summit (2012).[22]

It is a challenge for universities and investigators worldwide to embrace these potential obstacles to international collaboration and resolve them—or debunk them—in the case of inaccurate perceptions. The risk/benefit ratio must be considered in each case.

Collaborative Relationships between Developed and Developing Countries[23]

Science and technology in both developed and developing countries can address a nation's unique needs for economic growth, national security, human capital development, and public trust. The NSF Board Task Force on International Science and Engineering Partnerships[24] examined the role of the federal government in using science and technology to facilitate partnerships between developed and developing countries and raise the quality of life and environmental protection. While the recommendations and strategies were focused on governmental action, implementation through research and capacity building require the involvement and expertise of universities.

Scientific and technological aid to developing countries is a component of foreign policy and an issue of security, morality, and fairness. It helps partner governments improve law and order, recover from conflict, and manage a range of transnational issues. Science and technology must, therefore, become rooted in the social fabric of developing countries.

> *The biggest single factor limiting developing countries' potential for achieving sustainable economic growth—or even attaining the Millennium*

Development Goals—is their ability to access and apply the fruits of modern science and technology.[25]

Although both developed and developing nations face the same core research problems (energy, health, then environment, etc.), the effectiveness of working together can be stymied by disparity between them in physical and financial resources, time availability, and incentives within universities. Universities in developing countries may not have a culture of research or grantsmanship—or even of collaboration. Academic salaries are often vastly different; there may not be a research office to provide support; faculty time is limited and the benefits of the research to the advancement of a faculty member may differ.[26] Agreements need to avoid exploitation and paternalism if collaborators have different economic and cultural values and a power differential. Foreign students and postdocs can be very helpful in this context as they are already experienced in both cultures.[27]

The National Institutes of Health (NIH) Fogarty International Center is one example of a major program to support clinical, and applied behavioral and biomedical research and training for U.S. and foreign investigators who address global health issues and guide international health policies in the developing world. (See the discussion of NIH programs in Chapter 2 as well.)

The International Professors Project (IPP) is an independent, nonprofit worldwide organization that recruits academics (new graduates, midcareer switchers, early retirees, and professors emeriti) to engage in university teaching and mentoring, curriculum development, and global collaborations and alliances, and to conduct research on university campuses in the developing world. The goal is to internationalize college and university faculties in host countries and develop a cadre of new international professors as ambassadors who will further higher education across the globe that is free from bias or competing agendas. Those who join IPP must have the cultural sophistication and understanding of international relations to develop the curriculum and strategies to accommodate global pedagogy global.

Globalized research collaborations and partnerships are also tools of diplomacy[28] promoting democratic values, growing the economy, providing international aid, and building "relationships between countries that can be sustained regardless of the political winds."[29] Scientific diplomacy connects science and politics independent of national origin, age, ethnicity, gender, or politics.[30] Scientists and technologists are good "ambassadors and among America's most effective diplomats."[31] In 2009, President Obama began the Science Envoy program to improve foreign relations. Distinguished scientists were selected "to develop partnerships, improve collaboration, and forge mutually beneficial relationships between other nations and the United States."[32] This program follow on the earlier U.S. Embassy Science

Attaché program that ended in the mid-1990s and the United States department of State's Embassy Science Fellows Program of 2001.[33]

CRDF Global's tag line, "Peace and Prosperity through Science Collaboration," says it all.

International Interactions and Relationships in Research

Our international partnerships, like all of our work, arise from intellectual curiosity and research power, but are focused on creating imaginative, pragmatic, and enduring solutions to big issues.[34]

Cooperation, collaboration, partnerships, and alliances are terms that describe the relationships universities create with other universities, governments, businesses, nonprofits, and NGOs working together in general or on a specific project. These terms are used interchangeably in the academic setting, but they have more specific definitions and terms in business.

Cooperation and Collaboration

Cooperation and collaboration are not the same. Cooperation occurs when different teams or groups are congenial, cooperative and willing to share information, know-how, skills, and expertise, each contributing in different ways, to work on joint projects, share facilities, develop centers and virtual networks, and train and co-supervise students. Cooperation does not necessarily result in a productive collaboration.

Collaboration among engaged parties is characteristically well meshed and requires the "ability and flexibility to align goals, interests and assets with others in real time." A plan is developed for the entire project (versus sequential planning) that specifies the contributions of each team. Strategies are synchronized and performance measures agreed upon.[35] A collaboration is not typically codified in a legal contract and may not have equally distributed responsibilities among the partners, but to be successful, the plan and project must be mutually beneficial, complementary, not competitive, strategically located, leverage strong existing relationships, and expand upon existing strengths. It should be compatible with institutional core mission, philosophies, goals, and dominant research themes and set the stage for multilateral relationships. It often brings in new external financial sources, increases opportunities to establish linkages with industry and commercial enterprises, and needs to be sustainable.

> *Collaborations need to be grounded in authenticity. They need to take the heritage, the core values and the known strengths of the partner institutions and use these as a catalyst through which to realize global ambition. Collaborations should address real-world issues and partnerships characterized by pioneering ingenuity and practical application. Successful international collaboration requires resourcefulness, flexibility and proven expertise, enthusiasm, vision and commitment.[36]*

A successful collaboration requires the commitment and chemistry of people with different interests and benefits both. Methodologies for measuring various aspects of collaborations, including the impact, are included in Snowball metrics, the International Research Evaluations Metrics Study funded by the NSF (see Chapter 7). Nonetheless, as stated in the Universities UK document on international research collaboration[37] success still has a random quality:

> *part chance, part hard work, part good communication between institution level management teams and academics, a commitment to experiment and learn, and a willingness to recognise and respond to the aspirations and circumstances of one's partners.[38]*

Multicultural collaboration is the very nature of international research projects, bringing together individuals who most likely have different histories, traditions, racial attitudes, and sense of self and language. Conflicting values, especially, can make a project difficult. Why and how to build successful multicultural partnerships have been well documented in a public forum.[39]

Partnerships

A partnership is a voluntary collaborative agreement between two or more parties to work together to achieve a common purpose or undertake a specific task and to share risks, responsibilities, resources, competencies, and benefits.[40] Universities enter into many partnerships through virtually all of their colleges, programs, and administrative offices.

Partnerships are contractual and transactional relationships. They are real only when all partners contribute and gain from the relationship. True partnerships are deep and long lasting, thus in developing a partnership the players need to consider the real cost of the initiative, whether it adds value or is an opportunity cost, there will be a gain or loss to either party, and whether the values and a commitment to open communication are shared. Cultural factors can shape the success or failure[41] of a partnership.

A good partnership has the potential to "change the game." Parties with complementary expertise or skills, a record of successful partnerships, access to networks and money, a compatible academic culture, and the ability to adapt to changing circumstances are essential for success. Duplication of talents or imbalance in skills, competition for leadership, dissimilar reputations, failure to share risk, a "controlling" partner or a partner who "collects" partners (without true commitment), and misalignment with institutional mission will be unproductive.

Successful international partnerships require an investment of time at the outset to get to know and understand each other and their respective goals, and to build confidence and trust in one another. There will likely be differences in philosophies and cultures that will need to be accommodated, but working though such issues will build an even stronger relationship.[42]

One partnership can stimulate additional partnerships with the institutions and serve as a template for replication. A dual degree can lead to other interactions/collaboration with the partner institutions such as research projects. For example, the relationship between the University of Birmingham and the University of Illinois in a cultural heritage project was broadened to include other research relationships, as well as clinical, public health, and training interventions in China including the Birmingham Guangzhou Biobank Cohort Study of chronic disease, the largest medical intervention in the world.[43]

Partnerships were the foundation for the creation of King Abdullah University of Science and Technology (KAUST). The Global Research Partnership program and the Academic Excellence Alliance were designed to bring together the "best of the best" among universities worldwide to develop research partnerships in the disciplines germane to KAUST's mission and to develop curricula of the quality of the partner university to initiate KAUST's academic programs.

Each year, the U.S. Department of State, in collaboration with Concordia, USAID, and Peace Tech Lab (of the United States Institute of Peace) organizes the Global Partnerships Week celebration to recognize the important role public–private partnerships play in promoting diplomacy and development worldwide. The theme in 2016 was "Leveraging Innovation in Partnerships." Public and private organizations around the world are encouraged to develop their own activities to showcase their existing collaborations through conferences, panels, network gatherings, and webinars, and to create new collaborations as well. The one-day opening event of the week is arranged through the U.S. Department of State's Secretary's Office of Global Partnerships for partnership practitioners and leaders to come together to discuss common challenges and best practices, new partnership opportunities, and how to develop collaborative solutions.

Alliances/ Strategic Alliances

An alliance is usually an informal arrangement for purposes of cooperation that leads to the mutual benefit of like-minded organizations with common values. An alliance is not necessarily focused on a specific project and may have an uncertain time span or be a onetime event. Universities have entered into a number of global alliances.

The University of Birmingham (UK) and the University of Illinois (U.S.) alliance, known as the Birmingham Illinois Partnership for Education, Discovery and Engagement, began when the two universities recognized a shared civic mission, complementary research expertise, and similarities between Ironbridge Institute for Cultural Heritage (University of Birmingham) and Collaborative for Heritage and Management Policy (University of Illinois).

The Alliance for Global Sustainability is a cooperative venture with universities in the United States (Massachusetts Institute of Technology [MIT]), Switzerland (ETH Zurich), Sweden (Chalmers University of Technology), and the University of Tokyo (the initiator).

The University of Tokyo has established the International Alliance of Research Universities, including Yale; University of California, Berkeley; Peking University; National University of Singapore; Australian National University; ETH Zurich, Copenhagen, Cambridge; and Oxford. All are committed to educating future world leaders with joint degrees and research collaborations.

Consultancies

A consultancy can be an activity promoted by a research and innovation office in the United States and may be a specific program in the UK and Australia for faculty, students, and staff who wish to engage in this practice for personal gain or income to the university. Such offices help with negotiations, contracts, arrangements for use of university facilities, invoicing, debt collection, and income distribution.[44]

Consulting Programs and Services Offered by International Universities:

Universities may provide consulting on specific topics: The University of Edinburgh, University Consultancy provides the expertise, commercial services, high-tech equipment, and facilities of the university to outside organizations and governments around the world. Oxford University Consulting provides service and expertise in the energy sphere to companies in this sector on topics including storage systems, electric vehicles, smart meters, tidal energy, nanotechnology, and power conversion. The Institute for Economic Development Policy at the University of Birmingham provides assistance to European, national, regional, and local policymakers in businesses, universities, and governmental agencies on the development and evaluation of policies responding to economic changes affecting them.

Some universities assemble a general consulting practice: Cambridge Enterprise's Consultancy Services offer technical and creative solutions to specific business problems; expert reports on technical, economic, and commercial issues; expert witness advice; service to scientific advisory boards; reviews of government strategy and policies; art restoration; social housing assessments; development of training programs; and service for and appearances in film and TV documentaries.

Students, especially in colleges of business, may provide consulting service as part of their experiential learning—and be paid for their efforts. The students in the business policy and decision making course at the College of Business, Embry-Riddle Aeronautical University in Daytona Beach, FL, developed a report for the Kennedy Space Center (NASA) to document successes and failures in national and international partnerships for the space industry and government regulated industries. Their assessment of the purpose of the partnerships, structural arrangements, risks, and advantages and disadvantages provided significant benefit.

Northumbria University in Newcastle provides international development and advisory work for a wide range of international and national academic institutions, NGOs, and policy think tanks.

While consulting is clearly a practice at universities in the United States, it is rarely managed through a central administrative office, but may be a component of a specific unit or center, engaged in by university researchers independently or through their involvement with a for-profit organization. Universities recognize the practice and have administrative guidelines about the time commitment to this activity in order to protect their investment in educational and research activities. Academic consulting offers new insight into contemporary problems that can lead to research questions and even collaboration. Both the advantages and the downsides of this activity are well known within the academy.[45]

International Research Agreements

A number of agreements are signed routinely between collaborating universities and faculty at home and abroad.[46] These typically relate to a specific project and involve the university's international and research offices. The ritual of signing agreements with foreign universities acknowledges cooperation and demonstrates a sense of openness, collegiality, and willingness to engage with others, but only a portion of them become truly active. The terms of commitment should be clear from the outset, and the agreement categorized as to whether it is university, a college, department, or research group commitment—or simply ceremonial.

Most universities have developed a template or templates for creating an agreement or an memorandum of understanding (MOU) depending upon the level of the interaction and the activity or activities (education only, or research and education) to be covered. Others have a single document with a series of options that describe the goals of the relationship. Many agreements are only "enabling," and a specific research agreement follows up with details of how the relationship or engagement will function. The agreements are signed by university officials on both sides (typically the provost, general counsel, and the international office) and by the collaborating partners.

The important elements for international research agreements were covered with particular attention in the published proceedings of a meeting sponsored by the National Academies of Science[47] and thus will be discussed only superficially in this section, with the intention of merely drawing attention to them.

To avoid misunderstandings that may arise from possible different expectations of the partners (university, business, government), the topic of research ethics[48,49,50] and integrity and the standards of research compliance must be addressed when the collaboration is formed. It is important to assure mutual interests and benefits at the outset and ensure that the collective resources are adequate to achieve the objective. Technical issues such as authorship, data management, collection, storage, and analysis; management and storage of research materials (e.g., tissue cell lines, reagents); conflict of interest and conflict of commitment of faculty; and expectations of the roles, provision for dispute resolution, and responsibilities in research and timelines need to be addressed. The research team should consider the impact of the research inasmuch as the anticipated "improvement" or development may disrupt the currently accepted and perhaps traditional way of life for a group or community.

Legal issues in international collaboration require the involvement of the university counsel on both sides of the partnership[51] to evaluate whether the objectives of all parties are realistic, understood, and aligned—or at least compatible. If there is commitment to a long-term relationship, a substantial amount of money involved, and a high level of certainty that the relationship will be successful, the U.S. and foreign universities may consider developing a new corporation. A formal, legal partnership or entity, however, will have joint liabilities for torts, debts, contracts, and other obligations. MIT and Cambridge, for example, set up a separate entity to undertake a collaborative program that was funded for more than $100 million. The issue of U.S. campuses on foreign soil adds important responsibilities on each side in formalizing the relationship. Other areas where legal advice is essential relate to tax liabilities; transfer of money; overseas employment; immigration and employment overseas (work visas); facilities and administration cost of awards and subawards to foreign universities; shipping of research materials; and rules for disposition of assets, equipment, and vehicles when the project concludes.[52]

It was suggested that a major partnership should begin with a one-year pilot project to determine mutual interest, expectations, and objectives. If the venture goes smoothly, it can be extended.

University Research Cooperation, Collaboration, Partnerships, and Alliances

Individual to Individual Relationships

Investigators often create collaborative arrangements with overseas colleagues that involve the exchange of faculty and students. The relationship is formalized when a grant is involved, but there can be other less formal relationships. An interesting model of individual global partnerships is the establishment of satellite labs of U.S. investigators overseas in which the American faculty member and colleagues at one or more foreign universities create a new laboratory with resources from the foreign university, expanding the research and accessing students. Such arrangements work best when the faculty at the different sites are already working together and the expansion augments existing research capabilities and talent.[53]

University to University Partnership Strategies

Groups of research universities[54] around the world have signed the Hefei Statement on Concurrence pledging closer collaboration between groups of research intensive universities. The distinctive characteristics, roles, and contributions of research universities are itemized, supporting their mutual commitment to the breadth and depth of collaborative research and research training and the highest standards of research integrity, advancing their international reputation, welcoming different views and perspectives, supporting local and national communities, and contributing to international well-being.

Universities may develop partnerships anywhere the faculty have colleagues and the potential for relationships that support their research or connect the university in student exchanges—in other words, "establish as much collaboration with as many universities from diverse, regional, economic, and geographic background(s) as practical."[55] This has not necessarily been a "strategy," but what has accrued through years of interactions *without* a strategy. Many universities are paring down these relationships and adopting criteria for prioritization in accord with their strategic plans so as to pursue collaborations that augment, or complement, existing research strengths or bolster compatible but underrepresented areas.

The University of Exeter's internationalization strategy seeks parallel partnerships underpinned by multiple bottom-up links with a limited number of leading universities around the world.

European universities have established international offices and a culture that promotes cross-country collaborations within the European Union (EU) and elsewhere. The European University Association reports that 85 percent of institutions responding to a survey indicated that they had an internationalization strategy and 8 percent more were developing one.[56]

Strategic research partnerships may take the form of joint ventures, cooperative research and development (R&D) agreements, strategic technology alliances, or other more formal interactions. Some universities focus primarily on certain areas of the world:

- Rutgers has focused its relationships on China, India, Brazil, Indonesia, and Liberia.

- The University of South Florida has identified locations of emphasis and locations of opportunity. These were not decided a priori but were determined by learning where the faculty were already working.

- The Ohio State University has established seven Global Gateways in countries of cultural and economic importance to the university and Ohio companies.

- The University System of the North Carolina Universities (UNC) has created a multilateral, global University Partnership Network (University of North Carolina Exchange Program, UNCEP) of global "preferred partners,"[57] and UNC has developed strategic partnerships,[58] emerging partnerships[59] to promote joint research, course development, and other collaborative activities. The UNC-NUS partnership is a one of six strategic partnerships that gives UNC students access to research opportunities not available at UNC (see also Chapter 3).

- Vanderbilt University's "Core Partner Strategy" engages in "broad and profound institutional partnerships with a small number of peer institutions in strategic locations throughout the world."[60] Agreements commit logistical and financial resources (a small grant program) for research cooperation.

- Oregon State has developed an Asia Strategy program that focuses on university and industry partners in China, Hong Kong, Indonesia, Taiwan, Thailand, and South Korea.
- Systematized cooperation between universities around the world with Chinese universities has been established through the creation of Confucius Institutes (CI)[61] whereby one U.S. university develops a formalized relationship with one or more Chinese universities to establish teaching programs, exchange programs for students, faculty exchanges to aid teaching, and the administration of the CI. Many of the CIs have a specific academic focus (e.g., music) but all of them have developed a unique identify and programs to expose students to Chinese language and culture. CIs are also valuable to K–12 Chinese language and culture programs, train teachers, sponsor delegations of educators to China, provide cultural programming to communities, and promote business and cultural exchange between the United States and China. There are presently at least 350 CIs around the world.

And, some universities focus on priority research themes:

- UNC is one of eight global, core research universities that participate in an international consortium dedicated to the study of biodiversity, climate change and the environment (iCUBE).
- Australia's Higher Education for Development Partnerships connect institutions and individuals in more than 60 nations to build human capital, strengthen economic capacity, support agricultural productivity, improve health, and develop access to clean water through field work, exchanges, and other joint research opportunities.

Partnerships are not new for Asian universities.[62] International collaborative research has been one of the top priorities of university development strategies. A policy of Fudan University is to create more opportunities for internationally competitive research collaboration with foreign research foundations and companies.[63] The UK and China have created UK-China Partners in Science, Innovation, China-UK, and the Interact Supergen Group—a collaboration between seven UK and Chinese institutions to conduct research on sustainable energy. Still another collaboration focuses on the role of genes within crop plants, especially rice.

Northwest University in Xi'an, Shaanxi Province initiated collaborative research with Western Michigan, Michigan State Universities and universities in Japan in the 1980s, and the University of Tokyo has created the East Asia Liberal Arts Initiative with universities in China (Peking, Nanjing), South Korea (Seoul National) and Vietnam (Vietnam National University) to share resources, knowledge, and develop joint projects that engage students.

While many countries have a published strategy for international research collaboration, a 2008 study published in the UK[64] found that a minority of UK universities had an international research collaboration strategy. International collaboration was done best at the individual level. Only a few institutions had a dedicated budget to support international research collaboration and developed internal management capabilities for this purpose.

International University Consortia

There are countless university consortia established to solve common research problems and to develop big projects. A request for proposal (RFP) that announces a significant level of funding tor a project that requires cross-national borders and opportunities for student academic experiences can be a stimulus for the development of a consortium.

University Consortia Focused on Research Themes

USAID funds numerous consortia of university and other partners focused on themes such as the Millennium Development Goals. The Global Center for Food Systems Innovation at Michigan State University, for example, was established through USAID's Higher Education Solutions Network. It involves research partners in Africa, Europe, India,[65] and elsewhere[66] to seek solutions to the most critical problems facing the developing world's food systems. A Translational Scholar Corps engages students in the sharing of new information on global food security trends and supporting the education of development professionals.

The College of Food, Agriculture and Environmental Sciences at The Ohio State University manages a $24 million USAID consortium that prepares farmers and practitioners in Tanzania to address needs of small farm holders and agricultural business, and the University of Florida Institute of Food and Agricultural Sciences has recently received a USAID five-year cooperative agreement to establish the Feed the Future Innovation Lab for Livestock Systems.

Fifteen universities[67] belong to the U.S./Indonesia Teacher Education Consortium (USINTEC), whose goal is to improve Indonesian education, teacher preparation, and teacher quality. The program grew out of a 20-year relationship between Ohio State College of Education and Human Ecology and teacher education institutions in Indonesia.

Consortia of U.S. and International Universities:

The Global Enterprise for Micro-Mechanics and Molecular Medicine (GEM[4]) is a consortium of core[68] and partner institutions[69] around the globe that have developed a strategic international partnership to conduct collaborative, interdisciplinary, interinstitutional, basic, and clinical research on some of the major health challenges (e.g., malaria, cardiovascular disease). The consortium was initiated in 2005 among investigators in the fields of engineering, life sciences, technology, medicine, and public health. The program began with an emphasis on cell and molecular biomechanics, and public health in the context of select human diseases, and it has expanded to areas such as synthetic biology and cellular machines. The consortium organizes one- to two-week summer courses and winter programs on topics such as mechanobiology, developmental biology, biology machines, pediatric sciences and applications, enabling technologies, cancer, and infectious disease.

The Ibero-American Science and Technology Education Consortium (ISTEC) was started at the University of New Mexico in 1990 with the goal of forming strategic alliances among academia, industry, government agencies, and multilateral organizations. These alliances use science and technology as catalysts to foster socioeconomic development in Ibero-America by creating prosperity and improving the quality of life in the region. The organization provides an emphasis on entrepreneurship, consulting services, business development, and strategic alliances or joint ventures. Partner universities are connected with more than 100 other universities and industries in Bolivia, Brazil, Colombia, Panama, and Venezuela. The programs of ISTEC focus on the following:

- Advancing the state of higher education in STEM fields
- Generating and disseminating knowledge and information
- Establishing cost-effective vehicles for technology transfer
- Encouraging joint international R&D
- Fostering an environment for entrepreneurship and collaboration
- Promoting leadership models that adhere to the principles of responsibility and accountability

ISTEC Salud began in 2002–03 with telemedicine and today includes the objectives of integrating sustainability and health, education, engineering, computer science, anthropology, sociology, the humanities, and other disciplines. There are 46 colleges of medicine among the ISTEC members.

The largest higher education consortium is the Foundation for International Cooperation in Higher Education of Taiwan, representing 116 member universities through cooperative agreements in the UNC System; Florida's State University

System; and in universities in New Zealand, Austria, Korea, Japan, and India. The government of Taiwan founded the consortium to promote international cooperation to advance the globalization of higher education in Taiwan, enhance communication, and plan assemblies of international educators in Europe, America, and Asia. Future plans should foster international research collaboration.

George Mason University established the Global Problem-Solving Consortium in 2012 to learn how major societies approach solutions to global problems, and to develop networked courses with seven international universities.[70] The consortium has conducted intensive summer workshops on global water management and environmental sustainability, food security, and conflict resolution; developed the Global Problem Solving Fellows program, which prepares Mason students to address these global challenges; and created the "Confronting Global Challenges" MOOC (massive online open course) shared among the consortium partners.

Six Lasallian colleges in the United States and a total of 73 participating universities across the globe have established a consortium to promote leadership and global civil engagement through an interdisciplinary minor and a civic engagement experience for undergraduates to become socially conscious civic leaders with an international perspective.

North Carolina State University established the University Global Partnership Network[71] to develop global sensitivity and employability of students and to work on global themes and "innovation partnerships" with universities and industry through (1) joint research; (2) academic program development; (3) student and faculty exchanges; and (4) innovation, entrepreneurship, and technology transfer. Fields for joint engagement that were determined by mutual strengths include biosciences, energy, the environment, engineering, mathematics, chemistry, tourism, management, and veterinary medicine.

The Global Innovation Initiative (GII) between the United States and UK[72] was created to support multilateral research collaboration among members of a UK consortium of universities, the United States, and partner universities in Brazil, Indonesia, China, and India. The research must focus on cutting-edge multidisciplinary research on the topics of climate change and the environment, global health, energy, food security, water, and the urban environment, as well as strengthening international partnerships. The goals were to do the following:

- Forge university and business linkages that create a globally mobile talent pool and a multinational base for innovation and discovery.

- Increase the global mobility of students, researchers, faculty, and higher education administrators.

- Develop a cadre of investigators who will approach global challenges and operate in a global context.
- Encourage collaborations that develop capacity across a range of universities.

Beyond research, the benefits of GII are new web-supported global classrooms, virtual research seminars, interactions with local governments, increased funding, language and leadership programs for students, development of certificate programs and educational materials, workshops, new partners, and new centers of collaborative research.

The Network for European and U.S. Regional and Urban Studies (NEURUS) is an international, 13-university consortium established in 1998 by faculty from the Vienna University of Economics and Business, the Humboldt University-Berlin, the Rijksuniversiteit Groningen, the University of North Carolina at Chapel Hill, the University of Illinois at Urbana-Champaign, and the University of California, Irvine, to develop a new model for internationalizing collaborative research and education in urban and regional development in the context of the global economy. The strategies used include transcontinental seminars, student and faculty exchanges, distance learning, and research collaboration.

Faculty who participate in NEURUS have expertise in economic development; sustainable development; innovation; science policy, infrastructure; land use and management; environmental regulation and control; community development; housing; geographic information systems; and economic impact methods and modeling from the disciplines of business administration, public policy, city planning, geography, sociology, economics, and political science. The consortium was funded initially by the U.S. Department of Education Fund for the Improvement of Post-Secondary Education and the European Commission, Directorate General XXII (Education, Training, and Youth). Consortium members are exploring partnerships with universities and colleagues elsewhere in North America, Asia, and Latin America.

The Open University is an international partnership composed of 153 universities in 29 countries, 33 companies from the top 100 companies around the world, and 57 joint laboratories and joint research/training centers from Europe, Asia, Oceania, and North America.

University Partnerships with Bricks and Mortar: The Export of U.S. Education

A strong commitment to international partnerships is reflected in the many examples of bricks and mortar created by U.S. universities with a foreign university and/or government, and while many of these are for the purpose of educating the students in the region, they also enhance the local and collaborative research capacity and make inroads into regional, national, and global problems. Many of the relationships were established expressly to boost research for the country. This is especially true of those that feature—or are uniquely—graduate programs.

Colleges, medical schools,[73] dental schools,[74] hospitals,[75] and even entire universities have developed offshore facilities to offer their own degrees or dual or joint degrees and to conduct research with partner universities. MIT began to help other nations by expanding their educational partnerships in the 1960s and 1970s,[76] and New York University (NYU) has developed The Global Network University with 14 campuses on all continents. Duke has also developed a global network, entering into a partnership with the National University of Singapore Graduate Medical School, and has developed a new campus in partnership with Wuhan University in Kunshan, China, which began programs by offering MS degrees in 2012. Songdo Global University Campus in South Korea is a partnership among the University of Utah, Ghent University, Belgium, SUNY Stony Brook, and George Mason University.

The University of Warwick (UK) and Monash University (Australia) established another model of "networked universities"[77,78] and developed partnership initiatives through joint graduate degrees and research in "world-relevant and strategically important" areas. Both universities bring their own international networks into the partnership.

UC Berkeley's College of Engineering and the Shanghai Zhangjiang Hi-Tech Park jointly developed the Z-BEI Center to expand industrial and academic research collaborations and create global learning opportunities for Berkeley students. The facility was funded largely by the Shanghai government and companies. Stanford University and Peking University have been collaborating since 1970, and more recently opened the Stanford Center at Peking University to expand upon global education and research.[79] Georgia State is the first U.S. research institution to offer degrees in Africa with an in-country presence,[80,81] and both BS and MS degrees in engineering, business, and computing are offered in Dubai by the Rochester Institute of Technology. The list of examples of such partnerships is nearly endless, and new opportunities to establish campuses and design new universities and site programs outside the United States continually increase.

Some U.S. universities place their facilities adjacent to companies. Georgia Tech, for example, has a partnership with Infosys Technologies in Hyderabad, India, and the University of South Florida has developed a Management Information Systems program for Infosys employees in Bangalore, India. The Colorado School of Mines signed a 10-year agreement with the Abu Dhabi National Oil Company to develop the Petroleum Institute in Abu Dhabi that will offer undergraduate degrees in engineering fields.

Education City—now called Hamad bin Kalifa University—was established in Qatar primarily by U.S. universities,[82] and American universities have established joint research centers with partners abroad, such as Singapore CREATE. Research centers abroad are especially valued when the offshore programs allow research activities that are (or were) problematic to conduct in the United States (e.g., stem cell research). Yale University, for example has created three research centers in China,[83][84] and Columbia University has created at least seven global centers around the world to "promote and facilitate the collaborative and impactful engagement of the University's faculty, students, and alumni ... to enhance understanding, address global challenges, and advance knowledge and its exchange."

KAUST (see also Chapter 1) is an example of a Global Research University that is without parallel. Created in Saudi Arabia through the vision of the late King Abdullah, KAUST was designed in 2006 to become a world-class, graduate-only, coeducational university in the Kingdom focused on high-tech research to sustain the economy when oil is no longer the major economic driver. KAUST is organized around centers and research topics. Faculty, curricula, and research programs were recruited through a process in which the most prestigious universities around the globe were invited to compete to develop curricula and research programs. Individuals were enticed to become distinguished faculty with offers of impressive levels of research support, travel allowances, graduate students, and houses or villas at no or minimal cost. Progress in research and innovation is measured by publications, patents, and commercial potential. A research park at KAUST includes major multinational companies,[85] and an entire community was created for the university.

American universities also help countries upgrade their own institutions by developing programs to expand their offerings and reputations. Faculty from MIT, for example, helped to develop the Masdar Institute of Science and Technology in the UAE,[86] a graduate-level institution focused on advanced energy and sustainable technologies (water delivery, energy, and transportation).[87] MIT has also partnered with the Skolkovo Institute of Science and Technology (Skoltech) in Russia in biomedicine, space, and nuclear science, and Purdue, UCLA, the University of Maryland College Park, and the University of Washington have helped Skoltech gain proficiency in technology transfer.[88] Carnegie Mellon University, Harvard Medical School, MIT, and University of Texas at Austin have entered into partnerships with

Portuguese universities to help them expand their research and educational programs, connect with industry partners and international scientific networks.

Many of the GRU offshore establishments were created with the noble goals of cooperation in helping to build capacity in the partner country, preparing global citizens and leaders on both sides, pursuing solutions to universal problems, and assisting their partners in capturing the advantages of regional innovation for economic development. They build credibility for the country and legitimize the global footprint of the U.S. university on foreign soil. These relationships are also of significant value to the U.S. university in situations where the foreign government contributes substantial resources to build the partner university programs back home.

It is uncommon, however, for a foreign institution to establish a university in the United States,[89] although many of them have U.S. offices to recruit students and develop cooperative activities, including research. The Technion-Israel Institute of Technology and Cornell University are equal partners in establishing a world-class applied science and engineering campus in New York City.[90] SKEMA (School of Knowledge Economy and Management) Business School at the Institute d'Administration des Entreprises at Aix-en-Provence opened a new campus on North Carolina State's Centennial Campus in 2011 to offer a dual degree in Global Innovation Management. Perhaps more of these program and offices (even campuses?) will be established in the future and may be an opportunity that U.S. research universities might embrace.

International Virtual Research Partnerships among Universities

Technology is an essential component of global research collaboration, and the virtual research environment has been continuously developing to build communities, share and manage equipment, conduct projects and research centers through virtual networks, share data and develop publications, videoconference, organize virtual libraries, and a multitude of other research-related activities.[91,92] The cloud promotes collaboration by making the storage and synching of information across multiple devices easier and sharing information seamless, underpinning cross-border coordination. With this comes the need for a new set of standards, management capabilities, software, policies, and legal frameworks.

Business has entered the virtual collaboration space with companies such as Science Exchange, a science services marketplace that links a network of more than 400 top U.S. institutes and researchers in academia and business (e.g., Harvard University, NYU, Johns Hopkins, the Mayo Clinic, and Sigma) that make special services such as DNA sequencing available to researchers worldwide saving both cost and time.[93]

A PowerPoint presentation developed by a team from NIAID (National Institute of Allergy and Infectious Diseases) and the NIH[94] summarizes the many ways collaboration can occur among investigators virtually and the services that are provided in support. The presentation lists nearly 25 global, scientific, and collaborative networks[95] that connect investigators performing different tasks of research (data validation, bioinformatics, high-performance computing, specimen collections, patient volunteer activities, etc.) from their sites by various tools and services that employ the cloud. The presentation also addresses, and then resolves, the many challenges of creating virtual research organizations among universities around the world, foundations, and the government sponsor (NIH)—security of using the cloud, blending identities of the partners, and variability in technology capabilities, to name a few.

The virtual collaboration among Researchers at Oncology Research Information Exchange Network,[96] for example, has created a collaborative, "rapid learning" environment for sharing de-identified data to accelerate development of targeted treatments.[97] The Total Cancer Care® protocol, established by Moffitt Cancer Center, Tampa, FL, tracks patients' molecular, clinical, and epidemiological data in the participating centers and follows the patient throughout his or her lifetime. Thus researchers and clinicians at other institutions in the cancer network can more quickly match eligible patients to clinical trials and conduct larger and richer analysis.[98]

The NSF has created the Science Across Virtual Institutes (SAVI) program to accelerate research collaboration, networking, and technical exchanges between U.S. students, post-docs, and junior faculty with their international partners. It is intended to be a catalyst to bring leading researchers together from different countries, virtually and physically, and to leverage funding from the NSF with new international sources to address global scientific challenges (see Chapter 8) in sustained, collaborative partnerships. SAVI seeks to create "research hubs where new ideas originate, multi-disciplinary research is fostered, the next generation of globally engaged STEM researchers is nurtured and long-term professional relations are developed." An example of a SAVI pilot projects is the Wireless Innovation project, which involves nine U.S. institutions with NSF awardees and a counterpart Finnish team that is supported by the Academy of Finland and the Finnish Funding agency for Technology and Innovation. The Finland–U.S. (Wi.Fi.US) project is a platform to build a long-term research and education collaboration in the area of dynamic radio spectrum access.

Domestic and International University–Corporate/Business Partnerships

International university–industry research collaborations occur through individual relationships, contract research, and equipment sharing, with and without government and foundation funding. A survey conducted annually by the Industrial Research Institute 2015 R&D Trends Forecast[99] estimates that the strength of industry's collaboration with universities and federal labs in the United States and with countries outside the United States is favorable and stable. Companies responding to the survey listed their top concerns as "balancing short term and long term goals, attracting, developing and retaining talent, integrating technology planning and business strategy, and building and maintaining an innovation culture and measuring R&D processes, outputs, outcomes, and value (performance)."

Monash University's Graduate Interdisciplinary Research Program (GRIP) is an incubator of industry-relevant research programs in plastics and chemical industries that involve government (EPA, CSIRO) and industry partnerships (P&G, BASF, KPMG, 3M, PerkinElmer). The PhD projects are industry-focused and aimed toward commercialization. A second GRIP program is focused on sustainable water management in Asian cities.[100]

International Training and Professional Studies at Bloomfield College has created partnerships with more than 90 tertiary institutions, including corporate clients such as JPMorgan Chase and Bank of Tokyo. Vendor and nonvendor certified courses are offered through these relationships. Industry connections with universities in commercialization are particularly notable through their in work in incubators and accelerators (see Chapter 5).

International Megascience University Collaborations and Partnerships

Big science, or megascience, refers to worldwide projects that extend beyond the capabilities and budgets of single countries and are conducted more efficiently on a global scale. Most of these projects also require extraordinary equipment and must, therefore, be supported by scientists from many nations. University scientists not only use the equipment in many of the facilities, but also participate in developing it. And big science with its often extensive network of collaborators contributes to science diplomacy around the world.

CERN, the European Organization for Nuclear Research, Geneva, Switzerland, is dedicated to the study of the fundamental particles of matter. CERN houses particle accelerators, including the Large Hadron Collider—the world's largest and most powerful particle accelerator—operates with about 3,000 staff and boasts of 6,500 researchers, representing 500 universities and 80 nationalities—about half of the world's particle physics community. Twenty member states and 289 nonmember countries are affiliated with CERN.

The Human Brain Project, focusing on neuroinformatics and brain simulation, is also located in Geneva, Switzerland. It is directed by scientists at the École Polytechnique Fédérale de Lausanne and co-directed by scientists from the University of Heidelberg (computer focus), the University Hospital of Lausanne, and the University of Lausanne (medical focus) and engages researchers from 135 institutions in 26 countries.[101]

The goal of the project is to model the human brain to better understand its functions, development, and healing in order to identify disease signatures, discover the impact of certain drugs, and design diagnostic and treatment methods.

The computational aspects of this biological project can also lead to the engineering of computer chips and the development of new supercomputing and energy-efficiency techniques, all of which can be utilized in other realms such as data mining, telecommunications, appliances, and industrial uses.

The Human Brain Project is largely European funded with more than €1.19 billion from the European Commission[102] through its "Future and Emerging Technologies Flagship" grant, and the 113 partner institutions across Europe and another 21 collaborating partners will contribute up to an additional €1 billion in funding over 10 years.

The Gemini Project is a partnership among the United States, Australia, the United Kingdom, Canada, Chile, Brazil, and Argentina that provides researchers access to optical and infrared telescopes in Chile and Hawaii. The consortium shares the cost of building and maintaining a facility. Astronomers in the partner countries can apply for time on Gemini in proportion to the partner's financial investment. The Gemini Observatory is operated by the Association of Universities for Research in Astronomy, under a cooperative agreement with the NSF on behalf of the Gemini partnership

The Large Binocular Telescope (LBT) is an international collaboration of the University of Arizona, Italy (Instituto Nazionale di Astrofisica), Germany (LBT Beteiligungsgesellschaft), The Ohio State University, and the Tucson–based Research Corporation, representing the University of Minnesota, the University of Virginia, and the University of Notre Dame. The LBT was intended to be the first Extremely Large Telescope. The team seeks to develop new technologies and deliver high-quality data in scientific areas ranging from exo-planets to the high-redshift universe. The LBT observatory is a "community observatory" with observing programs that draws on the telescope's unique capabilities based on multiplex gain from its binocular nature and high-resolution from its interferometric modes.

The Laser Interferometer Gravitational-Wave Observatory (LIGO) is a large-scale physics project and the largest project ever funded by the NSF with supplementation with contributions from the UK Science and Technology Facilities Council, the Max Planck Society of Germany, and the Australian Research Council. More than 1,000 scientists worldwide have been involved in the work to validate Einstein's general theory of relativity presented in 1916. The project has gone through several phases since the 1960s, with NSF becoming involved in the 1980s to fund research on a large interferometer. After several rocky starts, with off-and-on funding from Congress and the NSF, the observatories and the collaboration were established in the mid-1990s, followed by additional development and improvement. Scientific runs were made in the early years of the new century without success. After a major overhaul completed in mid-September 2015, additional scientific observations were initiated, and in February 2016, the first observation of a gravitational wave was made. The LIGO Scientific Collaboration and other contributors were awarded a Special Breakthrough Prize in Fundamental Physics in May 2016 for contributing to the direct detection of gravitational waves. Expansion of this work will continue globally with a roadmap developed by the Gravitational Wave International Committee (e.g., LIGO-India). Many students were involved in this groundbreaking research.

The Integrated Ocean Drilling Program (IODP) began in 2003 when officials from Japan's Ministry of Education, Culture, Sports, Science and Technology (MEXT) and NSF signed an MOU to form and jointly operate IODP as a 10-year Earth science and research program that allow scientists from different disciplines to conduct investigations of the Earth deep below the sea floor.

Scientific ocean drilling is the longest running and most successful international collaboration among Earth scientists, contributing significantly to scientific understanding of Earth history, climate change, plate tectonics, natural resources, and geohazards. Continued scientific ocean drilling augments the information about Earth's dynamic nature and critical processes related to short-term change and long-term variability.

The European Consortium for Ocean Research Drilling was also established in 2003 and is currently a collaborative group of 17 European nations,[103] Canada, and associate members[104] that comprises an IODP-funding agency and provides access to mission-specific platforms.

The web-based Site Survey Data Bank is available to aid investigators in preparing proposals for drilling at specific sites. Core repositories based on geographical origin are located in Bremen, Germany; College Station, Texas; and Kochi, Japan. Scientists may conduct on-site research or request a loan of materials for teaching or analysis.

Future Earth is a 10-year, international collaborative research initiative to address global environmental change and sustainability. It was created from a number of existing international science organizations[105] and funded from international science funding agencies and other public and private sources.[106] Future Earth is based in Paris and organized through five global hubs and several regional hubs. The U.S. global hub[107] is located in Boulder, Colorado, and managed jointly by

Colorado State University and the University of Colorado–Boulder as part of a new Center for Global Environment within the Sustainability, Energy and Environment Complex at University of Colorado–Boulder and at the School of Global Environmental Sustainability at Colorado State University. The U.S. hub works closely with Colorado research institutions such as the National Center for Atmospheric Research, the National Oceanic and Atmospheric Administration's Earth Systems Research Laboratory, the National Renewable Energy Laboratory, other federal agencies, and national groups such as the Consortium for Ocean Leadership, all of which have relationships and/or cooperative agreements with universities and the state of Colorado.[108]

Future Earth is expected to engage about 60,000 scientists and students around the world, of all disciplines, natural and social, as well as engineering, the humanities, and law, who will monitor and forecast changes including climate, atmospheric chemistry, water, ecosystems, and biodiversity. They will work with decision makers, business leaders, and other stakeholders in the private sector to design and develop activities to coordinate new, interdisciplinary approaches to research on the themes of dynamic planet, global sustainable development, and transformations toward sustainability. International engagement will ensure that knowledge is generated in partnership with society and users of science.

The One Health Initiative is a worldwide strategy for expanding interdisciplinary collaboration and communication in all aspects of health care for humans, animals, and the environment. Cooperation and collaboration among health care professionals and their professional organizations, regional institutions, international technology agencies, NGOs, and civil society will result in better understanding of cross-species disease transmission, surveillance, and control, as well as the development and evaluation of new diagnostic methods, medicines, and vaccines. One Health provides information for political leaders and the public sector.

University Partnerships with the Military

Partnerships between universities and the military can be traced back to the Morrill Act of 1862 when the land-grant colleges were started for the purpose of agriculture and engineering training and to provide military education and the teaching of military tactics.[109] Today we connect research, science policy, technology, innovation, and cooperation with national security and international intelligence, continuing the connection with the military. A significant amount of research support to university campuses comes from the U.S. Department of Defense (DOD), and various centers and institutes on university campuses have strong DOD connections, often with industry as a co-partner. At the University of South Florida, for example, the Office of Military Partnerships, Center for Strategic and Diplomatic Studies, Global Initiative on Civil Society and Conflict, and Florida Center for

Cybersecurity all maintain alliances with MacDill Air Force Base in Tampa. Many of these relationships focus on activities that are matters of global security, in the sense that they are broader global challenges of energy, health, climate, and the environment, and so forth, that affect the security of society.

The University of South Florida is uniquely positioned, geographically and in terms of activities, to develop strategic partnerships in research, service, and education with U.S. Central Command and U.S. Special Operations Command at MacDill Air Force Base. The goal of the Office of Military Partnerships was to advance global activities through military relationships, to be certain the University of South Florida was a strong presence when MacDill is seeking partnerships, and to serve as a portal for those who are seeking entrée into MacDill. The program was led by a retired three-star Marine Corps general.

An MOU signed in 2011 between the University of South Florida Office of Military Partnerships and MacDill CENTCOM formalized the collaborative relationship and consolidated various existing relationships between the two organizations,[110] with the anticipated result that there would be more opportunities for education and training, enhanced operational effectiveness, greater shared subject matter expertise, joint research, and professional exchange. A similar MOU between the University of South Florida and U.S. Special Operations Command was signed a year later to empower each institution to seek meaningful interagency, military, and academic collaboration.

Military installations located at six universities[111] in the nation are designated Senior Military Colleges. They provide a university education along with military training. The university is required to produce graduates with professional language competence in strategic languages and cultural competence. The University of North Georgia is an ROTC Language Hub,[112] an ROTC Language Flagship, and a DOD Language Training Center focusing on the strategic languages: Arabic, Chinese, Russian, and Korean. Project GO (Global Officer) funding has been awarded to the University Corps of Cadets for eight weeks of intensive language immersion. The University of North Georgia has organized the Summer Intensive Language Program for language and culture in Chinese and Arabic. Other language initiatives at the university include Middle School Day Camp and Military Academy Exchanges.

The United States Army Research Laboratory (ARL) and academic partners engage in their own international R&D cooperative programs, bilateral agreements, and collaborative activities with allies where strengths are complementary. For example, there are agreements with Germany to work on tactical information processing, with Israel on solid-state laser research, and with Singapore on fuel cell development. ARL also supports the Department of the Army, the DOD, and other organizations and agencies[113] in their cooperative activities. Through a cooperative research program jointly created and funded by the UK and the United States, a consortium of industry and academic partners was designed to conduct research that transitions programs beyond basic research, and benefits from and shares intellectual property.

University–Government Partnerships (Often Including Industry and NGOs)

Universities partner with governments at all levels in a multitude of countries, through bilateral and multilateral agreements, typically in response to funding opportunities. Organizations such as USAID, the World Bank, the NSF, and the U.S. Department of State promote national and international science by coordinating and supporting more than 20 technical agencies that implement collaborative programs. This is a vast topic mentioned in other chapters and thus will be touched on here with only cursory examples.

USAID develops partnerships with universities, industry, NGOs, diaspora groups, and other groups, to address issues of global relevance (Millennium Development Goals, Sustainability Development Goals; see Chapters 2 and 9) using the mechanism of global development alliances. All partners in such an alliance work together to design, fund, and manage the partnership. The criteria for these to become established include the following:

- Leveraged funds (1:1 in-kind and cash)
- Common goals
- Jointly defined solution to the problem
- Nontraditional resource partners, risks, and results
- Innovation and sustainable approaches to development

The Asia-Pacific region is the fastest growing region of the world and today includes half of the world's population. It is also a region with challenges in managing the environment, natural resources, infectious diseases that cross national borders, and disaster risk reduction—all requiring science, technology, and innovation—and partnerships. USAID held an interactive summit in March 2015 in Bangkok, Thailand, that focused on "partnering to scale innovations to achieve, sustain and extend development impacts." Academics, entrepreneurs, private-sector partners, and development professionals came together to brainstorm potentially game-changing innovations that could address these challenges and devise ways to work together to implement them. USAID also sponsors the Association of Southeast Asian Nations (ASEAN)-U.S. Science and Technology Fellows Pilot Program, which places a class of fellows in ASEAN ministries to help the countries make greater use of science, technology, and objective analysis on policy issues related to biodiversity, climate change, reducing disaster risks, health, and water management.

The Alliance for System Safety of Unmanned Aircraft Systems (UAS) through Research Excellence is an FAA-sponsored Center of Excellence for Unmanned Aircraft Systems headquartered at Mississippi State University. Twenty-two Research institutions (one international partner)[114] and 100 leading industry and government partners are members of this alliance. The core university members have expertise in air traffic control and interoperability, covering a range of issues such as detect and avoid, human factors, unmanned pilot training and certification, system engineering, low-altitude operations and safety, airport ground operations, spectrum management, command and control, communications, and noise reduction. In all, 146 projects command $148 million of external funding.

Country-to-Country (Government-to-Government) Relationships Based on Academic Research and Capacity Building

The United States supports the efforts of all countries to create economic growth and prosperity through policies that promote innovation on terms that are fair and equitable to all and respect the principles of nondiscrimination, intellectual property rights, market competition, and no government interference in technology transfer.

The Partnership in Applied Sciences, Engineering and Technology is an initiative of African governments in partnership with governments of Brazil, China, India, and Korea; the private sector; education and training institutions; and regional organizations. The partnership's goal is to boost scientific knowledge and research in key sectors[115] to improve the economy, build human capacity, and align the work of universities with those areas that will promote development in Sub-Saharan Africa. A scholarship and innovation fund has been created, along with an action plan that benchmarks criteria, workshops, and "learning events."

Austria, France, Belgium, Finland, Norway, and Sweden have published strategy on international research collaboration. The government of Australia established the Group of Eight (Go8) Australian Universities which join partner countries via their governments in formal agreements. For example, the Go8 and DAAD (German Academic Exchange Service) cooperate to support research exchanges and cooperation between academic and PhD student research groups within both countries to develop early career researchers; the Go8 and Latin America have common research interests in tropical and subtropical agriculture, mining, environmental management. A Go8 office in São Paulo, Brazil, supports research and academic exchanges, encourages greater numbers of Brazilian students in Australian universities, and organizes workshops and conferences to explore new opportunities for collaboration. An agreement with the Chilean government stimulates exchanges, internships, and education (MS, PhD, and English language) in Australia for students with Chilean scholarships and works to develop research in priority areas: offshore technologies, mining, agriculture and the food industry, aquaculture and fishing, tourism and hospitality, information and communications technology, energy, environmental issues, health, education, housing, and public security.

Canada and International Research Collaboration[116]

Canada has worked with colleagues in the United States, UK, EU, and Japan for many years and more recently with the BRIC (Brazil, Russia, India and China) nations. The government published the document "Mobilizing Science and Technology to Canada's advantage" as a guide for increasing partnerships that promote R&D and talent in those fields. The investment at that time is shown in the following table:

Program	Grants Funded
Canadian Institutes of Health Research	230 grants and awards
Social Sciences and Humanities Research Council of Canada	Seed money for 112 projects, workshops, seminars, and planning meetings
Natural Sciences and Engineering Council of Canada	$8 million awarded for international collaborations
Department of Foreign Affairs and International Trade	Helped 170 private sector companies and universities to identify new collaborative initiatives with international partners
Canadian Foundation for Innovation	$200 million to Canadian institutions to participate in international research collaboration
Research Chairs Secretariat	Funding of up to $10 million to national researchers over seven years in areas of strategic importance to Canada; graduate fellowships to attract the best PhD students from Canada and the world to study at Canadian universities
International Development Research Centre	Investment in collaborative research that focuses on the Millennium Development Goals (MDGs), applied research, and the development of research capacity; to catalyze research consortia

In spite of the numerous initiatives outlined, the conclusion from this report is that "international research collaboration is rather limited and, according to some, is lacking coordination."

The U.S. India Cooperation Agreement of 2010 has been described as a "defining partnership of the 21st century" by President Obama. It has widely reaching tentacles into virtually every area of social and political concerns: diplomatic, defense cooperation commerce, space, agriculture, and people-to-people ties.

The United States–Israel Binational Agricultural Research and Development endowed fund (BARD), created in 1978, provides competitive funding for mission-oriented, strategic, and applied research on mutual-interest agricultural problems, conducted jointly by American and Israeli scientists. Each country made initial contributions of $40 million, augmented in 1984 by $15 million from each. In 1994, Israel agreed to match any U.S. supplement with $2.5 million annually, but this supplement has been substantially reduced since 1998.

The funds support projects to increase agricultural productivity and emphasize plant and animal health, food quality and safety, and environmental issues. BARD also supports international workshops; offers fellowships for postdoctoral research, senior research scientists, and graduate students; and encourages the exchange of agricultural experts.

BARD has awarded more than $270 million for 1,300 joint projects between Israel and nearly every U.S. state, as well as Canada and Australia. It has sponsored 185 post-doctoral fellows since 1985. Eleven senior research fellows have been appointed since 1991, and 45 scientific workshops and joint programs have been organized with universities in Maryland, Texas, and New York State.

BARD established the MARD (Multinational Agricultural Research and Development) program to promote cooperative agricultural R&D activities among scientists in Israel, Jordan, the Palestinian Authority, and the United States. MARD has funded successful regional workshops, mutual visits, training seminars, and other activities that have enhanced collaboration. MARD offers facilitating grants to enable small, multinational, research groups to prepare a research proposal for other international granting organizations.

The United States-Israel Collaboration in Computer Science is a joint program of NSF and the US-Israel Binational Science Foundation to support research projects that develop new knowledge in the theory of computing; algorithm design and analysis; design, verification, and evaluation of software systems; and revolutionary computing models based on emerging scientific ideas. NSF supports the travel of U.S.-based researchers to interact with their Israeli counterparts.

U.S.-China Relationships

The United States and China have been collaborating in the areas of science and technology for decades via the U.S.-China Agreement on Cooperation in Science and Technology, first signed in 1979 and renewed a few years ago. The collaborations are in the fields of fisheries, Earth and atmospheric sciences, basic research in physics and chemistry, a variety of energy-related areas, agriculture, civil industrial technology, geology, health, and disaster research.

In 2002 a cooperative agreement was signed to promote research by U.S. graduate students in China, and in 2006, NSF established an office in Beijing to promote and strengthen the collaboration of U.S. scientists and engineers. Numerous other agreements were signed to foster joint work in energy efficiency and renewable energy, green buildings, and a joint consortium on clean energy (U.S. China Clean Energy Research Center) supporting more than 1,100 U.S. and Chinese researchers partnering entities in areas of strategic importance to both countries: Joint Work Plan Research Areas: Public Private Partnership Advanced Coal Technology Consortium, Clean Vehicles Consortium, Building Energy Efficiency Consortium, and Energy-Water (to begin in 2015).

The United States and China have agreed to conduct intensive high-level, expert discussions on innovation issues under the U.S.-China Joint Commission Meeting on Scientific and Technological Cooperation, co-chaired by the director of the White House Office of Science and Technology Policy and the Chinese Minister of Science and Technology.

Innovation China-UK is a multimillion-pound, jointly funded, research partnership of the two governments with the goal of bringing more products of research to the marketplace. Five UK universities and approximately 20 Chinese universities are working together.

Partnerships with Diasporic Communities

As diaspora populations grow in the United States and internationally, so has the scope of their contributions beyond individual remittances. Diaspora Communities are important because:

- They innovate—Diaspora scientists and entrepreneurs have long been among the most influential innovators and change makers in their countries of origin. They are creating innovations and growing the U.S. economy and directing investments toward their countries of origin. Immigrant-owned businesses generated an estimated $67 billion in U.S. business income in 2011.

- They give back—Diaspora scientists and entrepreneurs often have the connections, linguistic and cultural competence, knowledge, and drive to serve as volunteers worldwide. About 200,000 first- and second-generation immigrants volunteer abroad each year.

- They invest—Diasporas create economic opportunities in the United States and abroad. Diaspora investors in the United States from India, Mexico, Ghana, and elsewhere provide much needed capital to home economies through various financial instruments.

- They are engaged—Diasporas make significant contributions to their ancestral homes. USAID's Diaspora Networks Alliance framework guides its work with diaspora communities to promote economic and social growth in multiple countries.

The United Nations created the TOKTEN program (Transfer of Knowledge Through Expatriate Nationals) in 1977 to aid in the development of the countries of origin of diaspora community members on a short-term (2–12 weeks), voluntary basis. USAID also seeks short-term, voluntary, commercial agriculture development and environmental recovery for post-earthquake rebuilding efforts through USAID's Washington contractors in Haiti. Some believe the success of these programs is limited because of the short duration of commitment. The American Association for the Advancement of Science (AAAS) and others have worked to organize and strengthen international networks of expat scientists and engineers with the objective that such networks could help drive innovation, solve problems in scientists' home regions, and improve diplomatic relations between countries.

Measuring the Success and Impact of International Partnerships

The University of Queensland's Partner Engagement Framework, coupled with the university's Country Engagement Framework, measures the effectiveness and success of international engagement with clearly defined, data-driven metrics. The university's international engagement profile focuses on regions and countries that have been given priority status due to their potential for deep and productive relationships and is the result of strategic partnerships with people and organizations across industry, government, philanthropy, alumni, and higher education. The effectiveness of this engagement strategy is measured using indicators related to various aspects of institutional collaboration and linkages. The framework allows the university to assess areas of current strength, potential for future initiatives, as well as areas where further development is needed to maximize mutual benefit. Thirteen indicators within three categories—discovery, engagement, and learning—inform partnership evaluation including the volume, impact, and breadth of joint publications; funded joint research projects; the recruitment of staff; student exchange; and inbound study abroad. The use of a sophisticated process for evidence-based decision making allows the university to continually identify highly engaged partners, the degree of partnership engagement across a given country, how best to leverage existing partnerships, as well as how to broaden and/or deepen engagements including whether to invest in new partnerships.

NOTES

[1] International Research Collaboration: Opportunities for the UK Higher Education sector (2008), p. 12. https://globalhighered.files.wordpress.com/2008/08/uukreportmay2008.pdf.

[2] Ottino, J. M., & Morson, G. S. (February 14, 2016). Building a bridge between engineering and the humanities. *Chronicle of Higher Education*, A 26–27.

[3] The Go8's international collaborations. (2014). Group of Eight (Go8).

[4] Chubb, I. (2012). Speech delivered by Australia's Chief Scientist at the Australia-Israel Chamber of Commerce (SA), Adelaide, Australia, May 17.

[5] Adapa, P. K. (2013*)*. Strategies *and factors effecting internationalization of university research and education*. Global Institute for Water Security University of Saskatchewan, National Hydrology Research Centre. Saskatoon, Canada: University of Saskatchewan. Retrieved from http://www.iau-aiu.net/sites/all/files/Adapa_Internationalization_0.pdf

[6] *McGinn, S.K. (2015).* Barbara Schaal chosen president-elect of AAAS. Will lead world's largest general scientific society in 2016. https://source.wustl.edu/2015/01/barbara-schaal-chosen-presidentelect-of-aaas/

[7] Guimón, J. (2013). *Promoting university-industry collaboration in developing countries. The innovation policy agenda* (Policy Brief). World Bank, pp. 1–11. http://innovationpolicyplatform.org/sites/default/files/rdf_imported_documents/PromotingUniversityIndustryCollaborationInDevelopingCountries.pdf.

[8] Sloan, S. S., & Arrison, T. (2011). *Examining core elements of international research collaboration: Summary of a workshop*. Washington, DC: The National Academies Press.

[9] Independent Expert Working Group. (2003, April). *Working Paper Expert Group report on role and strategic use of IPR (intellectual property rights) in international research collaborations* (Final Report). Directorate-General for Research, European Research Area: Research and Innovation, p. 23.

[10] Guimón, *Promoting university-industry collaboration in developing countries*, pp. 1–11.

[11] National Science Board. (2008, February 14). *International science and engineering partnerships: A priority for U.S. foreign policy and our nation's innovation enterprise*.

[12] Grumbiner, L. (2011). *Chapter 2. Creating an Environment for Productive International Collaboration. 2.1 Research Collaboration, U.S. Foreign Policy, and the Global Context*. In S. S. Sloan & T. Arrison (Eds.), *Examining core elements of international research collaboration: Summary of a workshop* (pp. 7–10). Washington, DC: The National Academies Press.

[13] *International Research Collaboration: Opportunities for the UK Higher Education sector,* Universities UK (2008), Woburn House, 20 Tavistock Square. p. 12. https://globalhighered.files.wordpress.com/2008/08/uukreportmay2008.pdf.

[14] Adapa, P. K. (2013). *Strategies and factors effecting internationalization of university research and education.* Global Institute for Water Security University of Saskatchewan, National Hydrology Research Centre. Saskatoon, Canada: University of Saskatchewan. Retrieved from http://homepage.usask.ca/~pka525/Documents/Internationalization.pdf

[15] Lane, J. E., Owens, T., & Ziegler, P. (2014). *States go global: State government engagement in higher education internationalization.* Rockefeller Report. Albany, NY: State University of New York, Nelson A. Rockefeller Institute of Government.

[16] Makki, R. (2011). Abu Dhabi Education Council. In S. S. Sloan & T. Arrison (Eds.), *Examining core elements of international research collaboration: Summary of a workshop* (pp. 11–12). Washington, DC: The National Academies Press.

[17] *Internationalization of Australian science.* (2010, February). Position paper, Australian Academy of Science.

[18] Suresh, S. (2012, May 25). Cultivating global science (editorial). *Science, 336,* 802.

[19] NextGen VOICES: Results. (2014, October 3). *Science,* 346, 47–49.

[20] Divergent perceptions of the same idea, concept, or information.

[21] Mpako-Ntusi, T. (2011). Chapter 3. *Cultural Differences and Nuances. 3.3 Perspective of a South African Institution.* In S. S. Sloan & T. Arrison (Eds.), *Examining core elements of international research collaboration: Summary of a workshop* (pp. 23–24). Washington, DC: The National Academies Press.

[22] Suresh, S. (2011). *Moving Toward Global Science.* Science 333 (6044): p. 802.

[23] Kirkland, J. (2011). *Chapter 2. Creating an Environment for Productive International Collaboration. 2.3 Clarifying Commonalities and Differences.* In S. S. Sloan & T. Arrison (Eds.), *Examining core elements of international research collaboration: Summary of a workshop* (p. 15). Washington, DC: The National Academies Press.

[24] National Science Board. (2008, February 14). International Science and Engineering Partnerships: A priority for U.S. foreign policy and our nation's innovation enterprise.(NSB-08-4). pp. 1–50.

[25] Dickson, D. (2010, July 16). *Science, communication, aid and diplomacy.* Retrieved from http://www.scidev.net/en/editorials/science-communication-aid-and-diplomacy.html

[26] Guimón, *Promoting university-industry collaboration in developing countries*, pp. 1–11.

[27] Sloan, S. S., & Arrison, T. (Eds.) (2011) *Examining core elements of international research collaboration: Summary of a workshop.* Washington, DC: The National Academies Press.

[28] Fedoroff, N. (2011). *Chapter 2. Creating an Environment for Productive International Collaboration. 24 Examples of U.S. International Engagement in Science and Technology.* In S. S. Sloan & T. Arrison (Eds.), *Examining core elements of international research collaboration: Summary of a workshop* (pp. 15–16). Washington, DC: The National Academies Press.

[29] Chubb I: Chief Scientist for Australia. (2012). Talk to Australian-Israel Chamber of Commerce.

[30] Grumbiner, J. (2011). *Chapter 2. Creating an Environment for Productive International Collaboration. 2.1 Research Collaboration, U.S. Foreign Policy, and the Global Context.* In S. S. Sloan & T. Arrison (Eds.), *Examining core elements of international research collaboration: Summary of a workshop* (p. 9). Washington, DC: The National Academies Press.

[31] Lord, K., & Turekian, V. C. (2007). Time for a new era of science diplomacy. *Science, 315,* 769.

[32] Announcement of U.S. Science Envoys, Media Note. (2014, December 4). Washington, DC: Office of the Spokesperson.

[33] Linkov, I., Trump, B., Tatham, E., Basu, S., & Roco, M. C. (2014). *Diplomacy for science two generations later.* Science & Diplomacy. Retrieved from http://www.science&diplomacy.org/print/149.

[34] Eastwood, D. (2015, May 29). Imaginative alliances: the key to a successful global research agenda. Advertising supplement to the *Chronicle of Higher Education*, p. 7. http://chronicle.texterity.com/chronicle/birminghamglobal20150529?folio=7&pg=7#pg7.

[35] Ashkenas, R. (2015, April 20). There's a difference between cooperation and collaboration. *Harvard Business Review*. https://hbr.org/2015/04/theres-a-difference-between-cooperation-and-collaboration

[36] Eastwood, D. (2015). Imaginative alliances: the key to a successful global research agenda. Advertising supplement to the *Chronicle of Higher Education*, p. 7. http://chronicle.texterity.com/chronicle/birminghamglobal20150529?folio=7&pg=7#pg7.

[37] *International Research Collaboration: Opportunities for the UK Higher Education sector*, Universities UK (2008), Woburn House, 20 Tavistock Square. p. 12. https://globalhighered.files.wordpress.com/2008/08/uukreportmay2008.pdf.

[38] Ibid., p. 22.

[39] Chapter 27, Section 8. *Multicultural collaboration community tool box. Cultural Competence in a Multicultural World*. Retrieved from: http://ctb.ku.edu/en/table-of-contents/cultural/cultural-competence/multicultural-collaboration/main.

[40] Kotelnikov, V. Retrieved from http://www.1000ventures.com/business_guide/partnerships_main.html.

[41] Riall Nolan, R. (2011). *Chapter 3. Cultural Differences and Nuances. 3.1 The Impact of Culture on Research Collaborations*. In S. S. Sloan & T. Arrison (Eds.), *Examining core elements of international research collaboration: Summary of a workshop* (pp. 21–22). Washington, DC: The National Academies Press.

[42] Chase Commercial Banking. (2011). *Education as an export: The globalization of U.S. higher education and the emergence of the overseas branch campus*. pp. 1-9. https://www.jpmorgan.com/jpmpdf/1320603368639.pdf.

[43] Eastwood, D. (2015). Imaginative alliances: The key to a successful research agenda. Advertising Supplement to the *Chronicle, Birmingham Global*, p. 7.

[44] Activities of Cambridge Enterprise's Consultancy Services.

[45] Shugan, S. M. (2004). Editorial: Consulting, research, and consulting research. *Marketing Science 23*(2), 173–179.

[46] Material transfer agreements, confidentiality and nondisclosure agreements, and data use agreements (among others).

[47] Sloan, S. S., & Arrison, T. (2011). *Examining core elements of international research collaboration: Summary of a workshop*. Washington, DC: The National Academies Press

[48] Discussion notes. In S. S. Sloan & T. Arrison (Eds.), *Examining core elements of international research collaboration: Summary of a workshop* (pp. 33–34). Washington, DC: The National Academies Press.

[49] Butts, S. (2011). *Chapter 4. Ethics. 4.1 Ethical Issues in International Industry-University Research Collaboration*. In S. S. Sloan & T. Arrison (Eds.), *Examining core elements of international research collaboration: Summary of a workshop* (pp. 27–28). Washington, DC: The National Academies Press.

[50] Bird, S. (2011). *Chapter 4. Ethics. 4.3. Ethical Considerations in Science and Engineering Practice*. In S. S. Sloan & T. Arrison (Eds.), *Examining core elements of international research collaboration: Summary of a workshop* (pp. 30–33). Washington, DC: The National Academies Press.

[51] Keith, J. L. (2011). *Chapter 9. Legal; Issues and Agreements. 9.1 Collaborative mechanisms: Pros and Cons of Various Approaches for U.S. Universities*. In S. S. Sloan & T. Arrison (Eds.), *Examining core elements of international research collaboration: Summary of a workshop* (pp. 63–74). Washington, DC: The National Academies Press.

52. Ferreira, W. (2011). *Chapter 9. Legal; Issues and Agreements. 9.1 Collaborative mechanisms: Pros and Cons of Various Approaches for U.S. Universities.* In S. S. Sloan & T. Arrison (Eds.), *Examining core elements of international research collaboration: Summary of a workshop* (pp. 63–74). Washington, DC: The National Academies Press.

53. Service, R. P. (2012). Satellite labs extend science. *Science, 337,* 1600–1603.

54. The Go8, the China 9, the League of European Research Universities (LERU), AAU, the Hong Kong 3, the Russell Group (UK), the U-15 (Canada), the U-11 (Japan) and the Association of East Asian Universities (ALEARU).

55. Adapa, *Strategies and factors effecting internationalization of university research and education.*

56. Sursock, A. (2015). *Trends 2015: Learning and teaching in European universities.* Brussels, Belgium: European University Association. Retrieved from http://www.eau.be/Libraries/publications-homepage-list/EAU_Trends_2015web.pdf?slvrsn=18

57. Australia, Brazil, Canada, Denmark, Sweden, Finland, Germany, Mexico, Uruguay.

58. King's College London, Malawi Ministry of Health, National University of Singapore, Tsinghua University, Peking University and Universidad San Francisco de Quito/Galapagos Initiative.

59. Universidade de São Paulo, Brazil; Universität Bremen and Eberhard Karls Universität Tübingen in Germany; Fudan University, China and University of Havana, Cuba.

60. China, Brazil, South Africa, Australia, and Chile.

61. Confucius Institutes were established in 2004 by the Chinese Ministry of Education (Office of Chinese Language Council International, known as the Hanban).

62. Guanghua, F. (2007). *Advances, cooperation and innovation.* The 2nd University Administrators Workshop-Proceedings Kyoto University—The organization for promotion of international Relations. Session A-1: Promoting International research collaborations. Retrieved from: http://www.isp.msu.edu/globalengagement/partnership.htm

63. Liu, L. (2007). *Status quo and experience of international research collaborations at Fudan University.* The 2nd University Administrators Workshop-Proceedings Kyoto University—The organization for promotion of international Relations. Session A-1: Promoting International research collaborations. Retrieved from: http://www.isp.msu.edu/globalengagement/partnership.htm.

64. Ibid.

65. Sokoine University of Agriculture, Tanzania; Wageningen University and Research Centre, the Netherlands; and The Energy and Resources Institute, India.

66. CRDF Global, Lincoln University, QED, and the University of Pretoria.

67. Ohio State, Indiana University, University of Illinois Urbana-Champaign, and Indonesian universities.

68. MIT, NUS, UIUC, Caltech, UCSD, Georgia Tech, Harvard, University of Cambridge, Imperial College, Tohoku University, Erasmus Medical College, CIBER BBN Spain.

69. Brown, Institute Pasteur, UT Austin, Texas A&M, UC Berkeley, U Minnesota, U Penn, Columbia, CMU, U Michigan, Stanford, Weitzmann, ETH Zurich, Chulabhorn Institute.

70. The University of Brasilia, University of Delhi, Higher School of Economics in Russia, Istanbul Sehir University, Kenyatta University in Kenya, Yonsei in South Korea, and Tsinghua University.

71. The University of Surrey, UK; the Universidade de São Paulo, Brazil; and North Carolina State University, USA.

72. The GII is funded by the U.S. Department of State's Bureau of Educational and Cultural Affairs (ECA) and the UK government, and administered by Institute of International Education and the British Council.

[73] Johns Hopkins Singapore International Medical Centre, a new Johns Hopkins Medical School and Teaching Hospital in Malaysia and Johns Hopkins Management of Tawam Hospital associated with the United Arab Emirates University in Al Ain, UAE, Harvard Medical School-Dubai Center—a joint development between Harvard Medical International and Dubai Healthcare City, Duke School of Medicine at the National University of Singapore (Duke-NUS Graduate Medical School), and Cornell Weill Medical School Qatar are five examples.

[74] Boston University and Dubai Healthcare City have opened a dental school.

[75] Cornell Weill Medical School and the Hamad Medical Corporation are developing the Sidra Medical and Research Center in Qatar to "promote healing, inspire learning and advance scientific discovery" (Sheikha Mozah, Qatar).

[76] Fischer, K. (2012, Oct. 26). MIT adopts a quiet global strategy. *Chronicle of Higher Education*, A10–12.

[77] Morgan, J. (2012, Feb. 2). Warwick and Monash team up for global strategy. *Times Higher Education*. https://www.timeshighereducation.com/.

[78] Roginski, A. (2013, June). Perfect match for global learning. Special Advertising Supplement, *Chronicle of Higher Education*, 24–25.

[79] Barboza, D. (2011, Nov. 17). Berkeley reveals plans for an academic center in China. *New York Times*, p. 8.

[80] Foderaro, L. W. (2010, September 13). Yale plans to create a college in Singapore. *New York Times*. http://www.nytimes.com/2010/09/14/education/14yale.html.

[81] Wilhelm, I. (2011). Duke faculty question the university's global ambitions. *Chronicle of Higher Education*, Nov. 4, A8.

[82] Northwestern University, Cornell Weill Medicine School, Carnegie Mellon University, Texas A&M, Virginia Commonwealth University, Georgetown University, HEC Paris (a business school) and University College London are all established at Hamad bin Kalifa University which is operating as a single multidisciplinary institution, but each institution has its independent quality standards.

[83] Yale has established the Biomedical Research Center in Fudan, The Peking Plant Molecular Genetics and Agro-Biotechnology, and the Peking Microelectronics and Nanotechnology Center.

[84] According to H. D. Madame Liu Yandong, State Councilor, People's Republic of China, Yale has more extensive contacts with Chinese universities than any other institution of higher learning in the United States. Yandong, L. (2009, April). *Deepening people-to-people exchanges and cultural cooperation, opening up new horizons for Sino-US relations.* A speech delivered at Yale University.

[85] Among the companies located at KAUST are IBM, GE, Schlumberger, Sabic, Rolls-Royce, Shell, Boeing, and Dow Chemical, to name only a few.

[86] Masdar is located in Masdar City, near the Abu Dhabi Airport. Masdar City is a hub for research in renewable energy, the world's first city aiming for zero carbon status.

[87] MIT received $35 million in research funds to help develop Masdar Institute of Science and Technology in partnership with Abu Dhabi Future Energy Company to focus graduate-level programs on clean energy technology and to aid capacity building in the UAE. MIT will help train faculty in the UAE and will connect with corporations in the region. A $250 million clean-tech private equity fund has also been established in concert with Masdar. This partnership follows upon the success and experience MIT gained in the Singapore-MIT Alliance which began as a partnership with the National University of Singapore and Nanyang Technological University to offer master's degrees. The initiative then advanced to a bricks and mortar research complex (SMART = Singapore-MIT Alliance for Research and Technology) that included other universities as well. Today, dual PhDs are also offered at the three universities.

[88] Fischer, K. (2010, Sept. 12). Portugal aims to modernize with help from the U.S. *Chronicle of Higher Education*. http://chronicle.com/article/Portuguese-Universities-Turn/124364/.

[89] Brewer, P. E. (2012). *International virtual teams: Engineering global success.* Hoboken, NJ: Wiley. Manchester Business School has opened a campus in Miami, FL, recognizing that Florida is the gateway to Latin America.

[90] *Cornell and Technion will partner in a groundbreaking NYC Tech campus.* Retrieved from www.news.cornell.edu/stories/Oct11/NYCpartner.html

[91] Whalen, C., & Koranda, S. (2014, April 30). *Building virtual research organizations across international borders.* Office of Cyberinfrastructure and Computational Biology, NIAID/NIH.

[92] Brewer, P. E. (2015). *International virtual teams: Engineering global success.* Hoboken, NJ: Wiley.

[93] Harmon, A. (2014). *Will market-driven collaboration enable new virtual research models?* Retrieved from Science Node website, https://sciencenode.org/feature/will-market-driven-collaboration-enable-new-virtual-research-models.php

[94] Tartakovsky, M., Erickson, J., Flanagan, H., Oshrin, West, A., Scavo, T., Krienke, J., Klingenstein, K., & Economou, M. (2014). Participants at ACAMPO 2014 Internet2 Technical Exchange.

[95] Based in Baltimore, Maryland, U.S.A. (Howard Hughes Medical Institute, University of Maryland School of Medicine), Navrongo Health Research, Ghana, Wellcome Sanger Institute, Wellcome Trust for Human Genetics, University of Oxford, UK to Malaria Research and Training Center, Faculty of Pharmacy, University of Science, techniques and Technologies, Bamako, Mali, and others in Australia, Thailand, Paris, Ho Chi Minh City, and other locations.

[96] City of Hope, University of Virginia Cancer Center, University of Colorado Cancer Center, University of New Mexico Cancer Center, Rutgers Cancer Institute of New Jersey, Morehouse School of Medicine and the University of Southern California (USC) Norris Comprehensive Cancer Center, Henry M. Jackson Foundation for the Advancement of Military Science, Murtha Cancer Center.

[97] Moffitt Cancer Center News Release. (2014, May 28). *Ohio State and Moffitt Form World's Largest Cancer Research Collaboration for Big Data; More Than 100,000 Patients Already Participating.* https://moffitt.org/newsroom/press-release-archive/2014/ohio-state-and-moffitt-form-world-s-largest-cancer-research-collaboration-for-big-data-more-than-100-000-patients-already-participating/.

[98] From Dr. Mike Caliguiri, The Ohio State University Comprehensive Cancer Center–Arthur G. James Cancer Hospital and Richard J. Solove Research Institute.

[99] The Industrial Research Institute 2015 R&D Trends Forecast: results from the Industrial Research Institute's annual Survey, Retrieved from http://www.iriweb.org/Public_site/RTM/Volume_58_2015/January-February_2015/2015_RandD_Trends_Forecast.aspx

[100] Nogrady, B. (2015, October). Chemical attraction: Science and industry both stand to gain from an innovative program that brings their interests together. Special advertising supplement, *Chronicle of Higher Education*, 29.

[101] European projects to model human brain, explore graphene win up to €1 B each. (2013, Jan. 28). *The Washington Post.* Available at: http://articles.*washingtonpost*.com/*2013-01-28*/world/.

[102] Nikolic. D. (2013, Oct. 30). "Genève récupère le Human Brain Project, au détriment de Lausanne," *Le Temps*, p. 7.

[103] Austria, Belgium, Denmark, Finland, France, Germany, Iceland, Ireland, Italy, The Netherlands, Norway, Poland, Portugal, Spain, Sweden, Switzerland, and the UK.

[104] Associate members include the People's Republic of China (2004), the Republic of Korea (2006), and the Government of India (2008).

[105] International Geosphere-Biosphere Programme, the International Human Dimensions Programme, Diversitas, the World Climate Research Programme, and the Earth Science System Partnership.

[106] The Science and Technology Alliance for Global Sustainability, comprising the International Council for Science (ICSU), the International Social Science Council, the Belmont Forum of funding agencies, the Sustainable Development Solutions Network (SDSN), the United Nations Educational, Scientific, and Cultural Organization (UNESCO), the United Nations Environment Programme (UNEP), the United Nations University, and the World Meteorological Organization.

[107] Other global hubs are located in Canada, France, Japan, and Sweden. Regional hubs are planned for Latin America, the Middle East, Asia, and Africa.

[108] Dennis Ojima, lead scientist for the Colorado State University, part of Future Earth, and professor of ecosystem science and sustainability in the Warner College of Natural Resources.

[109] Downs, D. (2015, July 24). Don't cut research ties with the military, *Chronicle of Higher Education*, A29.

[110] There are strong connections between MacDill Air Force Base and the Colleges of Engineering, Arts and Sciences, Behavioral and Community Sciences, Marine Science, Public Health, Medicine, Joint Command, the Veterans Reintegration and Resilience Initiative, the Center for Strategic and Diplomatic studies, and University of South Florida World.

[111] Texas A&M University, Norwich University, The Virginia Military Institute, The Citadel, Virginia Polytechnic Institute and State University (Virginia Tech), University of North Georgia, and the Mary Baldwin Women's Institute for Leadership.

[112] Designated by the Army Cadet Command.

[113] The Technical Coordinating Panel, North Atlantic Treaty Organization (NATO) Research and Technology Organization, and the five Country Senior National Representative—Army (SNR(A)) Working Groups.

[114] Mississippi State, Embry-Riddle Aeronautical University, Drexel University, University of Alaska Fairbanks, Kansas State, Montana State, North Carolina State, University of Kansas, Auburn University, Ohio State, Wichita State, UC Davis, University of Alabama Huntsville, University of North Dakota, Oregon State, New Mexico State and affiliate members: Indiana State, Concordia, Louisiana Tech, Tuskegee, University of Southampton, and Sinclair Community College.

[115] IT, construction and extractive industries, manufacturing, agriculture, and energy.

[116] Association of Universities and Colleges of Canada, International Research Collaboration, June 2009, AUCC. http://www.usask.ca/secretariat/governing-bodies/council/committee/international/reports-archive/International-Research-Collaboration2009.pdf.

Chapter Five
International Research, Innovation, and Entrepreneurial Ecosystems

Introduction

Research at universities has been focused primarily on generating new knowledge for the public good. Ideas and inventions were passed on to the private sector to produce marketable products. University leaders then began to realize that research and innovation could generate revenue for their institutions, investigators, their state, and the nation. Thus they began to develop an infrastructure to make this a reality.

Research and innovation go hand-in-hand, so much so that many offices of research have amended their titles to include research and innovation, research, innovation, and economic development (and sometimes outreach and engagement). The names of these offices capture the content of this chapter, but their focus is typically more national. The goal is to help them recognize the advantages of adding the international perspective.

We are only beginning to understand the challenges of working in this arena with international partners, especially in entrepreneurial activities, even though countries and universities abroad embrace research, innovation, and entrepreneurship in much the same way as our universities. They also have goals to generate intellectual property that lead to commercialization of products and the formation of companies. Universities across the globe are creating "spaces and places" to support entrepreneurs and are working with their institutions and communities to create entrepreneurial ecosystems and innovation zones.

Innovation

Research, innovation, entrepreneurship, collaboration, productivity, and prosperity are about policy, strategy, people, facilities, and resources. Research is linked with innovation to drive economic growth. Productivity depends upon innovation, and prosperity depends upon productivity. Innovation is global and interactive and is the key driver of global competitiveness, economic growth, and prosperity.

> *The world is dramatically being reshaped by scientific and technological innovations, global interdependence, cross-cultural encounters and changes in the balance of economic and political power.*[1]
>
> *Innovation is breaking down walls that have kept people apart for centuries.*[2]

Innovation is one of today's buzzwords in business, education, and manufacturing. Innovation is advancing the economy; improving our cities; and making inroads into solving local, national, and global problems. It is a strategy for thriving in a world of challenge and transformation, and it underpins our economic future in today's knowledge-based (also called innovation-based) economy.

Innovation is the intentional exploitation of new ideas and breakthroughs that are borne of creative passion to create new value for customers and the responsible organizations. Open innovation involves searching the world for ideas and engaging networks of people who collaborate. Closed innovation occurs when connections are made only within the organization. The philosophy in this case is, if you hire the right people, it will happen!

The U.S. Council on Competitiveness sees innovation as "i5"—imagination, insight, ingenuity, invention, and impact. An even simpler definition for innovation is "fresh thinking that creates value people will pay for."[3] Or, as the University of Georgia printed on a T-shirt, innovation is "make something work, then make it work better!"

Innovation is a "system" that consists of partnerships among the public sector (universities), private sector (businesses and industry), and economic development agencies. It is influenced by government policies and practices that protect intellectual property, and it requires investment in research and development (R&D), talent, access to education, physical facilities and sophisticated information and communications technology (ICT) infrastructure.

Innovation is encompassed in the cluster strategy,[4] in which the most prominent areas of expertise and strength of a region are built upon as priorities for economic development. Cluster strategy is also a way to focus the university's research enterprise to ensure that it is built upon the strengths of programs and investigators.

The life sciences, information technology, medical devices, aerospace technology, renewable energy, and chemicals and advanced materials dominate innovation clusters across the United States.[5]

Ingredients for Successful Innovation

Successful innovation requires openness to change, flexibility, talent, and a clear and simple concept to convince the world of its value. These fit into the ingredients for successful innovation stated previously: policy and strategy, people, and facilities and resources.

Policy and Strategy: Institutional, National, and Global
Institutional Strategy

Institutions that embrace innovation must have a high tolerance for creative people who are looking for better ways of doing things and who are prepared to fail. Universities can stimulate innovation by creating an atmosphere that encourages and promotes innovation and developing multidisciplinary, experiential opportunities such as internships, workshops, and seminars that integrate business enterprise and university research. The Henry Samueli School of Engineering at the University of California, Irvine, conducted a schoolwide "innovation caucus" to drive idea generation, intellectual property placement, and research development to promote these activities across disciplines. Few universities have an innovation strategy; it is simply assumed that it will happen!

National and Global Innovation Agendas

The future will belong to countries that are engines of innovation.[6]

Innovation Strategy of the United States

Innovation is what America has always been about.[7]

The Council on Competitiveness defined innovation goals for the United States in 2004.[8] Although more than 10 years old, these goals are as relevant today as they were when they were developed. They could also serve as goals for any U.S. or international university:

- Educate the next generation of innovators.
- Deepen science and engineering skills.

- Explore knowledge intersections.
- Equip workers for change.
- Support collaborative creativity.
- Energize entrepreneurship.
- Reward long-term strategy.
- Build world-class infrastructure.
- Invest in frontier research.
- Attract global talent.
- Create high-wage jobs.

In 2005, the Council on Competitiveness rolled out the National Innovation Act 2005 with a 10-year focus on innovation. According to the Council:

Innovation will be the single most important factor in determining America's success in the 21st century.[9]

This has not gone unheeded by other nations, many of whom have been developing innovation agendas over several years and especially in the last few decades; governments have recognized innovation is the engine of economic growth, prosperity, and competitive advantage. The leaders of competitiveness councils around the world have formed a network that is the Global Federation of Competitiveness Councils, to provide a platform for sharing best practices to promote national and global prosperity.

President Obama has asserted that U.S. innovation is a foundation of U.S. power.[10] In his 2015 State of the Union address, the president included discussion of the first ever *Strategy for American Innovation,* issued in 2009, updated in 2011 and renewed 2015 with nine key innovation investments[11] to ensure that the United States remains an innovation superpower.

The United States has not had a national strategy for innovation, and it has been argued that there should be a cabinet-level office to focus governmental emphasis on innovation and deployment of new technologies to meet critical national needs. The argument for such an office was reinvigorated at the time of the federal stimulus (2009) when an Office of Implementation was also envisioned.[12] Such offices, or another office with the responsibility to promote a national innovation agenda, would help to stabilize the U.S. competitive position with other nations.

The U.S. Department of Commerce describes itself as "America's Innovation Agency" and in 2012, published a report entitled, "The Competitiveness and Innovation Capacity of the United States,"[13] indicating that the United States is "waking up" to the urgency of the global innovation challenge and must abandon its complacency. The report underscores the need for federal investments in (1) research, (2) education, and (3) infrastructure. It warned that failure to respond to these needs will erode our competitive position. The report includes 10 policy proposals. Several of them are relevant to the roles U.S. research universities play in developing and translating basic research, preparing individuals for careers in the STEM fields, fostering entrepreneurship, and establishing regional clusters of technology commercialization.

> *The greatest long term threat to U.S. national security is not terrorists wielding a nuclear or biological weapon, but the erosion of America's place as a world leader in science and technology.*[14]

The Regional Innovation Strategies Program, run by the Department's Economic Development Administration's (EDA)[15] Office of Innovation and Entrepreneurship, provides the i6 Challenge grants, Cluster Grants for Seed Capital Funds, and Science and Research Park Development Grants, to assist entrepreneurs, innovators, and innovation organizations in moving their ideas and inventions to market, thereby strengthening the U.S. economy and global competitiveness.

- The i6 Challenge is a multiagency competition[16] that began in 2010 by awarding funds to develop proof-of-concept centers to help entrepreneurs and innovators at universities and research centers who have projects ready to commercialize or to begin a startup company with professional and financial assistance.
- The U.S. Cluster Grant for Seed Capital Funds competitively awards a plan or effort to create university commercialization seed funds, startup programs, and city and county development and innovation seed and venture funds that will help form or launch cluster-based, seed capital funds for entrepreneurs and startups.

The National Science Foundation (NSF) created the Innovation Corps (I-Corps) in 2011 to foster entrepreneurship leading to the commercialization of technology supported by NSF-funded research. Awards of $100,000 per year for three years were first made in 2013 to provide infrastructural support to selected innovative teams. The I-Corps program helps students create a startup company, develop a business model for review by third-party investors, and gain faster access to technology licenses.

Innovation Strategies Abroad

Many countries around the globe understand how innovation policies and programs that coalesce the perspectives and talent of researchers, innovators, inventors, and entrepreneurs in academia and business create solutions to local and global issue; enhance productivity and higher standards of living; promote growth; and increase the competitiveness of their nation and/or the region. These policies focus on R&D, science and engineering workforce development, entrepreneurship, health care investment, protection of intellectual property and technology transfer, education, business–university collaboration, regional economic development, and manufacturing. Nearly all of these agendas and strategies position university–industry–government partnerships in a central role.

Many of the top 40 countries ranked by R&D investment as "innovation-oriented" economies have a formal, innovation strategy, and a number of them began this effort far ahead of today's "innovation thrust."

Singapore began its National Innovation System in the 1960s with an emphasis on manufacturing and communications, and China developed its National Innovation System in 1979, providing a framework for enhancing universities and university research. In 1958, the Department of Science and Technology of the Philippines (DOST) realized that protection, development, management, and commercialization of high-impact technologies and new startup companies created by Filipino inventors and students promoted the growth and advancement of the region and country. They created the Technology Application and Promotion Institute (TAPI) to showcase inventors and their products through local and national contests, exhibitions, fairs, and hosted national and international conferences. A culture of innovation, entrepreneurship, and interaction was established among scientists and engineers in Filipino universities, R&D institutes, and the private sector, often in partnership with the government. Legislation similar to the U.S. Bayh-Dole Act was introduced to promote patent and licensing opportunities for research funded by the Filipino government.[17]

TAPI also provides training programs in enterprise development at colleges and universities and competitive funding to students and other inventors for startup companies, fabrication and testing of prototypes in a common service facility, and printing of technical and promotional material. The results of projects and products from TAPI-assisted work are displayed in an exhibition center sponsored by DOST.

Former Prime Minister Manmohan Singh of India declared 2010–2020 to be India's Decade of Innovation, with science and education at the center of their ambitions.

The British Government prepared a 10-year Science and Innovation Investment Framework for 2004–2014[18] to guide the UK to become one of the most competitive countries in the world for research and innovation. Higher education is recognized to be important in driving the nation's prosperity through cutting-edge research, innovation, and enterprise; through stronger links with industry; and by producing graduates with desirable skills for employment.[19] Several of the six major goals featured in the UK plan reinforced this statement and signaled government investment in universities.

Similarly, the government of France published a National Research and Innovation Strategy in 2009, with the understanding that research and innovation "are the main and sometimes the only—tools available to build tomorrow's world.["][20]

The priority areas for France's efforts included health care; nutrition and biotechnology; environmental urgency and eco-technology; and information, communication, and nanotechnology. Higher education is a top priority and is receiving significant government investment in both education and research.

European Union (EU): Lisbon Strategy, the European Institute of Innovation and Technology (EIT), Innovation Union, and Horizon 2020

The European Union (EU)[21] began the new century by recognizing that knowledge and innovation are the key resources of nations, companies, and people. The EU thus crafted the Lisbon Strategy, whose innovation agenda was to make the EU, by 2010, "the most competitive and dynamic knowledge-based economy in the world capable of sustaining economic growth with more and better jobs and greater social cohesion."[22]

By 2005, it was evident that the goals of the Lisbon Strategy were not being met, and a midcourse correction refocused the agenda on growth, jobs, and sustainable social and environmental goals. A separate thrust brought information and communication technologies into the plan[23] as core to accomplishing the objectives, but by 2009, the outcome was still considered unsuccessful.

The European Institute of Innovation and Technology (EIT) was created in 2008 and implemented in 2010 to bring together academia and business to reinforce innovation among EU Member States, develop entrepreneurs, train 10,000 PhDs, and create 600 new companies by 2020. In March 2010, the European Commission launched Horizon 2020, Framework Program 8 (FP8), which focused on the development of a smart, sustainable, and inclusive economy[24] for growth and prosperity in the coming decade.[25] In 2013, the EIT developed a Strategic Innovation Agenda within the Horizon 2020 Framework (see below), contributing to the overall goals of the initiative. Part of the strategy was to build five thematic Knowledge Innovation Communities (KICs)[26] over these years to share knowledge, information, and skills and to develop innovative products and services that will build jobs and opportunities for growth.

An alliance of top European universities, companies, and research institutes[27] participates in the KIC PhD programs. A Young Leaders Innovation and Entrepreneurship Training Program brings 30 young professionals, entrepreneurs, and academics together from across Europe to address big challenges with fresh new ideas, solutions, and recommendations. The EIT has more than 800 partners in Europe and makes numerous awards.

The Innovation Union[28] and Horizon 2020 of the EU

The Innovation Union is Europe's 2020 10-year, flagship strategy to enhance global competitiveness, economic growth, and jobs. Excellent science, industrial leadership, and tackling societal challenges are the three strategic priorities to create a single market for knowledge, research, and innovation.

Horizon 2020 is a pillar of the Innovation Union and the largest EU Research and Innovation program ever, with nearly €80 billion of dedicated funding over seven years (2014–2020), plus private investment to be attracted. Europe's leaders and Members of the European Parliament agreed that research is an investment in the future and the heart of EU's blueprint for smart, sustainable, and inclusive growth and jobs.

Progress toward the Horizon 2020 goals is measured annually through the Innovation Union Scorecard. The Scorecard is a comparative assessment of the research and innovation performance of the EU28 Member States and the relative strengths and weaknesses of their research and innovation systems, and it identifies areas of needed improvement in performance. The scoreboard also covers Serbia, Macedonia, Turkey, Iceland, Norway, and Switzerland, and based on a limited number of indicators, Australia, Brazil, Canada, China, India, Japan, Russia, South Africa, South Korea, and the United States are included. EU Member States are grouped into the categories of Innovation leaders, Innovation Followers, Moderate Innovators, and Modest Innovators. Great Britain may now need to separate from or position itself differently within this innovation scheme for the EU with the 2016 passage of Brexit.

Saudi Arabia's National Science, Technology and Innovation Plan (NSTIP)

Saudi Arabia's knowledge- and innovation-driven strategy is focused on entrepreneurship and inclusive growth through an ecosystem of universities, government, firms, and funding, and based on skilled manpower and research. The NSTIP is a stepwide roadmap to develop local strategies in key sectors where the Kingdom of Saudi Arabia has a competitive advantage to gain prominence, first in the region, then Asia, and then globally. Of the respondents to a survey,[29] 90 percent revealed that research and educational institutes and their external collaborators were either the top, or one of the top five, drivers for successful innovation. Other factors cited were infrastructure for technology transfer, internal research, foreign collaboration, and the development of human capital and technology.[30]

Kazakhstan—The Kazakhstan Technology Commercialization Project

In 2010, the government of the Republic of Kazakhstan and the World Bank launched the five-year, $75 million[31] Technology Commercialization Project for an "innovation ecosystem"[32] to support an innovation-driven economy that would be less reliant on oil and extractive industries; bolster other industry sectors such as transportation, pharmaceuticals, telecommunications, petrochemicals, and food processing;[33] and improve scientific performance through cross-disciplinary, problem-oriented research with commercial relevance. To strengthen the science base, funds were made available through a competitive, merit-based grant program to support high-quality R&D by Senior Scientist Groups, Junior Researcher Groups, and graduate students; develop a world-class instrumentation center; and to link science to markets. The International Science and Commercialization Board was selected to oversee the project, and the Technology Commercialization Office[34] was established to provide services for commercializing research and connecting Kazakh scientists to local and international markets. CRDF Global assisted in this project to provide training, policy and capacity building, grant programs, a technology management team, and commercialization of technologies.

In 2013, the project organized a workshop entitled "Innovative Economy in Kazakhstan: Instruments of Technology Commercialization" for high-level government officials, R&D institutions, academics, international organizations, and the media to showcase successes and exhibit grant projects. The plan to establish a research park in Astana with academic and corporate partners was also revealed. Microsoft, Samsung, and Hewlett-Packard signed memoranda of understanding (MOUs) to create research centers in the park. Although the plan was developed with sound intentions, the political and economic situations within and surrounding the country have placed Kazakhstan in a less favorable situation, where this economic initiative appears to be eclipsed by the downturn in the oil economy in the region.[35] The success of the work thus far has been in commercialization of technologies (revenue from sales $2,639,050), new laws regarding commercialization enacted in 2015, grant programs, and seminars to teach business skills. A follow-on project also funded by the World Bank ($80 million) and Kazakhstan ($30 million) was initiated in 2016.

People: Innovators and Entrepreneurs

The Council on Competitiveness characterizes successful innovators as individuals who

> *are not born with inherent skills, but can learn them. They can acquire social skills to work in diverse, multidisciplinary teams, to communicate their innovations, and garner the resources to see their innovations through to completion. They are comfortable with ambiguity, recognize new patterns within disparate data; they are inquisitive and analytical. They see challenges as opportunities and understand how complete solutions must be built from a range of resources. These skills are best acquired by actually experiencing innovation first-hand. This builds the confidence that underpins future success.*

Courses to promote Innovation are organized by U.S. and international partners. The "Oceans of Transformation Course" was developed by Georgia State University and Harry Manchester College at Oxford University with facilitation and support from Harvard University and Coca Cola. This five-day program for 24 potential leaders, innovators, and change agents is about building a culture of innovation and change; technology; mastering the art, science, and discipline of transcending innovation; developing an innovation action plan.

Companies, universities and other organizations are recruiting Chief Innovation Officers (CIOs or CINOs) who may be an innovation or idea person or an individual who recognizes potential within the organization and has the leadership and people skills, technological wisdom, business sense, and ability to develop cross-company collaboration and create an environment that promotes and supports innovation by operating tactically in the short term and strategically for the long term. Roles for the CINO have been defined.

Universities recruit CINOs with backgrounds in business, startup formation, strategic partnerships, innovation management, law, and government. Medical schools and hospitals have been leaders in adopting this position. The Association of American Medical Colleges has prepared a handbook for CINOs entitled *Chief Innovation Officer Primer: Key Elements for Success*.[36] Universities and professional organizations have organized or participated in summits for CINOs, futurists, and other professionals who work in innovation, R&D, product development, marketing, and technology.[37]

Entrepreneurs and entrepreneurship extend beyond the research programs of universities and are included in the academic programs, degrees, minors, certificates, and co-curricular programs of many disciplines. The University of North Carolina at Chapel Hill has even created a Special Assistant for Entrepreneurship and Innovation within the Office of the President.[38] Entrepreneurship thrives within an ecosystem of support, physical resources, and interaction. Entrepreneurship stakeholders are individuals, organizations, and institutions such as governments, schools, universities, private sector investors, family businesses, research centers, the military, banks, private foundations, and international aid agencies—virtually every field, discipline, and profession includes entrepreneurs and values entrepreneurship.

Entrepreneurship is global and has been organized and partitioned into activities that help people develop their ideas into new ventures, create jobs, and strengthen the economy. Global Entrepreneurship Week has been celebrated in November since 2008 when three million people in 77 countries joined the activity initiated by the Kaufman Foundation. Today, 10 million entrepreneurs, innovators, investors, researchers and policymakers in about 157 countries are involved. Events are organized in each partner country, some on a specific topic such as the challenges for women entrepreneurs, or to develop masterclasses on entrepreneurship for secondary school children, stimulate high-level policy discussions, make new cross-boundary connections, arrange a significant series of events (240 in London, for example), or even extend the week to a month (Peru).

The successful 2014 Global Entrepreneurship Congress engaged more than 6,000 people from 153 nations and prompted the development of the Global Entrepreneurship Network (GEN) to increase the numbers of people involved in start-ups and connect them with others who have similar interests worldwide.[39] GEN works with governments and the private sector, organizing competitions, summits, and round tables. GEN has taken on major development projects such as the program with the U.S. Department of State and the Templeton Foundation to expand the opportunities and resources that will advance African entrepreneurs across the continent.

Startup Nations began as a small, informal community in 2013, and today it is part of GEN and a network of startup policy advisers to governments in 49 locations. A Startup Nations Summit was held in 2014 to bring together community and government leaders.

The Global Entrepreneurship Research Network was formed to generate joint research projects such as the ecosystem mapping project that involves 100 cities globally and a Global Entrepreneurship Index that monitors the performance and the health of entrepreneurship ecosystems in 130 countries through a combination of data on opportunity recognition, risk perception, depth of capital markets, globalization, and R&D spending. Not surprising, the data revealed entrepreneurship to be the highest in richer countries, with the top five being the United States, Canada, Australia, UK, and Sweden.

The 6th annual Global Entrepreneurship Summit (GES) Youth was held this past year in Sub-Saharan Africa for 300 young people who have started new firms around the world. They shared their successes and learned from global innovators how to seek investment and broaden their businesses. GES Youth and Startup Experience were both developed in partnership with the White House.

The Global Entrepreneurship Library was established by the Kaufman Foundation and the World Economic Forum to curate information needed by entrepreneurs in each country.

Facilities and Resources

Environment: Ecosystems—Innovation Spaces

An innovation or entrepreneurial ecosystem is an environment with well-designed research facilities, compact geographic area, "collaboration stations" and resources to support and stimulate Innovation. It includes talent, expertise, and investment; promotes interaction through networks and online resources; and embraces diversity among disparate knowledge fields and cultures. A healthy ecosystem presents few bureaucratic obstacles and is accepting of failure.

Many different environments have been designed for students, faculty, staff, and often community members to become innovators and entrepreneurs through hands-on practice. Makerspaces, hackerspaces, and fab labs are set up within universities, communities, and public facilities. Incubators and accelerators, research parks, and community and regional innovation districts or zones involve universities and business partners in the United States and abroad.

Makerspaces, Hackerspaces, and Fab Labs

The concept of makerspace came from the technology-driven "maker culture," a do-it-yourself (D.I.Y.) culture associated with *Make* magazine, and the Maker Faires that stimulate interaction among "makers" and display the results of their projects. These kinds of facilities have become more visible in recent years in the United States and around the world. Makerspaces are arenas for informal, project-driven, and self-directed learning. They provide space to tinker, try out ideas, and interact with colleagues who have similar interests. Hackerspaces have been around since the mid-1990s, when they started as computer innovation centers. There are nearly 2,000 makerspaces spaces internationally. They are especially prominent in the United States and the EU, but much less so in South America, Africa, and Asia. Makermap.com shows a near absence of facilities from most countries of the former Soviet Union.

Fab labs are often associated with universities in the United States and are catalogued in more than 30 countries. MIT created the nonprofit Fab Foundation to provide education, service, and business assistance to users of fab labs.

Universities, alone, and in partnership with their communities have created makerspaces as physical locations (specially created buildings, libraries, museums, community centers, etc.) that provide tools and assistance to students, faculty, staff, and community members to connect with other similarly minded individuals to translate their ideas into a model, pilot, or product. Although these spaces are characteristically associated with fields such as engineering, computer science, and graphic design, individual inventors and teams in other (often artistic) fields are using them increasingly.

The labs are open for informal, unscheduled activity, or an organization may schedule classes in spaces that may focus on a single skill, such as coding, soldering, or woodcarving. Supplies such as cardboard, plastic, metal, gears, wood, and batteries may be available, and tools vary from a welding machine, to a laser cutter, and microcontrollers to 3D printers. College credit for the work is typically not offered although it is recognized that makerspaces at colleges and universities are important learning environments. Advisers may be present at certain times, but often users gain advice from other users. Some universities have even developed residence halls for entrepreneurs (University of Maryland).[40]

The WHALE Lab (Wheaton Autonomous Learning Lab) at Wheaton College is an interdisciplinary makerspace where students embroider, solder, weld, sculpt, or otherwise design and manufacture creative projects. ThinkLab (University of Mary Washington), Headquarters (Rutgers University), the Garage (University of Maryland) and the FabLab at Stanford are a few other innovation spaces by name. The ThinkBox Invention Center at Case Western Reserve University has become so important that it is being expanded to a seven-story, 50,000 sq. ft. building. The Invention Studio at Georgia Tech is student-run, design-build-play space for students, faculty, and staff. University Lab Instructors and student volunteers help to turn ideas into reality using machinery and equipment, sharing ideas through classes, workshops, and seminars and vendor networks. The lab has an ethic of responsibility, safety, and student ownership. Members manage the facility and are responsible for scheduling and monitoring.

Public makerspaces are also available. The Tinkering Studio at the Exploratorium Museum for Science, Art, and Human Perception in San Francisco allows museum visitors to test their ideas, and the Co-working Space in Oslo, Norway was developed for city planners and developers, government workers and international partners to work together. Similar facilities have been created in Norwegian science parks in conjunction with universities, and the Oslo International Hub serves international clients who plan to set up business in Oslo. Following the 2010 earthquake in Haiti, a makerspace was created for local and international aid workers and developers to recreate together some of the physical infrastructure of the country using recycled trash.

Clearly, innovation underpins all of the many facilities that have been created to take advantage of, improve, or stimulate action that promotes change.

Incubators and Accelerators Assist Startup Companies

At least 400 of the more than 7,000 accelerators and incubators located in "core cities"[41] around the globe help launch and sustain startup companies and are frequently linked with universities and colleges[42]. Although there are some differences in the activities each supports, "incubator" and "accelerator" are often used interchangeably—even when describing the same organization. Generally, however, an incubator supports earlier stage companies than accelerators in which participating companies may already have a client base.

Incubators

Incubators are spaces, typically within a research park, office or park business complex that provide support services for a year or more to startup and nascent companies to begin operations and become successful. Incubator personnel may recruit an external management team with the business expertise if it is not already present within the company's development team. A membership fee for incubation assistance is usually charged.[43] Incubators encourage employment, private investment, and public recognition of the role small businesses play in the economy of the region.

The majority of companies within incubators are developed around their own ideas and technology. Some incubators (Y Combinator, Mountain View, CA), however, accept entrants who do not have a startup idea,[44,45] and the staff of IdeaLab in Pasadena, CA, generates the ideas then recruits outside talent to put them into effect. Incubators can also have a specific business focus, for example, m:lab in Nairobi, Kenya, provides support to developers and entrepreneurs of mobile apps. A number of incubators in Africa are designed for technology developers, in general.

Companies that begin their operations in an incubator have a greater chance for success. According to a survey from the National Business Incubation Association (NBIA), 87 percent of the companies that started in an incubator and graduated were still thriving five years later, and 78 percent of them stay in the community.[46]

U.S. Incubators

The IC² Institute in Austin, TX, is an interdisciplinary research unit of the University of Texas that works to catalyze regional economic development through collaborative, technological innovation among the university, government, and private sector. IC² draws upon the theory and practice of entrepreneurial wealth creation to help Austin grow as an innovation and technology center and to develop knowledge-based economies in over 30 countries. IC² includes the Austin Technology Incubator, Bureau of Business Research, and the Global Commercialization Group, which provides technology commercialization training and international business development programs around the world.

Incubation Abroad

The Kiev Incubation Program

The Business Incubator Development Program in the Ukraine was created in September 1997 by the International Technology Research Institute of Loyola College in Baltimore, MD. A grant from USAID supported the establishment of incubators to provide consulting services, access to office equipment and training, assistance in accessing credit, and physical building space to promote small business growth. The project was also supported by the Ukrainian Government and local organizations. There are offices in Kiev and Kharkiv and plans to add incubators in other Ukrainian cities. An office in Slavutich, the town where the Chernobyl workers live, has been part of an effort to close the plant. Ukraine's many R&D centers, industrial centers, the Ukrainian Academy of Science Institutes, and national and polytechnic universities provide a rich talent pool of qualified entrepreneurs.

MENA Incubators[47]

Governmental entities, corporations, and individuals support entrepreneurs to improve the economies in the Arab world. Toward this objective, 15 incubators for startups have been established in the MENA region[48] to provide coaching, training, and mentoring; managing media relations; intellectual property (IP) protection and patent assistance; advice and consultation on business and subject matter; project management; investments and banking, accounting, and legal services; recruitment; connections to the global markets and networking; market validation; and business plan development and seminars and workshops—among many other resources.

Virtual Incubators

Virtual incubators have also been created across the globe, in the United States, the EU, India, Chile, Africa, Costa Rica, and the Netherlands, to mention a few. These provide cost-effective, geographically unlimited, one-on-one ICT-based exchanges and online communities that can serve a far greater number of entrepreneurs than on-site incubators. Some are for-profit, others are free, or free to up to a limit, then charge for expanded and personalized services. Virtual Incubators offer the same services to early-stage entrepreneurs as the traditional incubators except that interaction with mentors and peers around the world.[49]

FledgeX, a Seattle Incubator, was announced in 2015 with online versions in cities around the globe.[50] Zana[51] was founded as a free, peer-education incubator available to anyone, anywhere in the world, with a laptop. Five-minute or even shorter videos are targeted to early and midstage businesses in all sectors. One Million by One Million (1M/1M)[52] is a for-profit technology-based incubator and online educational program with a range of free services. Additional services that are specific for a startup company are offered at a cost.

Global, Real-Virtual Incubator Networks (G-RVINs) link entrepreneurs with local, regional, and global networks, and a series of e-implementers, e-government, e-learning, e-finance, and so forth. Virtual Incubation in East Africa occurs through a consortium of regional partners: a pan-Africa network (Afrilabs), and in Kenya (m:lab and Nailab), Uganda (Hive Colab), Rwanda (Technology and Business Technology Incubation Facility), and Tanzania (Dar Teknohama Business Incubator).

Accelerators

The accelerator model was started in 2005 by Y Combinator and expanded by TechStars in 2006. Accelerators, like incubators, promote the growth of externally developed startup companies, but on a faster time scale. Cohorts of highly selected, relatively mature companies that are close to market entry and typically start and leave the program at the same time.

Pre-accelerator programs work with a team that has an idea to be developed into a company and, through a seven- to eight-week series of workshops and coaching, prepare them to enter a full-time accelerator. Government, corporations, investors, and accelerators offer these programs.

Accelerators provide some or all of these elements: small amounts of capital, mentorship, educational programs, support services, networking, and free or subsidized space, in exchange for 6–12 percent (or more) equity in the company. Accelerators can be publicly or privately supported, often backed by a significant number of well-funded, well-recognized companies so that the programs are relatively cost neutral to the startup companies until they "graduate" in three to four months and move to their own location and independence. More long-term accelerators also exist.

The International Accelerator in Austin, TX, for example, has a 12-month program consisting of two phases. Companies are evaluated after participating in Phase 1. They, in turn, evaluate the accelerator program, before continuing to Phase 2. The first phase requires an 8 percent equity payment to the accelerator. Those who complete Phase 2 pay another 7 percent.

Niche accelerators are designed, for example, around health care,[53] technology (CANVS in Orlando), to help companies that have female founders or cofounders (Women Innovate Mobile), minorities (NewMe), and non-U.S. citizens (International Accelerator).[54] Those which cater to companies coming from overseas require the accelerator personnel to be versed in visa issues, incorporation abroad as it pertains to investment from U.S. sources, and to include mentors who understand the needs of international companies and can provide legal and banking intelligence, IP expertise, and communications—especially regarding the marketing of the companies. Many accelerators that deal with international companies provide online training to jump start their education before the company leaves its home country.[55]

Starburst Accelerator is a niche accelerator focused on startups in the aerospace industry. It has connections with more than 100 laboratories and universities in Europe and the United States and more than 20 well known industry partners[56] around the world and U.S. government sponsors (NASA, FAA, DOD). A satellite site will be launched in Asia in 2016. In addition to programs in the immediate aviation space, it also supports companies that develop sensors, antennas, software, AI, and so on. Starburst calls itself a "technology middleman broker."

U.S. Accelerators

Two new, large, innovative U.S. accelerators are MassChallenge in Boston and Grand Central Tech in New York City. Both offer space and services to startup companies at no cost and no equity is taken from the company. The MassChallenge Entrepreneurship Accelerator is based on the concept that "Modern entrepreneurship is a global endeavor ... [that] spans geographic and cultural boundaries." Based in Boston, Israel, and the UK, MassChallenge is a not-for-profit organization and the world's largest accelerator program and annual competition for startup companies. It is open to all entrepreneurs who need education, mentorship, space, and networks to develop their company. Accelerator companies are entered into an annual competition, and if successful, garner resources for further development. In 2015, 128 startups competed in Boston and another 89 in the UK in the fields of energy or clean tech, general, health care and life sciences, high-tech, and social impact.

Grand Central Tech is located in the former Facebook Midtown headquarters adjacent to Grand Central Station. It supports 12–18 startup companies every year by providing the best services New York City (NYC) offers, including relationships with eight NYC high schools and local universities, and benefits from the talent and mentorship of individuals in Fortune 500 companies and a global network. Startups have a corporate partner and are provided free space and services for one year, requiring only that they settle their company in adjacent space for a few years thereafter. The goal is to build upon the NYC talent to contribute to the NYC economy.

Accelerators Abroad

TechStars, a U.S.-based accelerator system located in several major U.S. cities, created the Global Acceleration Network, a global ecosystem for entrepreneurs, with programs in 600 cities, 120 countries, and six continents. Mentoring is a cornerstone of the TechStars program; as many as 10 mentors assist a single company. The program usually selects only one small cohort each year.

Another worldwide accelerator network, Startupbootcamp, has offices in global innovation hubs. A three month program engages investor and mentor talent from over 30 countries to assist a class of 120 startup companies.

Chinaccelerator, located in Shanghai, is Asia's number-one startup accelerator. A 90-day program serves a small number of handpicked companies, each awarded $30,000 and provided intensive mentoring from entrepreneurs and company founders, CEOs, and managers from a wide range of business and professional services, investors, and university leaders. All new companies begin the experience with an eight-day trip, modeled after the "Geeks on a Plane" for-profit tours (geeksonaplane.com), to visit successful Chinese startup companies. At the close of the session, the companies pitch to selected investors at Demo Day for further support.

In 2015, five Russian research universities[57] and the Russian Venture Capital Association signed on as members of an international accelerator, International Proof-of-Concept Association (IPOCA), that connect proof-of-concept centers. It was originally started by Skolkovo in 2013 in partnership with MIT Deshpande Center for Technological Innovation, the Masdar Institute of Science and Technology (UAE), the University of ITMO (Saint Petersburg), and subsequently, with three additional universities.[58] IPOCA will accelerate advanced technologies in Russia through international cooperation, networking, and data sharing among entrepreneurs, researchers, investors, government agencies, and corporations.

There are well over 100 startup local and regional accelerators across the EU,[59,60] with some belonging to international accelerator networks (e.g., TechStars, YCombinator), some pan-European, and others corporate backed. iMinds is a digital research institute in Flanders, Belgium, that created the iStart incubator supporting digital entrepreneurs. University-based accelerators have been ranked among some of the best accelerators by UBI Global and the FUNDACITY European Accelerator

Report, 2014. Incubators located in the UK, Spain, and Germany, in that order, have the greatest amount of financial investment. The top four fields for investment are in the IT sector.

Research Parks—U.S. and International

Research parks, science parks, and technology parks are ecosystems that attract like-minded organizations, research groups, companies and governments which are anxious to collaborate in shared physical space with university faculty and students who bring talent, skills and creative thinking, and access to the technology transfer infrastructure to aid commercialization. Parks typically include business and professional services, incubators and accelerators, and have amenity programs and recreational space. The development of research or technology parks and their means of support is highly variable in both the United States and overseas. Ideas for park initiation, progress and development are shared at national and international meetings organized by the Association of University Research Parks (AURP) and International Association of Science Parks (IASP) (see below).

Some parks have a single theme such as energy or biotechnology, whereas others—especially those such as Research Triangle Park,[61] that have been in existence for a significant period of time may house companies focused around cluster themes such as life science, information sciences, and clean tech.

Research Parks typically develop around universities that have recognized the potential of their research to create economic value, especially in collaboration with the private sector. A park may recruit and grow around an anchor tenant company or develop clusters of companies that match a particular university strength. Many university parks recruit international companies as partners. The Research Triangle Park (founding partners North Carolina State, University of North Carolina, and Duke University), for example, has international companies which began as U.S. companies, then expanded internationally, as well as those which are foreign-based. Talent at Research Triangle Park is also international as the three universities have a vast number of partnerships with universities and companies abroad. Research Triangle Park is described as a place to "explore bold ideas." This is the goal of most parks—to provide the freedom to innovate, produce, and grow.

Extremely large research parks are developing in China, India, and the Middle East, where oil money is invested in research, industry, and government clusters of innovation. Biopolis in Singapore has 12 million square feet of research space, 2,500 researchers from 70 countries, 10 research institutes, and nine government agencies. Vedanta Research links university students with commercial enterprise focused on the pharmaceutical and health care industry in India. At least 30 multinational companies such as IBM, Shell, Dow, GE, Siemens, Boeing, and Schlumberger that have committed to a presence in the research park at the King Abdullah University of Science and Technology (KAUST) in Saudi Arabia.[62]

The Dhahran Technology Valley (DTV) Science Park is an open innovation ecosystem for entrepreneurial activities established in 2006 by the King Fahd University of Petroleum and Minerals (KFUPM) to align economic policy, higher education, innovation, and industrial research; to commercialize technology-based products; and to create innovative companies in the energy sector.[63] The DTV includes the King Abdullah Science Park, an innovation center at KFUPM, a liaison office, business incubator, an industrial consulting office, and a science and technology exhibition. Labs, offices, social areas, and spaces for business incubation, prototyping, and product development are available to researchers, technology innovators, entrepreneurs, venture investors, product designers, developers, and multinational and Saudi Arabian industries.[64] A multinational board supports and makes recommendations on park operations.

Startup Village, Kerala, India, is an ambitious, vibrant, technology business incubator located at the Kinfra High-Tech Park in Kochi, Kerala. Startup Village seeks to become Asia's Number One startup destination and, with at least 46 multinational and Indian companies, there is success is toward this goal. The Village has an array of programs that provide support, especially, for young entrepreneurs to develop cutting-edge technology, telecom innovation, and startup companies. The ambition is to create 1,000 startups over the first 10 years of operation. The motto for the park is "Build. Break. Innovate," sending the message of taking risk, learning from failure, and bouncing back.

The park features education campaigns and initiatives. A Startup Playbook compares what Startup Village offers to prepare an entrepreneur versus a traditional school or college. The Intel Tech Challenge is organized for young children interested in design, discovery, coding and advancing their computational skills (see precollegiate programs in Chapter 3), and in 2013, Startup Village and the Kerala government launched SVSquare to fund a trip for selected young entrepreneurs to Silicon Valley to learn from that startup environment.

A biotechnology park with a 50,000-square-foot incubator and a patent facilitation center is also located with Startup Village at the Kinfra High-Tech Park.

Techno Lodges are being established in rural areas of Kerala as low cost versions of the IT parks to assist local startup companies.

Support for Research Park Development and Management

The Association of University Research Parks (AURP) is a 25-year-old professional association that provides support to more than 700 research and science parks worldwide. It was developed to foster "innovation, commercialization and economic growth in a global economy through university, industry and government partnerships," and has become the world's largest association to assist park leaders, architects, master planners, financial organizations, government, industrial partners, and academic institutions. AURP offers educational programs and modules for industry and universities and annual meetings are opportunities to share experiences and learn from experts about building and growing a successful park. An interactive seminar on "Creating Communities of Innovation" is held at each of the meetings, and numerous awards[65] are given annually to recognize research parks and their leaders for innovation and success.

AURP received its first federal grant in 2014 to support research parks, and in the same year held a symposium with the U.S. National Academy of Sciences on the importance of research parks to innovation districts. AURP and Battelle produced a report entitled "Creating Communities of Innovation" that highlights the economic advantages of research parks.

The International Association of Science Parks (IASP) and Areas of Innovation is an nongovernmental organization (NGO), a worldwide network of science parks and areas of innovation, founded in 1984 and headquartered in Malaga, Spain. IASP provides services that drive growth, effectiveness, and visibility to member activities and marketing for its nearly 400 members in 70 countries who manage science, technology, and research parks and other areas of innovation. Publications, networking assistance, conferences, workshops, and seminars are organized for members around the world to advance the "competitiveness of companies and entrepreneurs of their cities and regions, and contribute to global economic development through innovation, entrepreneurship, and the transfer of knowledge and technology." IASP maintains statistics on science parks and organizes regional events and its Annual World Conference. IASP has Special Consultative Status with the Economic and Social Council of the United Nations.

State, Regional and City Innovation Zones and Districts[66]

Innovation zones are being developed the world over as places where economic, networking, and physical assets converge around a strategy to recruit companies—or engage existing companies—that are anxious to collaborate with education and become part of a cluster to "supercharge" economic development and increase the number of high-tech jobs.[67] Innovation zones are typically located within a city, but may be equivalent to an entire city. An innovation zone may be a statewide initiative with sites dispersed among cities. Community leadership (mayors, city councils, economic development organizations), including university presidents, is critical for these collaboratives to develop and stabilize.

The difference between innovation zones or districts and research parks or campuses is often unclear. Both ventures may include social amenities, recreational facilities, and retail in addition to work spaces and become mixed-use, live-learn-work-create communities. Innovation zones and districts are often the beneficiaries of donated land and a shared commitment among cities, regions, governments, and private individuals to exploit the fruits of research and talents of university researchers or innovators to advance their economies.

Innovation zones are often developed around universities and colleges that produce world-leading research as well as technical schools and business schools, science high schools, hospitals, and companies. They offer common space, federal corporate R&D tax credits, low-cost energy, a skilled workforce, startup business incubators and accelerators, wired connections, and efficient transportation, including a local airport. Higher education, in partnership with industry, is typically the economic driver and the magnet for others to become members of the zone.

Innovation zones may focus on specific activities. For example, educational innovation zones link higher education institutions and schools in a state or city. "Digital Learning Now" in West Virginia, is a component of the state's Education Innovation Act. Health care innovation zones are designated geographic areas in which teaching and nonteaching hospitals, outpatient clinics and facilities, and community public health organizations collaborate, and even food innovation zones have been created.

City and Campus Located Innovation Zones

Virtually all of the major cities in the United States are repurposing industrial sites, warehouses, waterfronts, and other sites, especially around universities, to develop innovation districts. Seattle's South Lake Union, Cambridge's Kendall Square, South Boston's Waterfront, and San Francisco's Mission Bay are only a few of the most notable innovation districts. An example of a continually developing innovation zone located adjacent to the university campus is Technology Square (Tech Square), located on the Georgia Tech campus in Midtown Atlanta.

Tech Square is a mixed-use, full-service innovation district that supports entrepreneurship and innovation of students, faculty, and the community. It was founded in 2003 on an eight-block abandoned neighborhood adjacent to and across the freeway from Georgia Tech in Midtown Atlanta through a partnership of the university, its foundation, and the business community. Tech Square houses university programs,[68] spinoffs, centers of several Fortune 500 companies, venture capitalists, research labs, a business incubator and the Advanced Technology Development Center (ATDC),[69] an organization that assists technology startups with connections and coaching. Retail and restaurant space are also within Tech Square and a high performance computing center for Georgia Tech and company partners is currently under development.

Technology Enterprise Park is a cluster of four midrise, multitenant, technology development buildings near Tech Square affiliated with Georgia Tech, other universities and Atlanta hospitals, and numerous high-tech companies that have an emphasis on the biosciences. A new health biosciences live-work-play-create community is being developed[70] within Technology Enterprise Park to attract investment and create jobs in the life sciences, health services, medical device and pharma companies, and houses companies that spin off from Georgia Tech, Emory University, Georgia State University, Clark Atlanta, and Morehouse School of Medicine. The district will also include the Global Center for Medical Innovation (CGMI) and the Georgia Tech Research Institute, and it will provide land for Technology Enterprise Park tenants to expand their companies.

Numerous support programs developed by Georgia Tech for its faculty, students and community members to grow and thrive as entrepreneurs and transform ideas into startup companies augment the real estate aspects of this vast innovation ecosystem. The Integrated Program for Startups (GT:IPS) provides training and support to help those interested in launching companies based on Georgia Tech intellectual property. VentureLab helps to transform research into startups, complementing the work of ATDC.

Centennial Campus

One of the first all-inclusive R&D campuses connected with a university, was developed in 1984 on the property of a previous mental health institution adjacent to North Carolina State University. The land was donated by the government to become Centennial Campus, envisioned as a model community—a research park, an innovation destination, and a "self-sustaining city" to bring together government, industry, NGOs, and academia to promote economic development based on university and partnership research and technology. The first building opened in 1989 and the first company joined the campus in 1991.

Today, 30 years after its founding, Centennial Campus houses four colleges of North Carolina State University,[71] 70 industries, programs of several government agencies,[72] 75 academic research centers, institutes and departments, and two schools—a magnet middle school and an early STEM high school in which students can earn up to two years of college credit as they obtain their high school degree. Centennial Campus has apartments for workers, housing for students, and amenities such as a championship golf course, fishing ponds, walking trails, and retail shops. A research library and the Springboard Innovation Hub help students, workers, and entrepreneurs establish collaborations among partner groups and make global connections. Space for companies is available in the Centennial

Technology Incubator or in downtown Raleigh. Metrics to measure the success of innovation include disclosures, patents, commercialization agreements (and miscellaneous other agreements), revenue, and venture developments (startups and products). Each of these categories has several independent measures to document the success of Centennial Park. NC State has more than 700 research projects involving international collaboration.

Regional Innovation Zones

Silicon Valley, the first research park in the world started in 1951[73], is still recognized as the premier, regional, innovation zone[74] and epicenter for startups. It has evolved through several stages in developing innovation industries with IT industries being dominant. The success of Silicon Valley is partially attributed to the university R&D and related expenditures, STEM talent, and international and risk capital availability.

Cities in several states[75] have created their own versions of Silicon Valley. The Florida High-Tech Corridor, for example, extends from the Gulf of Mexico on one side of the state across 23 counties to the Atlantic Ocean on the other side, anchored by several major cities, three research universities, 14 community and state colleges, one specialty private university, more than 20 economic development organizations and workforce development boards, high-tech industry clusters, and literally thousands of innovative companies. The Corridor partnerships support research, entrepreneurship, marketing and workforce development and are linked through matching grants for research projects with Corridor universities and international companies and with the International Consortium for Advanced Manufacturing. The Corridor Council has supported the development of technology degree and certificate programs at the education institutions, created a Virtual Entrepreneur Center, and invested more than $60 million in projects that have benefitted the regional economy.

Israel is considered the Innovation Nation, or as described by authors Senor and Singer, Israel, "The Startup Nation,"[76] and is also called Silicon Valley: Part II, or the Other Silicon Valley. Israel is home to well over 250 multinational corporations.

Statewide Innovation Zones

Pennsylvania developed the Keystone Innovation Zone (KIZ) initiative in 2004 as a follow-on to the 1999 Keystone Opportunity Zone initiative, to improve entrepreneurial activity to increase the growth of the knowledge economy around Pennsylvania's R&D centers. The KIZ connects 28 KIZ zones in urban and rural regions where Penn State campuses are located and partners with local companies.

International Innovation Zones

Simon Fraser University, Ryerson University, and the University of Ontario Institute of Technology (Canada) have established Zones of Incubation and Innovation (ZI^2), the first pan-Canada incubator or accelerator program in digital technologies and a student-only incubator. The partnership has also created the first Canadian-led incubator or accelerator in India, Zonestartups, located in the Bombay Stock Exchange Tower in Mumbai.

King Abdullah University of Science and Technology (KAUST) in Thuwal, Saudi Arabia, is an example of a global live-learn-work-create community where the graduate-only University is the centerpiece. The KAUST community includes residences for the faculty and students of KAUST, houses of worship, medical and recreational facilities, a yacht club, retail, and a research park accommodating many multinational companies.

A parallel research, education and economic development community—an innovation zone—was developed in Russia. In 2010, then-President Medvedev established the Skolkovo Foundation through law and, in cooperation with the Russian Academy of Sciences and the Federation Agency for Scientific Organizations, began an effort to change Russia's dependence on an oil and gas economy through research, innovation, entrepreneurship, internationalization, interdisciplinary problem-based learning, and the development of a startup culture. Their tag line was "Reimaging the World."

Described as Russia's Silicon Valley, the Skolkovo Innovation Center is a city and an innovation ecosystem within 30–40 minutes of Moscow, accessible by several means of transportation. It houses Skolkovo Technopark, providing services to resident companies, common use and business centers, an Intellectual Property Center, venture investors, an International Accelerator,[77] the Skolkovo Institute of Science and Technology, and 336 participating companies[78] (27 international) organized in five clusters.[79] Skolkovo Innovation Center measures its success by counting 1,000 startup companies prepared to expand internationally. Russian scientists and technologists who earned their educations abroad and remained in professional careers overseas have been enticed to repatriate.

Skolkovo Institute of Science and Technology (Skoltech) was established in 2011 in partnership with MIT. It is a private, international graduate university that focuses its programs on Russia's economic priorities (see clusters). Like KAUST, the educational programs are organized in centers, each with a specific research mission and with collaborators from Russian and international universities. The President of Skoltech Institute, Edward Crawley, describes Skoltech as a different kind of university, emphasizing teaching, research and innovation, and industrial development. MIT and Skoltech have also initiated an industrial internship program (see Chapter 4).

Other education programs expand the goals of Scoltech to create entrepreneurs, beginning at very early ages. Skolkovo Open University was established in 2014–2015 to offer programs and competitions[80] for college grads and young entrepreneurs to become involved in the innovation ecosystem. An international school (preschool through secondary school) located in Innovation City offers programs in either English or Russian to foster innovation. The Skolkovo Foundation has created a branch in the Far East to build ecosystems similar to the one in Russia.

In accord with the national goal to increase innovation and R&D cooperation among local and global universities, research institutes, and corporations, China has developed three innovation zones of exceptional size as a strategy focusing on research universities as the drivers of economic development. Suzhou Industrial Park (SIP), Tianjin Eco-City, and Zhongguancun Sciences Park (ZGC) are all located in innovation development zones.[81] Both Suzhou and Tianjin began as collaborations between the Chinese and Singapore governments.

Twenty-seven domestic and international universities are housed at the Suzhou site. Suzhou has also created Nanopolis, the world's largest nanotech research and commercialization enterprise, housing more than 100 nanotech companies and 20 university research institutes. Suzhou started similar innovation zones at UCLA (now closed) and Monash University in Australia.

Tianjin Eco City has been described more as a "housing development" although more than 3,000 companies are registered at the site.

ZGC is considered the Silicon Valley of China. It is the most successful of the three zones, engaging 40 colleges and universities, including Tsinghau and Beijing universities, 200 national scientific institutions, and 100 national engineering and technology research centers. It hosts more than 20,000 high-tech enterprises, international incubators, venture firms, and the ZGC Private Equity and Venture Capital Association. Significant incentives were provided to entice ethnic Chinese who are educated and working abroad to return to China. ZGC has repatriated 15,000 Chinese through the Thousand Talents Program.

By 2015, China had created 219 Economic Technology Development Zones (ETDZ) and 53 high-tech industrial development zones (HIDZ).

World Innovation Cities

The concept of world innovation cities began in 2006 in Melbourne, Australia, through an innovation company called 2thinknow, which has assembled databases on innovation in cities and developed courses and service products that measure and deliver innovation to cities, businesses seeking new markets and growth, investors, and NGO or government clients.

The Innovation Cities™ Index uses 162 indicators and five categories[82] to measure and rank the innovation potential of 500 cities to become urban innovation economies. The Index classifies these cities in descending order of importance to the global innovation economy. In 2015, 40 cities were classified as nexus cities. San Francisco/San Jose was the top-ranked U.S. city (and #2 in the index) with 11 other U.S. cities in this category.

Support for Innovation, Entrepreneurship, and Technology Management at Home and Abroad

Protecting IP and Commercializing Products of University Research

The Stevenson-Wydler Innovation Act of 1980 made the transfer of federally owned technology produced in government labs an explicit mission, and the Bayh-Dole legislation, also in 1980, gave federal agencies the ability to transfer custody of patents of federally funded R&D to nonprofit organizations and small businesses and to allow universities to patent federally funded research. The NSF established Cooperative Research Centers between academia and industry in 1986 as part of the Federal Technology Transfer Act.

A new effort was announced by President Obama[83] in 2012 to expedite commercialization of inventions for humanitarian purposes, and in line with this goal, the University of California at Berkeley has developed a Socially Responsible Licensing program to target therapeutic, diagnostic, vaccine, sanitation, and agricultural biotechnology solutions for use in developing countries. The White House Fact Sheet cites several other examples of initiatives designed by federal agencies and national labs to promote product development, commercialization, and application of new technologies for humanitarian purposes (e.g., humanitarian apps and mobile devices for agriculture).

U.S. laws and regulations safeguard intellectual property (IP), protect personal information, and ensure that government funding protects national security, domestic business, and economic well-being. Many of the U.S. IP rules are codified in international treaties and trade agreements. The FBI collaborates with universities in areas such as cybersecurity, protection of students and faculty from recruitment by foreign intelligence services, identify theft, stolen research and fraud, campus safety and safety awareness by students abroad, animal and eco rights, and terrorism. The U.S. Departments of Commerce and State and the Treasury have established Export Controls to restrict the transfer of goods and technologies largely related to dual use or military use items and trade embargoes overseas (see Chapter 2).

The protection of IP rights has been frequently cited as a key factor in promoting innovation. Universities manage the ownership rights of IP generated by faculty, students, and staff within their own institutions through licensing of the technology, commercialization, and/or startup company formation. There are added layers of complexity when students are among the inventors, when the inventors work at multiple universities and/or when government and private sector (industrial) partners have rights associated with the research and in the creation of the IP. There is an additional challenge when the partners are international colleagues.

> *Intellectual property can be among the most contentious issues that must be addressed when putting together an international collaboration, but it is one that nonetheless must be solved for such collaborations to move forward with the necessary trust between collaborators.*[84]

Negotiating IP derived from international collaborations and managing background IP is difficult.[85] The collaborating partners may differ in their culture, type of organization they belong to, and in the share of project funding, making joint ownership of IP "fraught with danger and contrary to common perception. It is often unfair and, even worse, is usually unworkable."[86] An eligibility criterion for obtaining funds from certain European programs requires collaboration between universities and industries to stimulate technology transfer. Issues dealing with IP need to be agreed upon before the work begins.

During the 1990s, most OECD countries introduced legislation similar to Bayh-Dole, and since 2000 many other countries, including China, Brazil, Mexico, South Africa, Malaysia, and the Philippines, have followed suit. They have also instituted voluntary guidelines for IP management and codes of conduct in collaborative projects, and have established offices of technology transfer.

International patenting is complex. The Patent Corporation Treaty of 1970 among 142 countries is an agreement to international cooperation and coordination of filing, searching, and examination of patent applications, but it does not grant international patents.

> *There is no such thing as an international patent.*[87]

Inventors must decide in which nation(s) they will file the patent. To be protected worldwide, the patent has to be filed in all of the countries of interest and granted by their national offices. IP laws are still primarily national and not harmonized.

The European Patent Office grants "standard" European patents to all 38 European Patent Convention member states, but the patents need to be validated by the particular state to take effect. After four decades, the Unitary Patent Package was passed (2012–2013) providing for a pan-European patent that affords protection across the 28 EU states (with the exception of those states which have opted out) that can be applied for after the standard European patent has been granted. The application must be translated into numerous languages within a limited time frame. A Unified Patent Court (UPC) has jurisdiction over the standard European patents and Unitary Patents so long as they are assigned to member states. The UPC can decide questions of infringement and validity of patents, but numerous issues between the two systems remain unresolved.

Several initiatives have been developed to work around international patent barriers. The largest patent offices (U.S., Europe, and Japan) work together to accelerate consideration of a joint patent if two of the three offices agree that the claims are patentable. Several countries have also tested a peer-to-patent system whereby patent examiners use citizen experts to assess prior art. This has proven to be beneficial.[88]

The U.S. Department of Commerce advocates for the establishment of global IP norms, supports national and international IP enforcement efforts advocating protection for product or category-specific U.S. interests, works to build capacity in other nations to generate more effective IP regimes for their own benefit and the benefit of global commerce.

Support for Innovation, Entrepreneurship, and Technology Management Abroad

Technology transfer offices and the practice of technology transfer have been slow to become established in universities outside the United States. In many instances, it is the governments, companies, and stakeholders from the private sector that are developing organizations to transfer technology from a variety of sources, including universities. Foreign universities often call upon U.S. universities that have a strong record of success in capitalizing on the research produced by their faculty, students, and staff to turn early-stage innovations into products and start new companies, to help them establish offices of technology transfer, develop IP policies and practices, and draft collaborative research and license agreements and licenses.

Some international universities have very well established offices to commercialize university research. The Intellectual Property Management Office at the University of Nairobi, Kenya, for example, has an extensive program to serve the government of Kenya and the University of Nairobi's vice chancellor, innovators and inventors on issues of IP protection, and technology licensing and patenting. The office also helps researchers secure funds for their work and create mutually beneficial research collaborations. In all respects, the office mimics the range of responsibilities characteristic of sponsored research and technology transfer offices in the United States.

Imperial Innovations

Imperial Innovations is a technology commercialization company that began as the technology transfer office for Imperial College, London. It has an expanded role today, combining the activities of technology transfer, IP protection and licensing, incubation of and investment in companies and developing their management teams and boards, and commercializing products from a broad range of technology sectors. They have particular expertise in therapeutics, medical technology, engineering, and materials and ICT. Imperial Innovations also acts as the technology transfer office for several National Health Service Trusts and makes investments in opportunities generated by the University of Cambridge, the University of Oxford, University College, London, and Imperial College, London. Collectively, these universities have a research income of over £1.3 billion per annum.

Imperial Innovations manages an incubator and laboratory and office space in London where a number of portfolio companies are located. Since 2005, it has raised £206.0 million in net proceeds from investors allowing it to make substantial investments within its portfolio companies and to build and invest in new companies. Innovations also has a £30 million loan facility from the European Investment Bank.

Technovia—Saudi Arabia

Saudi Technology Development and Investment Company (Taqnia) was developed in 2011 to facilitate technology transfer, commercialize technology, support sustainable growth of the GDP, diversify the economy, and create high quality jobs and an innovative ecosystem in the Kingdom. Taqnia invests in local and global technologies which have promise to become economically sustainable enterprises. In 2012–13, a group of public-private partners[89] engaged RTI International[90] to streamline IP commercialization processes, and in 2014 they created the Saudi Arabia Advanced Research Alliance (SAARA) to connect academic research and industry and to turn research outcomes and early-stage innovations into economically viable products. SAARA, in turn, launched Technovia (2015) to become the national R&D center of Saudi Arabia and the hub of an emerging research ecosystem to support national strategic priorities.

Technovia is located at the Dhahran Techno Valley with offices in Riyadh and Thuwal (adjacent to KAUST). It works with stakeholders to screen ideas and assess IP for high commercial potential, prepare technologies for market entry, gain competitive investment and funding, conduct market research and competitive analysis, develop and test prototypes and field-able demonstrations, and prepare technologies for commercial launch. Technovia helps all research universities in the Kingdom develop a culture of entrepreneurship, provides training in technology development and commercialization, and promotes local workforce development so that Saudi-based and global companies become immersed in the knowledge economy.

Wamda is a grassroots ecosystem in the MENA region that is about "inspiring, empowering and connecting entrepreneurs" to transform small and medium-sized companies into successful businesses. It also supports community development by providing office space and support, advisory services, and networks. Wamda is managed by a team of entrepreneurs and experts and assisted by a board of leading serial entrepreneurs and investors.

Project Eureca, Enhancing University Research and Entrepreneurial Capacity,"[91] began in 2010 as a U.S.-International partnership pilot project of the Russian Government, the New Eurasia Foundation, and two American-based foundations. The project brought together Russian research universities and four American universities[92] to help Russian universities gain the confidence and experience to commercialize the products of their research. The U.S. universities that were engaged were highly productive in technology transfer, experienced in industry collaboration and economic development, and already had research ties with Russian universities. Eureka II (2013–2016) sought to increase the role of universities in economic development, promote an innovation and entrepreneurship mind-set, and to develop regional ecosystems among universities, regional authorities, and business.

Training Programs in IP Management for U.S. and International Professionals

Training programs have been developed to help technology managers, scientific professionals in universities and other public organizations or small- to medium-sized businesses and international lawyers, understand successful models of U.S. IP management.

The United States Patent and Trademark office (USPTO), for example, created an Attaché Program in 2006 that placed experts in countries[93] where challenges to U.S. IP were the greatest. The attachés work to strengthen IP protection and enforcement, advocate U.S. IP policies, coordinate training on IP matters, and assist businesses that rely upon IP protection.[94]

The USPTO has also created the Global Intellectual Property Academy (GIPA) to provide high level training related to patents, trade-related aspects of IP, trademarks and copyrights for foreign judges, prosecutors, customs officials, IP enforcement personnel and individuals from copyright, trademark, and patent offices around the world. GIPA also provides training for government officials, small business owners, and the general public in the United States.

The University of California, Davis organized a two-week Licensing Academy for international lawyers, technology managers, and scientific professionals in the public sector or small- to medium-sized enterprises. The course covered the essentials of IP protection and management, transfer of technology, and development of startups and spinoffs from public-sector institutions. Field visits to Silicon Valley and elsewhere exposed participants to practice.

The Global Commercialization Group (GCG) at IC^2 in Austin, TX, provides technology commercialization training and international business development programs around the world for tech transfer professionals, incubator managers, scientists, and researchers to help them commercialize their technologies. GCG has the tools, training programs, experience, and networks to move innovation into the international market place, create sustainable technology, and produce visible and measurable results in the near term as well as long term. The programs offered include the following:

- Technology Business Incubation Management
- Technology Transfer Office Management
- The Scientist's Role in Technology Commercialization
- Entrepreneurship Training, Including Training in Effective Presentations
- Technology Assessment
- Online Innovation Readiness™ Series

Twenty participants join the program each year, coming from at least 20 different countries and five continents. In recent years, GCG has worked with more than 1,000 technologies and innovators in 19 countries. It has facilitated $100 million in international business engagements, creating greater than $300 million in economic impact.

The IP Academy (IPA), Singapore, is a national initiative to deepen and broaden Singapore's knowledge and capabilities in IP services (protection, exploitation, management, and education) in line with the goal for Singapore to become an IP hub in the global, technology, and knowledge-based economy. The IPA organizes IP thought leadership activities through conferences and roundtables and sponsors a biennial Global Forum on IP. A network of prominent IP leaders and policy and decision makers from leading global IP institutions, international organizations, higher education, and industry participate in the forum and contribute innovative thinking and practice to the global IP arena. Research and certificate programs are offered in concert with the National University of Singapore.

The CRDF Global Technology Entrepreneurship Development Program has trained more than 200 Russian innovators through the Entrepreneurship Development Workshops under the Commercialization Pathfinder program, created in partnership with the University of Texas Austin's IC^2 Institute and cooperation with the Foundation for Assistance to Small Innovative Enterprises in Science and Technology in Kazan, Russia. The program is a six-week online training session and an intensive boot camp on technology commercialization.

The World Intellectual Property Organization (WIPO) is a global forum for technology transfer and economic development that runs workshops, seminars, and training courses throughout the year at its headquarters in Geneva and worldwide. WIPO Academy offers distance learning and face-to-face courses about IP and IP services, as well as policies and cooperation for development and global activities. The University Initiative Program[95] was established to develop expertise in IP protection and management, technology transfer policies, and commercialization. An online national, regional, or global forum is available to members to contribute best practices; facilitate collaboration among universities, governments, and industry nationally and globally; and provide mentoring by established tech transfer managers and other professional organizations. The University Initiative defined the factors for successful IP management and technology commercialization.[96] WIPO will also create a customized three- to four-year action plan for a member organization. More than 250 universities in over 65 countries have signed on to the University Initiative. WIPO became a specialized agency of the United Nations in 1974.

Nonacademic Organizations That Support Innovation, Entrepreneurship, IP Management, and Company Formation

CRDF Global is a Washington, DC-based, not-for-profit NGO created by Congress in 1995 to advance U.S. science, foreign affairs, and national security. It was chartered to undertake threat reduction work and to transition scientists researching the development of weapons of mass destruction to civilian research. CRDF Global provides services to support entrepreneurship, innovation, and collaboration through grants, technical resources, and training to accelerate growth of innovative, early-stage companies; support technical commercialization; and develop innovation ecosystems and startups. CRDF Global is committed to developing strategic partnerships in research, building entrepreneurial ecosystems, and promoting innovation that affects positive change and addresses global challenges.

CRDF has also established 21 shared equipment centers in eight countries that can be used by university, company, and research institute researchers. Professional skills curricula have been developed for scientists and engineers at all stages of their careers, and grant programs that are specific to the needs of the country have been designed.

The Association of University Technology Managers (AUTM) offers support for the globalization of startup initiatives worldwide—in the United States, Chile, South Africa, Turkey, China, Japan, South Korea, Russia, and Singapore. Academic research institutions, industry, technology transfer professionals, and entrepreneurs attend AUTM conferences and rely on AUTM for advice and assistance.

The International Intellectual Property Institute (IIPI) is a nonpartisan, nonprofit think tank and development organization in Washington, DC, that provides programs, seminars, and workshops to aid in the creation of modern IP systems and the use of IP rights as a means to promote investment, technology transfer, and wealth across the globe. For example, IIPI, along with the USPTO and the Intellectual Property Office of the Philippines, organized a workshop on commercialization that helped six Filipino universities learn about the commercialization process. One proprietary technology from each university was the subject of in-depth assistance to generate a product ready for commercialization. The IIPI hopes to use this model to help other countries build economic capacity through commercialization of university technology.

The Fraunhofer Institute for Systems and Innovation Research (ISI) is a public, contract research organization in Germany comprised of 67 individual institutes that help industry and academic and political decision makers increase their understanding of the scientific, technical, economic, social, legal, and political conditions for innovation, as well as the implications of research on society. Research is conducted in seven Competence Centers[97] to help clients create a favorable environment for innovation. ISI analyzes innovation systems at the national, sectoral, and technological levels; analyzes the diffusion processes of innovation; forecasts; and creates scenarios for future technological developments. It also investigates the regulation of innovation; evaluates specific innovations and their potentials in an economic, societal, and ecological perspective; assesses innovation-related policy; and advises on the introduction and implementation of innovative solutions.

The National Council of Entrepreneurial Tech Transfer (NCET2) is a network of more than 200 research universities that promotes best practices in entrepreneurship for entrepreneurs forming startup companies. NCET2 brings together members of the "research commercialization ecosystem"—angel and venture capital investors, Fortune/Global 1,000 companies, governmental science and technology agencies, and economic development organizations with universities—to build centers of innovation. These partners gather at an annual startup conference. The conference title for 2016, "A Venture Model for the National Research Commercialization Enterprise: Bringing Together Universities, Researcher-Entrepreneurs, VCs, Angels and Corporates," describes the overall intent of the organization. This conference will also announce the Global 1,000: Corporate Commercialization Center (CCC) developed by 20 corporate open innovation venture groups with input from universities, angel investors, and venture capitalists. The CCC will be an organization where select research universities and Global 1000 Corporations will work to create and fund startups. Numerous other topics at the conference relate to funding and commercializing research and developing startups companies.

Incentivizing, Recognizing, and Rewarding Innovation

Competitions for awards and prizes of various kinds acknowledge and celebrate innovation anywhere in the world. They range from local and national awards to major global awards, such as Nobel Prizes. Many prizes recognize innovation in business (e.g., Edison Awards) and international associations (e.g., Global Innovation Award for Excellence in media company innovation from the International News Media Association) but are worthy of review because they may stimulate ideas for universities seeking to add a prize or recognition for innovation-based on values a university wishes to recognize.

Tangible rewards (money, grants, travel awards, gift cards, plaques, certificates and medals) and intangible rewards (parties, galas, recognition videos, press releases) are offered to individuals, a team, organization, company, or a university—even a city—for outstanding effort in developing and/or implementing an idea for an invention, for innovation as a process, a ground-breaking advance in a field, an activity that has had major social or economic impact (commercial benefit), a technological advance that is delivering sustainable change (e.g., Millennium Technology Prize, Finland). The innovation may have transformed a culture, advanced valuable partnerships between a university and industry, and/or substantially benefitted a city, state, or nation. When crafting a new award, the objective needs to be considered carefully. Is it to recognize success? A final product? Ideation and effort? Innovation programs? Innovative behavior?[98]

Awards are made by federal governments (Japan Global Development Awards and Medals), state governments and government agencies (California Department of Finance Awards for Innovation in Higher Education policies, practices, and systems to community colleges, California State Universities, and University of California universities), NGOs (Institute of International Education [IIE] Andrew Heiskell Awards for Innovation in International Education); national higher education organizations (National Association of State Universities and Land-Grant

Colleges [APLU]), the Economic Prosperity Award, the International Education Organizations awards (NAFSA, Senator Paul Simon awards); NACUBO Innovation Award for innovation in process improvement or re-engineering and resource enhancement), companies (e.g., IBM Faculty Awards to stimulate innovation in curricula relevant to IBM), and universities.

Horizon 2020 offers very significant monetary prizes as inducements or in response to challenges that contribute important advances. For example, innovators were challenged to develop a food scanner that measures and analyzes food intake, a means to reduce particulate matter in the air (clean air), breakthrough digital technology transmission and spectrum sharing, vaccine technology, and methods to prevent antibiotic resistance. The theme of the most recent prize for social innovation was the challenge of the aging population.

The EIT offers awards to teams that have developed innovative projects (Innovators Award), successful startup companies (EIT Venture Award) that have been crafted through the Knowledge and Innovation Communities, and young entrepreneurs (EIT Change Award) in Europe, to recognize and award entrepreneurship and innovation and to celebrate success.

Cities that promote innovation—create an innovation ecosystem that improves the quality of life for their citizens—may compete for the European Capital of Innovation Award. The city that wins must be inclusive, inspiring, interactive, integrated, and impactful, and it reach out to its citizens to make the innovation evident.

Universities have added innovation awards to the typical end-of-the-year awards that recognize faculty, staff, administrators, and students for exemplary teaching and research, efforts in internationalization, and other innovative measures to improve university performance. For example, the President's Innovation Imperative at the University of Washington, announced in 2014, stimulates and rewards innovation among the faculty in engineering, health, and the natural and social sciences. Large monetary awards support innovative programs and faculty creativity.

The University of Kent, UK, offers innovation awards in the categories of: ICE (Innovation, Creativity and Enterprise), an Innovation Project, Impact through Knowledge Exchange, and for an Early Career Researcher. Bangor University in Wales makes annual Impact and Innovation Awards to recognize the importance of innovation to the economy and society, business, and contributions to the country, and Innovation awards at West Virginia University reward early career and established faculty, students, staff, and administrators who have made an impact on the public and support a 21st-century land-grant mission.

WIPO Awards:

- The WIPO Medal for Inventors has been offered by national and international organizations for more than 25 years to stimulate inventive and innovative activity around the world and to recognize outstanding inventors whose contributions, in particular, are significant to the economic and technological development of their countries. Candidates must have obtained or applied for a patent or utility model for their innovation. The medals are awarded at international exhibitions or competitions at the highest national level (such as the International Exhibition of Inventions, Geneva, or the Seoul International Invention Fair). Some 2,000 medals have been awarded from over 130 countries, the majority from developing countries and countries in transition.

- The WIPO Medal for Creativity recognizes outstanding authors, designers, performers and producers, including the creators of software, who have made a substantial contribution to cultural, social, and economic development in the field of copyright and related rights. The award recognizes artistry and imagination resulting in works, designs, performances, or productions that have had outstanding impact or have fostered greater respect for the creative output. The medal may be given in the context of a national award scheme.

- The WIPO Users' Trophy recognizes the early adoption or innovative use of WIPO services which include the PCT (Patent Corporation Treaty) System (patents), the Madrid System (trademarks), the Hague System (designs) and the Lisbon System (appellations of origin), together with the services of the WIPO Arbitration and Mediation Center. The Trophy is awarded at the discretion of WIPO.

- The WIPO IP Enterprise Trophy encourages businesses, including small and medium-sized enterprises, and institutions to make imaginative use of the IP system in their business activities, to recognize those that have undertaken successful activities to build public respect for IP, to publicize the role of IP rights as important business assets, and to recognize acts of good citizenship by IP-based businesses. The WIPO IP Enterprise Trophy can be given on the occasion of international exhibitions (industrial, technological, or commercial) or conferences of national importance.

GoAbroad.com makes several awards to universities and organizations for innovation in the categories of diversity; marketing and digital media; new programs—internships, study abroad; volunteer; philanthropy; sustainability; technology; travel; and student videos.

Other innovation awards honor:

- Outstanding woman innovators—Ohio University.
- State relations professionals who have shown exception effort, initiative, and innovation in achieving legislative goals for their institutions—CASE.
- Innovative partnerships between universities and industry—Synergy Awards, the National Science and Engineering Council of Canada.
- Programs that accelerate economic development—Excellence in Innovation and Entrepreneurship—University of Kansas.
- Young Innovators Awards for inventors from kindergarten through high school who have developed a functioning model or prototype—University of South Florida.
- The Schoolchildren's Trophy—to children in primary or secondary grades who have demonstrate outstanding innovation and creativity and have achieved distinction in a school activity related to the IP system—WIPO.
- Collegiate Inventors Competition—National Inventors Hall of Fame encourages undergraduate and graduate students to be creative and innovative with science, engineering, and technology in dealing with the problems of the world.
- Strategic Innovation in Internationalization of Higher Education—European Association for International Education.
- Entrepreneurs, inventors, researchers, and early-stage companies for innovations in the state of Florida—Cade Museum Prize.

The National Academy of Inventors® (NAI) and Fellows of the National Academy was started at the University of South Florida in 2010 to recognize individuals in universities and nonprofit research institutes to recognize and encourage inventors in the same manner that the U.S. National Academies recognize individuals for their accomplishments in science, engineering, and medicine. Chapters are established at universities in the United States and overseas (international affiliates) and individuals invited to membership have at least one issued patent from the USPTO. Each of the current approximately 150 chapters can organize its own activities and events. The national organization holds an annual meeting at one of the member universities. The NAI edits the international journal *Technology and Innovation—Proceedings of the National Academy of Inventors®*.

In 2012, the Fellows of the National Academy were added to recognize individuals "who have demonstrated a highly prolific spirit of innovation in creating or facilitating outstanding inventions that have made a tangible impact on quality of life, economic development, and the welfare of society." NAI fellows are nominated by their peers. The median number of patents for each fellow is 18.

The National Inventors Hall of Fame was founded in 1973 by the then National Council of Patent Law Associations, now the National Council of Intellectual Property Law Associations, and the USPTO. It was moved from Akron, OH to the USPTO campus in Alexandria, VA in 2008, and in 2014 a new Hall of Fame opened with a theater, a museum displaying artifacts, and interactive kiosks. Images of the more than 500 Inductees and each patent are displayed. The IP Hall of Fame was developed by Intellectual Asset Management[99] to honor the achievements of men and women who have made an outstanding contribution to the development of today's IP system and its role in enhancing lives across the world. Inductees are chosen each year by the IP Hall of Fame Academy (a body organized from the previous inductees) from nominations sent in by members of the global IP community.

NOTES

[1] Council of Graduate Schools. (2007). Graduate education: The backbone of American competitiveness and education, CGS Publications, Washington, D.C., pp. 1–36. http://cgsnet.org/graduate-education-backbone-american-competitiveness-and-innovation.

[2] Hirsch, A. (2014). *Professional development center at Webster University Vienna*. Retrieved from http://pdc.danesgar.net/PDC_Daneshgar?Arthur_Hirsch.html

[3] Innovation in China: From brawn to brain. (2012). *The Economist*, March 10.

[4] Porter, M.E. (1998). Cluster and the new economics of competitions. Harvard Business Review, Nov-Dec. pp. 77-90

[5] Porter, M.E. (2010). Cluster mapping project. Institute for Strategy and Competitiveness, Harvard Business School.

[6] Canada (CMEG), PowerPoint.

[7] Quoted in Gertner. J. (2012, Feb. 15). True innovation. *New York Times Sunday Review*. http://www.nytimes.com/2012/02/26/opinion/sunday/innovation-and-the-bell-labs-miracle.html.

[8] America's National Innovation Goals, Council on Competitiveness. (2004).

[9] Bergquist, K. (2005). Challenge to America: Innovate or fall behind. http://www.ur.umich.edu/0405/Jan10_05/06.shtml.

[10] U.S. White House. (2010, May). *National Security Strategy*, Obama Administration. (2010, May). President Obama's introductory letter undated.

[11] Advanced manufacturing, precision medicine, Brain Initiative, advanced vehicles, smart cities, clean energy and energy-efficient technologies, education technology, space, and new frontiers in computing.

[12] Block, F., & Keller, M. (2008, Dec. 1). Building on success: Reforming the U.S. innovation system. University of California Davis, White Paper. pp. 1-13.

[13] U.S. Department of Commerce in consultation with the National Economic Council (2012, January). "The Competitiveness and Innovation Capacity of the United States. http://www.esa.doc.gov/sites/default/files/thecompetitivenessandinnovativecapacityoftheunitedstates.pdf.

[14] Alden, E. (2010, 27 July). U.S. losing ground in competitive immigration. *World Politics Review.*

[15] The U.S. EDA leads the federal economic development agenda by promoting competitiveness and preparing the nation's regions for growth and success in the worldwide economy. (www.eda.gov).

[16] Support for i6 comes from the National Science Foundation, the US Department of Energy, the US Department of Agriculture and the Environmental Protection Agency with technical support from the National Institutes of Standards and Technology (NIST), the U.S. Patent and Trademark Office (USPTO) and the Small Business Administration.

[17] Guimón, J. (2013) *Promoting university-industry collaboration in developing countries. The Innovation Policy platform.* World Bank. https://www.innovationpolicyplatform.org/

[18] Science and Innovation Investment Framework, 2004-2014. HM Treasury, Department for Education and Skills, Department of Health. http://webarchive.nationalarchives.gov.uk/+/http:/www.hm-treasury.gov.uk/media/7/8/bud06_science_332v1.pdf.

[19] 2012 International Education Summit: A Call to Action. (2012). Washington, DC Policy Sessions: Economic Impact. Economic Impact of Higher Education. British Delegation, British Council. Washington, D.C. May 2-3, 2012.

[20] National Research and Innovation Strategy, Ministry for Higher Education and Research, Republique Francaise. (2009). p. 3. Retrieved from: http://www.ambafrance-uk.org/National-Research-and-Innovation.

[21] Lisbon Strategy, European Union. (2000). Retrieved from: http://ec.europa.eu/archives/growthandjobs_2009/documentation/index_en.htm. [22] European Union Parliament website. Lisbon European Council. (2000). Presidency Conclusion. *http://www.europarl.europa.eu/summits/lis1_en.htm.*

[23] European Commission. (2007, 14 March). Evaluation of the Information Society Technologies (IST) Event. Submitted to the Information Society and Media Directorate General. http://ec.europa.eu/smart-regulation/evaluation/search/download.do;jsessionid=222yTJSB0HjGczKzXMpPpk0FZG7mNYwlFcz2Vgy7dwBhKYLj5rJf!1601440011?documentId=773

[24] European Commission. Europe 2020.

[25] European Commission. (2011). *From Challenges to Opportunities: Towards a Common Strategic Framework for EU Research and Innovation Funding.* EN, Brussels, pp. 1-14.

[26] Climate change, sustainable energy future information, and communication, plus five others.

[27] EIT partners include 470 companies, 159 higher education institutions, 114 research programs, 72 cities, regions, and NGOs. (2015).

[28] European Commission. (2004). *State of the Innovation Union: Taking Stock 2010-2014, Research and Innovation as Sources of Renewed Growth, COM.* (2014). Commission Staff Working Document, RTD-Publications@ec.europa.eu p.300.

[29] Aranca research survey response (n = 231).

30 Jinal Mehta, J., Vaidya, J., Chaudhary, R., Ramamrajan, V., & Ranjan, A. (2014). *Saudi Arabia: Emergence of an innovative Kingdom* (An Aranca Special Report prepared for the Euromoney Saudi Arabia Conference). http://context.aranca.com/hubfs/Aranca_Reports/Saudi-Arabia-Emergence-of-an-Innovation-Kingdom-An-Aranca-Special-Report.pdf.

31 The total project support was $75 million, with $61.6 million from the Government of Kazakhstan and a $13.4 million loan from the World Bank.

32 The engaged components include government, industry, institutional investors, venture capital, media, service provides, entrepreneurs, universities, and research institutes.

33 Guimón, J. (2013). *Research centers of excellence in Kazakhstan: The Technology Commercialization Project, The Innovation Policy Platform.* (Policy Brief). World Bank, pp. 1–8. https://www.researchgate.net/publication/278962013_Research_centers_of_excellence_in_Kazakhstan_The_Technology_Commercialization_Project_Innovation_Policy_Platform_OECD_and_World_Bank

34 $21 million funded 21 grants for interdisciplinary, problem-oriented research to groups of senior scientists and junior researchers for three years at $1.5 million each, and a world-class, International Materials Science Center to be developed.

35 Stronski, P. (2016). *Kazakhstan at twenty-five: Stable but tense.* Carnegie Endowment for International Peace, Retrieved from http://carnegieendowment.org/2016/02/04/kazakhstan-at-twenty-five-stable-but-tense-pub-62642

36 Association of American Medical Colleges. (2013). *Chief innovation officer primer: Key elements for success.* Washington, DC: Author.

37 Chief Innovation Officer Summit, New York, December 7–8, 2016, organized by Innovation Enterprise.

38 McMurtrie, B. (2015, April 24). Now everyone's an entrepreneur. *Chronicle of Higher Education*, pp. 22–23.

39 GEN is a platform of programs and initiatives that also develops data that inform the best practices for developing new entrepreneurs.

40 Katz, B., & Wagner, J. (2014). *The rise of innovation districts. A new geography of innovation in America.* pp. 1–85. Retrieved from http://www.brookings.edu/about/programs/metro/innovation-districts

41 Silicon Valley, New York, Los Angeles, Boston, Tel Aviv, London, Chicago, Seattle, Berlin, and Singapore (as the top 10).

42 Prelude. (2015). *Virtual incubators for enterprise startup.* Heliotrope LLC. http://www.playprelude.com/virtual-incubators-for-enterprise-start-ups/

43 Carayannis, E. G., & von Zedtwitz, M. (2005). Architecting gloCal (global-local), real-virtual incubator networks (G-RVINs) as catalysts and accelerators or entrepreneurship in transitioning and developing economies: lessons learning and best practices from current development and business incubation practices. *Technovation, 25,* 95–110.

44 Geron, T. (2012, April 30). Top startup incubators and accelerators: Y Combinator tops with 7.8 billion in value. *Forbes.* http://www.forbes.com/sites/tomiogeron/2012/04/30/top-tech-incubators-as-ranked-by-forbes-y-combinator-tops-with-7-billion-in-value/#6ccafd4d6dfe.

45 Y Combinator receives one application per minute and accepts only a little over one percent of those who apply. Shoot, B. (2014, May 23). Can a virtual incubator democratize entrepreneurship? *Fortune.* http://fortune.com/2014/05/23/can-a-virtual-incubator-democratize-entrepreneurship/

46 NBIA has served over 35,000 companies; 19,000 of them were successfully established after the incubator experience.

[47] Maynard, A. (2014, August 6). 15 MENA incubators to help nurse your company. WAMDA. https://www.wamda.com/2014/08/incubators-in-the-arab-world.

[48] Algeria, Egypt, Jordan, Lebanon, Palestine, Saudi Arabia, Tunisia, UAE.

[49] Prelude. (2015). *Virtual incubators for enterprise startup.* Heliotrope LLC. http://www.playprelude.com/virtual-incubators-for-enterprise-start-ups/

[50] *FledgeX, the conscious company accelerator.* Retrieved from http://fledge.co/2015/introducing-fledgex/

[51] Shoot, B. (2014, May 23). Can a virtual incubator democratize entrepreneurship? http://fortune.com/2014/05/23/can-a-virtual-incubator-democratize-entrepreneurship/

[52] The name refers to the cost of serving one million entrepreneurs to reach one million or more in annual revenue.

[53] Shah, N. (2016) 5 accelerators healthcare startups san apply to in early 2016. Arkenea. http://arkenea.com/blog/healthcare-accelerators/

[54] Desmarais, C. (2012, Feb. 7). Accelerator vs. incubator: What's the difference? *Inc.* http://www.inc.com/christina-desmarais/difference-between-startup-accelerator-and-incubator.html.

[55] Hendricks, D. (2015, Feb. 17). 7 leading accelerators for overseas startups coming to Silicon Valley. *Forbes Entrepreneurs,* Retrieved from http://www.forbes.com/sites/drewhendricks/2015/02/17/7-leading-accelerators-for-overseas-startups-coming-to-silicon-valley/#1680b7dbf69e

[56] Examples include Boeing, United, Lockheed Martin, Airbus, GE Aviation, and Air France.

[57] Goren, I. (2015, May 5). Skoltech and partner universities form international proof-of-concept network. Retrieved from www.scoltech.ru

[58] Kazan Federal University, North-Eastern Federal University, Ural Federal University, Innopolis University, and Samara State Aerospace University.

[59] The numbers can increase significantly depending upon how accelerators are defined and counted. Moreover, articles from Europe often use the terms *incubator* and *accelerator* interchangeably.

[60] The rise of the UK accelerator and incubator ecosystem. (2014, November). Telefónica UK. http://cdn.news.o2.co.uk.s3.amazonaws.com/wp-content/uploads/2014/12/O2_WAYRA_Report_121214.pdf

[61] Research Triangle Park is one of the largest research parks in the world.

[62] Association of University Research Parks. (2008). The power of place. A national strategy for building America's communities of innovation, Washington, D.C., http://www.aurp.net/assets/documents/pop_npc_pres.pdf.

[63] Advanced materials, geosciences and petroleum engineering, refining and petrochemical processes, water management, production and treatment, energy efficiency and renewables, and advanced computing.

[64] Schlumberger, Yokogawa, Baker Hughes, Honeywell, GE, Emerson, Rosen, Argas, Sipchem, Weatherford, Halliburton, Amiatit, and Inverisms are residents of the park.

[65] Award of Excellence (outstanding university research and science parks, park directors and best practices); Emerging Research Park Award (to a park in operation less than 10 years); Leadership Award (business, university or governmental leader); Innovation Award (company within a university research park); Vision Award (individual); Career Achievement Award (individual).

[66] Katz, B., & Wagner, J. (2014, May). The rise of innovation districts. A new geography of innovation in America. *Metropolitan Policy Program at Brookings,* pp. 1–33. https://www.brookings.edu/wp-content/uploads/2016/07/InnovationDistricts1.pdf.

67. Katz, B. Rainwater, B. & Wagner, J. (2014, June 2). *Innovation districts are catalysts for urban growth.* Cities speak, National league of Cities. https://citiesspeak.org/2014/06/02/innovation-districts-are-catalysts-for-urban-growth/

68. Georgia Tech Scheller College of Business, the Economic Development Institute, and the Global Learning Center.

69. *Forbes* named ATDC as a "Top 12 Incubator Changing the World" in 2013.

70. A federal grant was made to Georgia Tech, "Invest Atlanta" (Atlanta's economic development group), the Atlanta Housing Authority, and the University Financing Foundation.

71. Colleges of Textiles, Engineering, Veterinary Medicine, and Education.

72. DOE, USDA, National Forest Service, and NOAA National weather service.

73. Association of University Research Parks. (2008). The power of place. A national strategy for building America's communities of innovation, Washington, D.C., http://www.aurp.net/assets/documents/pop_npc_pres.pdf.

74. Silicon Valley Leadership Group: Silicon Valley Competitiveness and Innovation Project—2015. (2015).

75. Southern California, Seattle, Boston, Austin, and New York City.

76. Senor, D., & Singer, S. (2009). *Start-up Nation: The Story of Israel's Economic Miracle*, the Hachette Book Group, New York.

77. A collaboration with the Houston Technology Center, MassChallenge, and others.

78. 30 of the world's most successful companies, including Boeing, Cisco Systems, EADS, GE, Johnson & Johnson, IBM, Intel, Microsoft, Siemens, Nokia, and Samsung, agreed to join Skolkovo at the outset.

79. The five technology clusters are space and telecommunications, information technologies, biomedical, energy efficiency, and nuclear technologies.

80. Nearly 900 events have been organized.

81. Krusekopf, C., & Du, J. (2015). *International collaboration and innovation: Comparing innovation zones in the Chinese Market. Asia Pacific Foundation of China* (Research Report). https://www.asiapacific.ca/sites/default/files/filefield/apfc_rr-pd08.pdf.

82. Nexus, hub, node, influencer, and upstart. Definitions for each of the categories are available online.

83. Office of the Press Secretary. (2012). *The White House Fact Sheet: Harnessing innovation for global development.* https://obamawhitehouse.archives.gov/the-press-office/2012/02/08/fact-sheet-harnessing-innovation-global-development.

84. Sloan, S. & Alper, J., Rapporteurs. (2014) *Culture matters: International research collaborations in a changing world.* Summary of a Workshop.Washington, DC: National Academies Press. https://www.nap.edu/read/18849/

85. Reingand, N., & Stech, M. (2011). *Worldwide scientific collaboration and national intellectual property: how to put those things together?* 2nd Congress of the International Commission for Optics: Light for the Development of the World, R. Rodrigues-Vera & R. Diaz-Uribe (Eds.). *Proceedings of SPIE*, 8011. http://www.patent-hatchery.com/Articles/Reingand-Stech-11-29-2011.pdf.

86. O'Connell, D. *Avoid jointly owned intellectual property.* IPEG (Intellectual Property Expert Group), an IP consultancy based in Europe. http://www.ipeg.com/avoid-jointly-owned-intellectual-property/

87   Fitzgerald, B. (2011). International cooperation in IP issues. In S. S. Sloan & T. Arrison (Eds.), *Examining core elements of international research collaboration: Summary of a workshop* (p. 51). Washington, DC: National Academies Press.

88   Ibid., pp. 51–53.

89   The partners in Technovia are the Saudi Arabia Advanced Research Alliance (SAARA), Saudi Aramco, (the world's largest energy company), KACST (King Abdullah City of Science and Technology—the Kingdom's Science & Technology agency), Taqnia (the technology arm of the Saudi Public Investments Fund development and knowledge-based industries incubator) and two research universities, KAUST (King Abdullah University of Science and Technology, and KFUPM (King Fahd University of Petroleum and Mineral Resources).

90   RTI International is a research institute based in the Research Triangle Park, North Carolina, but also located and serving clients in more than 75 countries around the globe.

91   Blumenstyk, G. (2010, Oct. 8). In new project, Russian Universities tap American expertise in tech transfer. *Chronicle of Higher Education*, A34.

92   The University of Maryland College Park, Purdue University, UCLA, and the University of Washington.

93   Brazil, Russia, China, India, and Thailand are examples.

94   Stoll, R. L. (2009, December 9). *Protecting intellectual property rights in a global economy: Current trends and future challenges, statement before the subcommittee on government management, organization and procurement, committee on oversight and government reform.* United States House of Representatives. USPTO. https://www.uspto.gov/about-us/news-updates/protecting-intellectual-property-rights-global-economy-current-trends

95   *IP policies for universities and research institutions.* Retrieved from WIPO website, http://www.wipo.int/uipc/en/

96   Adequate IP protection and enforcement of the legal framework at the national level; adequate IP and technology management infrastructure, guidelines and incentives at the university level; marketable technologies; funds for research, technology transfer office operation, IP protection, prototype creation, technology marketing and startup or spinoff launch, etc.; human resources with appropriate IP and technology management expertise; networking or collaboration with industry and other organizations.

97   Energy Policy and Energy Markets, Energy Technology and Energy Systems, Foresight, Industrial and Service Innovations, Sustainability and Infrastructure Systems, Emerging Technologies, Policy and Regions.

98   How Companies Incentivize Innovation. Insight Paper by SIT® (Systematic Innovative Thinking), April 2013. Retrieved from: http://he.sitsite.com/our-work/articles-publications/.

99   A British bimonthly magazine and online service that treats IP as a business asset and tool.

Chapter Six
Connecting University International Research Programs with the Community, Region, and State

Introduction

Universities, especially research universities, periodically develop publications documenting their economic impact on the community and region. One of the inputs to these documents is the financial benefit of the university's international programs and students, but there is rarely any significant information about how the international research agenda provides revenue, helps to recruit companies and increase the trade, benefits the cluster strategy, promotes the international reputation of the community, and stimulates the immigration of a highly educated working class.

University research and researchers can provide a connection to countries that the region and the state wish to exploit, for example, in establishing sister cities and trade partnerships. The university may even be out ahead of a community in guiding international ventures if there have been long-standing research and education exchanges in a region. For example, the University of South Florida has maintained Public Health and Medicine programs in the City of Knowledge in Panama for several years. Only recently has the State of Florida engaged in a trade mission to Panama. Ohio State has been connected in agriculture with Brazil for many years, including research to develop biofuel long before biofuel became part of the energy agenda. The University of the Pacific in Stockton, CA, is involved with the local community through agriculture. Stockton is located in one of the richest agricultural regions in the world and attracts farm workers, who are largely Hispanic and have little or no education and a major goal for the university's Inter-American Program to enroll these individuals in their global educational enterprise.

The benefits of international programs can be direct (fees, books, living expenses, travel, and visitors), indirect (multiplier impacts of employment, purchases of goods and services from local suppliers) and induced (employment and activity supported by those individuals directly or indirectly employed spending their incomes on goods and services in retail outlets, companies producing consumer goods, and in a range of service industries). There are also tangible and intangible benefits to individuals and society, measured in reputation, prosperity of the region, high-wage jobs, and business creation.[1]

Town and Gown Relationships

Colleges and universities are economic engines that help drive the quality of life in their host communities. As permanent neighbors, universities and cities (local governments) seek creative ways to collaborate and maximize financial and capital resources. University communities attract a diverse population, ranging from young domestic and international professionals to retired adults. They encourage research and development and provide opportunities in the arts and athletics.[2] There are many symbiotic relationships where universities and community organizations work together (see Chapter 5, innovation districts or zones) for mutual benefit. Successful innovative university–community partnerships require: (1) funding, (2) communication, (3) synergy, (4) measurable outcomes, (5) visibility and dissemination of findings, (6) organizational compatibility, and (7) simplicity.[3]

In some communities, however, town and gown relationships become stressed over the absence of taxes paid by the nonprofit institutions, safety concerns, noise issues, and traffic. The Clemson Joint City-University Advisory Board formed the International Town & Gown Association (ITGA) in 2008 as a nonprofit corporation to focus solely on establishing and improving better community relations and to create resources for civic leaders, university officials, faculty, neighborhood residents and students to collaborate on common services, programs, and citizen issues. The president of Clemson University and the mayor of the city were the founding organizers.

The ITGA is now helping more than 200 colleges, universities, and municipal governments address the challenges, emerging issues and opportunities between and among institutions of higher education and the communities in which they reside, and to engage in broader issues such as economic development, company recruitment, international trade, and so on. The Association provides a network of professionals and resources to help with professional development opportunities for municipal and university communities and to share best practices and innovative solutions that have worked elsewhere. ITGA ranks universities on their town and gown relationships. Top-ranking institutions are both small, private liberal arts colleges (e.g., Ripon College, Ripon, WI) as well as research universities (Clemson, Virginia Tech, and Kansas State).

Many of the community or regional organizations that support international relations include members of the university who are engaged in international activities and/or have come from another country and made their homes in U.S. university communities. Through their enthusiasm for international research, faculty and university leaders often insert themselves into community organizations with the city, county, region, and state, and into groups and activities that their communities plan overseas.

University Alignment with a State's Strategic Goals for Internationalization

Many states have developed strategic plans making international goals and linkages a priority. The 2010–2015 Strategic Plan for Economic Development in Florida, "The Roadmap to Florida's Future," for example, offers the recommendation: "Florida should strive to be a global innovation leader commensurate with its rankings" as the fourth largest state in the United States and the 20th largest economy in the world. The strategic priorities outlined in the plan, in short, include the following:

- Talent development—higher education and STEM.
- Innovation—expanding research and development.
- Growth of leadership or infrastructure.
- Improving the business climate including small business and entrepreneurship.
- Becoming a global hub—Florida is an international state.
- Enhancing the quality of life—creative class.

All of these statewide priorities mesh with the international partnership agenda of the state universities and pose questions for any university and state agenda that are in synch as to how to capitalize on this synergy even further and to engage the expertise and knowledge of Governmental Affairs personnel to expand the international efforts in new directions.

Global Washington is another example of a highly successful statewide organization that developed an agenda offering the consistent message that globalization is good for the state (see also Chapter 1). The three founding partners engaged leaders from other stakeholder organizations such as Boeing, Microsoft, the Bill and Melinda Gates Foundation, Laird Norton Company, the Trade Development Alliance, World Affairs Council, Starbucks, Pacific Northwest National Laboratory, Philanthropy Northwest, and PATH (a global health organization) and became a membership organization. Global Washington is a catalyst in leveraging resources; increasing visibility; sharing best practices; convening the sector by country, issue, and organization type; and advocating around education, global engagement, and foreign policy.

Global Washington draws heavily on the principles of the following:

- Grassroots leadership
- Cooperative community engagement
- Systemic cross-sector partnerships
- Open sharing of knowledge and best practices among member organizations
- The willingness to take a stand on critical issues
- Leveraging multiple sources of support and member organizations
- Enthusiastic outreach to diverse new audiences to increase awareness of, and engagement in, global development issues

Community and Regional Partnership Organizations to Support International Goals

Chambers of Commerce

Chambers of Commerce are not only prominent in local communities in the United States, but also around the world. The World Chamber of Commerce, located in Atlanta, GA, organizes and supports initiatives and events promoting global trade, cultural, educational, and humanitarian goals. The U.S. Chamber of Commerce is headquartered in Washington, DC. Other Chambers are located in 103 countries overseas (AmChams) and binational chambers (e.g., U.S.-Germany) are present in U.S. cities, where they encourage networking, social activities, and business development between cities of the two countries.

City Chamber of Commerce

The Chambers of Commerce in cities around the world have similar purposes. In some countries, businesses are required by law to become members of their local Chamber. "Public law" chambers are common in the EU and Asia. Voluntary chambers are characteristic of the United States, UK, Australia, and Eastern Europe. Both volunteer and public law chambers advocate for workforce and infrastructure enhancement, economic development, education, and community image.

Community chambers in the United States invariably include members from local universities and colleges, and academic leaders often assume elected leadership roles on the Chamber board. They, and other members of the university, may join trips overseas seeking opportunities in countries and sister cities (see below) for purposes of business and trade development. Some of the travel destinations have not been open to the general public (e.g., Cuba in the past) and give universities early insight into how they might establish research relationships in the future.

The Tampa Bay, FL, Chamber of Commerce has recognized the value of the local universities and established the Tampa Bay Chamber Education Connection. Resource pages designed specifically for members of the business community describe the array of opportunities for business professionals to connect with educators, researchers, and students in the Tampa Bay area, and enumerate the array of opportunities for university and business personnel to engage with one another. The Chamber's International Committee assists in promoting Tampa Bay as an international hub and works with member companies throughout the area in public policy, arts and culture, education, tourism, and building capacity in the trade arena.

The Local Chamber and the Military

Local chambers in communities that have military installations may have close and interactive relationships. The Greater Tampa Chamber of Commerce has worked with the MacDill Air Force Base since 1940 and organized the Chamber's Military Council, one of the largest and most active committees. The council seeks to foster the relationship between the Chamber and the men and women that serve at MacDill and the military, in general, and is comprised of four committees. Military policy, commerce, military and veteran support and recognition, and military workforce and retention. The Council involves representatives from every command at MacDill and every branch of service.

Binational Chambers of Commerce

Many cities have a few to several binational Chambers of Commerce established in parallel with the number and growth of international firms from that country.

Universities interact with these chambers to promote international research linkages. The University of South Florida prepares "Country Briefs," highlighting the University's interactions with those countries through research collaborations, international students, study-abroad destinations and agreements with the country's universities (Appendix), for these chambers and for other international community activities such as trade and scouting missions. These documents can be assembled using the University's international database (see Chapter 2) on short notice for visits from delegations and high ranking government and university officials, international universities, businesses, and so forth from other countries. The binational chambers in Florida are members of the Association for Bi-national Chambers of Commerce in Florida that has been organized to advance the goals of all commercial relations and exchanges overseas in the State.

U.S. Chamber of Commerce and American Chambers Overseas (AmChams)

The U.S. Chamber of Commerce also has offices in Belgium, Brazil, China, Ghana, India, and South Korea. The Chamber's International Affairs Division has 70 policy experts and advocates who work to promote investments and trade for the United States. They also work to modernize export controls that enhance national security and competitiveness, benefiting universities that must fall under these restrictions in some of their research involving international students (see Chapter 2).

International Business and Trade

Regional and Statewide Trade Missions

Members of international affairs programs and administrative officials at universities join trade missions abroad with local and state governments, particularly in cases where university research and education programs have extensive relationships. If university members are not included, it is important that information about the impact of the university on research, business, trade, and international student presence at the U.S. university is provided to those who are traveling. Local elected officials and economic development staff who do participate in the trade or study missions should also be briefed so that they can emphasize the opportunities available to foreign students, faculty and businesses at universities in the region or state represented by the delegation.

Higher Education Plays a Role in Foreign Direct Investment (FDI) and International Export Task Forces[4]

Universities partner with community working groups such as FDI and International Exports. Educational services are an export and universities help expand international business, promote multicultural activities and foreign language education, work with federal officials, conduct and participate in business seminars and conferences, and provide assistance through small business development programs and university partnerships. Research is connected to economic development overseas and university research parks are a venue for international companies to locate in a community (see Chapter 5). The Center for International Business and Research at The Ohio State University Fisher College of Business sponsors an internship programs to promote international business (see below).

The Global Cities Initiative

The Global Cities Initiative is a five-year program, sponsored by the Brookings Institution and JPMorgan Chase, to help leaders of metropolitan cities in the United States strengthen their regional economies to become more competitive in the global marketplace, boost exports, and advance the economic profile of the regions and states through practical knowledge, policy ideas, and networks that help them become more globally connected and competitive. An export plan is embedded in an innovation plan, workforce, trade and logistics strategy, immigration networks, and cultural literacy initiatives.

Pilot projects were started in 2012 in Los Angeles, CA; Portland, OR; Minneapolis-St. Paul, MN– and Syracuse–Central New York. Members of research universities in these cities joined project steering committees to draft the plans to "[groom] a globally fluent workforce" and develop "new programs to better leverage universities." International business and culture degrees were cited as means of engagement and benefits of the plan. Universities bring global networks to the communities that can be tapped into. CIBERs (Centers for International Business Education and Research) in business schools were involved. Undergraduate students from Ohio State's Fisher College of Business participated in its Export Internships Program and conducted research on international small and medium-sized companies to become involved in the initiative. The students learned how to analyze global markets; identify good export partners; and develop a market entry strategy, international pricing, logistics, and distribution patterns.

Resilient Cities

The Rockefeller Foundation is behind the 100 Resilient Cities (100RC) initiative to help cities around the world become more resilient to the physical, social, and economic challenges that are so evident in this century. Natural stresses such as earthquakes, fire, and floods, as well as a multitude of other stresses (e.g., high unemployment, chronic shortages of food and water, deficient public transportation) damage the fabric of a city and require the city to have a high degree of resilience to sustain the momentum. The 100RC initiative also helps to build a global practice of resilience among governments, nongovernmental organizations (NGOs), the private sector, and individual citizens. Three rounds of applications have been supported to reach the 100RC level.

Sister City Relationships

The sister cities program adds another dimension to universities international partnerships. The cities engage in international cooperation to promote cultural understanding and cultural and educational exchanges, business development and economic partnerships, training, research, and humanitarian assistance. They become connected based on similarity in industries, existing economic and cultural relationships established through state governments, local businesses and universities, and educational and cultural climates. Larger cities often have a number—even scores—of sister city relationships.

Sister Cities International (SCI) was started by President Eisenhower after World War II as a national initiative to develop economic, cultural, and technical exchanges between U.S. cities (or counties or states) and corresponding cities worldwide. The plan was to involve people and organized groups in establishing productive relationships through global community partnerships and volunteer or service learning opportunities. SCI has helped to create citizen diplomacy, initially meant to ease post-WWII tensions and improve diplomatic relationships and cross-cultural understanding. SCI today represents 1,200 U.S. cities, counties. and states and their 2,100 partners in 125 countries worldwide. Florida, Texas, and California have the most members in SCI.

Tensions still exist today, and these situations can also be eased through sister city relationships. The "Minneapolis–Najaf Sister City Relationship: A Model for Sister City Relationships between Iraqi and American Cities in Support of Reconciliation" offers a unique opportunity for citizens in both countries to support reconciliation and rebuilding after decades of war, sanctions, and occupation, repairing broken relationships and addressing past harm to a group. The University of Minnesota and the University of Kufa in the Najaf area exchanged "Letters of

Cooperation" and began faculty and administrator exchanges. In 2012 the president of the University of Kufa, met with faculty and administrators at the University of Minnesota, Augsburg College, the University of St. Thomas, and Macalester College. At the University of Minnesota, he discussed the possibility of establishing an Arabic language program at the University of Kufa for college students from the Twin Cities, collaborative faculty research opportunities, a joint scientific journal, and guest faculty lectures at his university.

Every U.S. president since Eisenhower has served as the honorary chairman of SCI, even though the sister city relationships do not always include a U.S. city. Ohrid, Macedonia, and Wollongong, New South Wales, Australia, for example, entered into a sister city agreement in 1999, which included a formal relationship between the University of St. Klimint in Ohrid and the University of Wollongong. Cultural artifacts on exhibit in Wollongong City Gallery are shared, and student exchanges and donations of surplus Wollongong City library books have been given to Ohrid.

Sister city relationships may initially involve universities through their business schools to support and grow business connections, then expand into additional programs. Albion College in Albion, Michigan, is such an example. The sister city relationship between Albion and Noisy-le-Roi, France, began as "intentional internationalization" in 1997 and engaged the college in the partnership. Business students became involved in an international business exchange with French business students, described as an entrepreneurial exchange, then education students developed an international practicum with a middle school at Noisy-le-Roi.

The Denver Sister Cities Program has partnerships with Kunming, China, and Axum, Ethiopia (among others). The Metropolitan State University (Metro) in Denver is central in these relationships, developing visiting professorships and student exchanges and conducting research. Metro and Denver Sister Cities have also collaborated in fundraising for community support in the two cities.

A new relationship between Spartanburg, SC, and Landshut, Germany, was created through SCI of Greater Spartanburg[5] to foster business relationships and economic development, promote the exchange of students and academics, and enhance cultural understanding through collaboration. Students from the University of South Carolina Upstate German-American Club promoted this relationship with the objective of growing an existing academic exchange agreement and a dual-degree program between the South Carolina University and the University of Applied Sciences, Landshut, that would allow students from both universities to obtain a degree from each.

Birmingham, England, West Midlands established a sister city relationship with Chicago, IL, based on their similar backgrounds, industrial heritage, and cultural and artistic contributions. As part of this relationship, universities in Chicago (University of Chicago, Northwestern University, and the University of Illinois at Urbana-Champaign); the University of Birmingham; and museums, charities, and government organizations began collaborating in the exchange of students, creation of high-technology solutions for industrial problems, and development of knowledge and practical ways to apply their joint research expertise. A network of faculty researchers is generating research results and funding.

Summits, Conferences, Initiatives, and Town Halls

Universities and communities co-host or at least co-participate in summits, town halls, and so forth, that deal with international relations and activities.

Economic Development and International Companies

International Business Connections

Research programs at universities are often involved in building a city's or region's economic development strategy. This is also true for an international strategy where their programs may entice companies to settle in the community and/or a university's research park. Universities, in metro areas and port cities, in particular, help recruit international businesses and increase trade. In some cases, the university may be the lead in making connections in countries where the state wishes to be more engaged in commerce.

Ohio State's Global Gateways are not only valuable for their connections with faculty and students, but are also important to the business community in forging new partnerships between international companies and Ohio-based companies that operate in global markets (see Chapter 1).

Industry Clusters and City–University Alignment

Many of the industry target sectors for a region are also priority programs for university goals and global priorities and often match global and sustainable development goals in the life sciences, defense, agricultural technologies, clean energy, and high-tech manufacturing (See Chapter 9).

Innovation Destinations—Innovation Ecosystems

This topic has been developed extensively in Chapter 5, but is mentioned here because it is reflects interactions among community organizations and universities that benefits research in general, international research, and economic development. Strategic partnerships need to be developed with many stakeholders in a community to create innovation destinations that become internationally recognized as centers for medical care, biomedical research and allied technology development, world-class entertainment venues, business creation, education training and employment, quality neighborhood redevelopment, and revitalized cultural identity.

University Engagement with Diaspora Communities

Like so much of American life, the story of innovation is a story of immigration.

William J. Burns, Science and Diplomacy

Diasporic communities,[6] especially from China, India, Africa, Caribbean Countries, and Iran are prominent in large U.S. cities.[7] According to the US Department of State, the United States is home to the largest number of global diaspora members of any country worldwide.

The individuals in these communities have often achieved high levels of education and, importantly, they retain strong social, cultural, intellectual, financial, and sentimental ties with their native countries.

In the context of this chapter, we highlight the importance of these communities to their host countries and cities, our universities, the workforce, and especially to entrepreneurial and startup activities.[8] Diaspora community members are transnational citizens who contribute to the scientific, technologic, administrative, and industrial development in their host countries. Many of them are our faculty members. They leave their native homes and come to the United States and elsewhere as students and remain to contribute to the high-tech and professional workforce.[9] They may also migrate because of wars or revolutions in their countries and the potential of being imprisoned or even killed if they do not leave their country (see Chapter 2).

Universities, especially urban research universities, call upon support from diaspora communities when developing or organizing projects for area study centers and other programs with an international thrust (e.g., Confucius Institutes), when making connections with universities and businesses overseas, assisting international students who have newly arrived from their countries, organizing fundraising activities and supporting cultural events, providing cultural knowledge and insight, and recruiting international companies (startup and established) to university research parks. In turn, our universities support concerns within diaspora communities that they identify. U.S. universities need to pay attention to the diaspora communities, per se, beyond the members of their faculties, and develop policies, infrastructure, and resources that can support their goals and capitalize on the benefits they bring.

Federal programs and Diaspora Advocacy Coalitions around the world—grassroots organizations and volunteer groups, have been created to connect scientific members (especially) of diaspora communities to their native countries through service in situations of disaster relief and resilience[10], and to work on global problems that affect their homelands disproportionately. These groups are also beneficial in creating international research collaborations and promoting scientific diplomacy. In some cases, foreign government agencies have been established (e.g., the Ministry of Overseas Indian Affairs) to retain relationships with their citizens. Agencies China, the EU, Japan, South Korea also work to repatriate faculty, IT workers, physicians, and the like, by offering various incentives.

The Organization for Diaspora Initiatives (ODI), based in New Delhi, India, for example, seeks to understand the domestic and international status and role of diasporic communities across the globe as a resource that serves international civil society with the host and the home countries. ODI focuses on the linkages between economic integration of communities in the United States and their potential to contribute to causes and development in their communities of origin and undertakes research projects on topics such as diaspora policies of different countries, utilization of diasporas as resource for the host countries, the role of diasporas in development and nation building, and the impacts of globalization on diasporic networks. ODI also publishes a research journal, *Diaspora Studies*.

"Knowledge networks," such as the Turkish American Scholars and Scientists Association, the Wild Geese Network of Irish Scientists, and the Ethiopian Physics Society in North America[11] are diaspora groups that organize opportunities for diaspora scientists to build capacity and encourage innovation in both the scientists' home countries and the United States.[12]

U.S. diaspora communities contribute to the development of their homelands and global prosperity through remittances,[13] investments in companies, real estate, trade and business, skills and knowledge transfer, education and scientific connections, goods and services, and other means of economic development). The Diaspora Engagement Alliance is a nonpartisan program that engages global diaspora communities, the private sector, civil society, and public institutions in collaborative efforts to support economic and social development. The organization promotes and supports diaspora-centered initiatives in investment and entrepreneurship, philanthropy, volunteerism, and innovation in countries and regions of diaspora origin (see below).

The Science, Technology, and Innovation Diaspora[14]

The science, technology and innovation diaspora has been described as "a vastly untapped resource"[15] for developing international partnerships that benefit science globally and a unique resource for bidirectional exchanges of U.S. universities with others overseas. According to a survey conducted by *Nature*, the United States, Switzerland, Canada, and Australia are top destinations for foreign scientists who become a strong force in forging collaborations with other faculty and universities from their home countries. The partnership is often lopsided, however, because of incompatibilities between the partners' universities and geopolitical and economic differences between the countries (see Chapter 4).

Two important diaspora fellowship programs seek to collect such a power imbalance. IIE manages both programs to reengage foreign-born academics currently working in U.S. and Canadian universities with universities in their home countries. The Greek Diaspora Fellowship Program (GDFP) and the Carnegie African Diaspora Fellowship Program (CDAFP) are scholar exchange programs designed for faculty to spend 14–60 (GDFP) or 14–90 (CDAFP) days in mutually beneficial collaborations to develop curriculum, conduct research, and work with graduate students. It is hoped that these short-term experiences will extend to longer, sustained relationships.

The GDFP at universities throughout Greece is supported by a sizable grant from the Stavros Niarchos Foundation and coordinated with the Fulbright Foundation in Greece to expand "Greece's human capital and [invest] in the country's long-term economic recovery."[16] The projects are designed by the Greek universities and submitted to an IIE web portal to be matched with a qualified Greek-born scholar. The program will fund 40 fellowships over two selection cycles.

The CDAFP is a partnership with the United States International University-Africa in Nairobi, Kenya, funded by a grant from the Carnegie Corporation of New York in 2013. It has already supported 110 African-born scholars to work in Ghana, Kenya, Nigeria, South Africa, Tanzania, and Uganda. A second phase of the program, also supported by Carnegie will support up to 140 additional fellowships and then seek additional support from other sources to expand diaspora sites globally. The program has also added multi-institutional projects and linkages with research organizations in addition to universities.[17] This is just the first phase of a vision[18] to sponsor 1,000 diaspora scholars each year for 10 years to visit universities in Africa.

The Network of Diaspora in Engineering and Science (NODES) is a partnership among the U.S. Department of State, American Association for the

Advancement of Science (AAAS), the National Academy of Science and the National Academy of Engineering. It supports diaspora communities by sharing knowledge and best practices, and convening diaspora groups and linking them with useful tools and institutions, and diaspora scientists with those in their native countries and communities.

Diasporas and Diplomacy

Diaspora networks are valuable in engaging scientists in countries where political relationships are strained or where there is great potential for opening doors through science. Research partnerships with Cuba, for example, are beginning, and researchers from the United States and Iran are collaborating on topics such as food-borne diseases, neuroscience, and drug abuse, noncommunicable diseases, health disparities, and bioethics.[19] A diaspora-related event organized by AAAS in January 2014 considered the potential for involving Iranian diaspora scientists in promoting science diplomacy efforts with Iran. The Malta Conferences which have brought together scientists from across the Middle East, including Israel, have led to important collaborations on issues of regional importance such as water and solar energy.

Universities develop specific strategies for advancing relationships between faculty members of diaspora communities and their home countries. Mini-sabbaticals and seed funding for collaborative program development allows U.S.-based foreign scientists or scientists from their countries of origin to come to the United States. The University of South Florida (USF) established a program for Ghanaian faculty members from two universities to come to USF for several months to finish their terminal degrees. The time without teaching responsibilities and the access to mentors allowed them to complete work that was not possible in their home universities.

University Academic and Research Programs Focus on Diaspora

University programs developed for the purpose of studying diaspora communities help build relationships between the university and the community. The Asian American and Diaspora Studies program at Binghamton University is an interdisciplinary approach to the study of Asian diasporic communities, especially those in the United States, Canada, Latin America, and the Caribbean. Students learn about the historical, cultural, and political dimensions of diaspora and minority experiences. The program also works to build beneficial relationships between academy and community.

The Rutgers Centers for Global Advancement and International Affairs have created a grants program that benefits both the state (government and business) and the institution in crafting cultural, economic, and social connections with local international and diaspora communities. The grants are to build partnerships that will promote interactions with these communities to advance research, internships, and experiential learning opportunities for students. The benefits to all concerned must be demonstrated and the intent is for these relationships to be sustained.

A National Science Foundation research grant awarded to faculty at Florida Atlantic University and Georgia State University seeks to understand the role of diaspora advocacy coalitions, NGOs, and networks after the 2010 Haiti earthquake. The objectives probe how diaspora groups influence long-term, post-disaster recovery and resilience through transnational advocacy efforts and organizational and social networks. The study area is South Florida, New York, Boston, and Atlanta, where there are large concentrations of Haitian American populations and diaspora groups. Studying diaspora networks in host countries and in the international community will advance scholarly and practical understandings of transnational social capital, capacity, and coordination in the continuum of disaster response to long-term recovery and rebuilding.

There are many examples where other diaspora groups across the nation and university colleagues from the social sciences, health sciences, and engineering have engaged with local community and advocacy groups, governmental and nongovernmental organizations, and international aid agencies to provide emergency management, evacuation, sheltering, housing recovery homeland security, infrastructure planning, and post-disaster economic development for relief and recovery from medical and natural disasters.

Celebrating Diaspora Communities

Global Diaspora Week is organized each year by the Diaspora Engagement Alliance to celebrate the dedication of diaspora communities and the contributions they make to global development. It also serves to create awareness of Diaspora groups and promotes collaboration and learning with these communities around the world. The 2015 event launched at the Department of State by Secretary Kerry, entitled "Partnering for Global Impact," featured panels, discussions and breakout sessions on topics such as diaspora entrepreneurship and science diasporas and their role in international engagement. As part of Global Diaspora Week 2014, ODI (New Delhi) in collaboration with *Diaspora Studies* and the School of International and Public Affairs at Columbia University organized a panel discussion on South Asian diaspora communities in the United States to highlight their value to social, economic, and political interactions in their countries and communities of origin. Also included were discussions of public policies in the exchanges and differences among regional groups, individual and collective actions, and the role of socioeconomic status and gender of migrants.

Local Councils on World Affairs

University members who are engaged in international research and consulting are frequently members of their community's Council of World Affairs and may contribute their own expertise in terms of presentations to the group, inviting new connections with individuals interested in the same region who may have different legal, business, and philanthropic perspectives. Around 100 such nonprofit, nonpartisan, autonomous councils in over 40 states are a forum for dialogue, a source of expertise, venue for the exchange of ideas and knowledge and understanding of global issues. The local groups are connected with the national World Affairs Councils of America. Some of the organizations, such as the World Affairs Council of Central Florida (WACCFL), have expanded their roles. The WACCFL has also become the home of the local branch of the International Visitor Leadership Program[20] which facilitates short-term visits of current and emerging foreign leaders who come to the United States to develop lasting relationships with their American counterparts.

University Interactions with Local Honorary Consular General Corps Members

There are more than 20,000 Honorary Consuls General around the world,[21,22] typically located in smaller cities which do not have professional consulates. Honorary Consuls General are recognized in international law and enjoy many of the privileges of career diplomats although most of them work without pay. They are intermediaries between U.S. government, business, political, and community leaders and the same leaders of the country they represent to promote and expand international relations and diplomacy, educational, intercultural, economic, and humanitarian relationships and exchanges. They welcome delegations from the foreign country and assist immigrants, businesses, university leaders, and academics.

Some Honorary Consuls General initiate new programs. Mona Diamond Sunshine, the Honorary Consul General for Turkey in the state of Georgia, for example, founded the American Turkish Friendship Council, a 501(c)3 organization, to promote education, trade, and cultural understanding between the United States and the Republic of Turkey.

The University Consortium for Liberia (UCL) was founded by the Honorary Consul General for the Republic of Liberia, Cynthia L. Blandford, and the Liberian Embassy in the United States. The UCL provides a framework for U.S.-based colleges, universities, and other academic-related organizations with an interest in

Liberia to pool resources; network; exchange information; collaborate on global initiatives and projects; establish research partnerships; and organize study-abroad and summer experience opportunities as well as student and faculty exchanges. In all, 20 institutions and organizations, including 15 colleges and universities in Georgia, are members.

Honorary Consuls General have backgrounds in business, culture, philanthropy, international service, and academia. They play roles in their communities that are valuable to students and research programs at local universities. University of Pittsburgh Chancellor Emeritus Mark A. Nordenberg, for example, was appointed British Honorary Consul in Pittsburgh in 2004 while still in office, and Dr. Sibrand Poppema, President of the University of Groningen was appointed Honorary Consul General of the Republic of Korea to assist Korean people in the Netherlands and promote relationships between the two countries. Korea is an important trade partner for the Netherlands. Groningen would welcome many more Korean students to the University. Dr. Poppema has also been active in teaching and research at several Korean universities and research institutions since 1990 and engaged more recently in institutional cooperation with higher education institutions and government bodies in Korea. A faculty member at the University of Michigan with an Honorary Consul General for Spain from the Detroit area designed an internship program for students in the South-East Michigan Consular offices.[23]

Barbro Osher, Honorary Consul General of Sweden in San Francisco, is a philanthropist with broad interests and reach. She chairs the board of The Bernard Osher Foundation, one of the nation's largest and most generous philanthropic organizations focused on higher education. The Osher Lifelong Learning Institutes is an expanding national network of ~120 classes and special programs for older adults on university campuses. The Osher Foundation also supports medical education centers that integrate conventional and alternative approaches to research and treatment at University of California, San Francisco (UCSF) and Harvard and the Karolinska Institute in Sweden.

In Florida, for example, Honorary Consuls General represent 81 nations with six international trade offices around the state.[24] Many of them connect with university activities and are a resource of expertise for faculty who wish to begin a relationship in a country that is not well linked with the university and its faculty. The Honorary Consuls General Program at Michigan State supports groups of Michigan State University representatives from different colleges to travel to India to discuss university-wide research initiatives and emerging opportunities for research collaboration.[25]

Citizen Engagement—Citizen Science

Citizen science is a grassroots activity—a tool for participatory democracy—that occurs around the world to engage citizens in collecting data, reviewing, assessing and monitoring public activities and policies and/or the activities of leaders and public officials in their respective communities. Technology has promoted online collaborative projects whereby citizens can act as sensors, interpreters, data collectors, and problem definers. In the case of "extreme citizen science" community members are empowered to "analyze, understand and ultimately take ownership of the issues that affect them, enabling them to propose concrete and actionable solutions to decision makers." One example of a global citizen science initiative is the "One Seventeen Challenge" in which citizens use open source data to develop crowdsourcing projects aimed at holding stakeholders (business, government, NGOs, media and organizations) accountable for working toward solutions to the sustainable development goals (see Chapter 9). The project "leverages the power of hyperconnectivity."[26]

U.S. Global Leadership Coalition (USGLC)

USCLC is a broad-based network of businesses and NGOs; national security and foreign policy experts; and business, faith-based, academic and community leaders in all 50 states that supports citizen diplomacy and development. The goal is to gain support from the American public and policymakers about the importance of America's civilian-led tools of diplomacy and development by doing the following:

- Protecting national security by fighting terrorism, stabilizing weak and fragile states, combating weapons proliferation, and promoting global stability.

- Building economic prosperity by developing international markets, driving economic development, building micro-enterprises, and expanding exports.

- Strengthening humanitarian values by saving lives, alleviating global poverty, fighting HIV/AIDS and other infectious diseases as well as hunger, expanding educational opportunities, and strengthening democratic institutions.

The Center for U.S. Global Leadership is the education arm of the USGLC. Members of International Affairs Offices in their states are often members of their state USGLC organization. The national group prepares an annual "International Affairs Budget" for each state with data citing the benefits to the state of its international activities in terms of job creation, exports, growth, education, research, and global engagement.

International Students

International students add significant academic and cultural value to our campuses and local communities and provide substantial economic benefit to the states and nation. The nearly 975,000 international students who studied at U.S. colleges and universities during the 2014–2015 academic year added $30.5 billion to the U.S. economy for living expenses, books and supplies, transportation, health insurance, and support for accompanying family members. Eight states each gained more than a billion dollars by hosting international students, with California and New York earning $4.6 billion and $3.7 billion, respectively. This revenue equated to more than 373,000 jobs. *Open Doors 2015* reports that 72 percent of all international students receive the majority of their funds from personal and family sources and assistance from their home country governments or universities.[27,28]

The University of Washington developed the Foundation for International Understanding Through Students (FIUTS) program to connect foreign students, local and global community members, and alumni. It is a center of international culture that delivers programs to promote global understanding and respect. International students provide interactive programs about their home countries to schoolchildren, exchange letters with fourth and fifth graders over a six-week period, then meet with the students directly at one of FIUTS's monthly Wednesday lunches with community members. The Homestay program for new international students helps students transition into their new environment during orientation week, often resulting in long-lasting relationships and friendships. FIUTS also sponsors a public Culturalfest with performances and booths to present information about the students' many cultures. Two thousand or more guests and local school children attend the event. The Department of State, local corporations, donors, and the university provide support for these activities.

Eastern Illinois University (EIU) Office of Special Services maintains a family and friends program to host international students. The office facilitates meetings between an EIU international students and an American families who then meet once a month throughout the semester to play sports, engage in hobbies and crafts, celebrate holidays and birthdays, and so forth. The Host Family Program provides an opportunity for students who are enrolled in the Language Company, an intensive English language center on the EIU campus, to experience the American culture by living in an American home.

Some cities have a specific program to welcome international students to their community. The City of Riverside, CA, for example, has an International Student Friendly Taskforce working with the International Relations Commission and the Mayor's office. The group reaches out to international students to welcome and assure them that the community is committed to making their experience as a student and resident in Riverside the best possible. They have developed helpful resources ranging from food to housing on a website to help students become more acquainted with Riverside and assist them in their transition.

In other communities, local officials show their appreciation of foreign students by hosting lunches or holding recognition ceremonies to celebrate them. Community groups and nonprofit organizations across the nation also participate in the lives of international students by inviting them into their homes over holiday breaks when they are unable to travel to their home or do not celebrate the holiday.

University Government Relations and International Offices

Many Government Relations Offices at universities are not only connected with legislative bodies at the state and federal levels, but also have members of the team involved in community activities where the university can play a significant role with government and business leaders. They, in fact, may carry the title of Community and Government Relations (e.g., University of Pittsburgh; UCSF), or Government Relations and Public Affairs. The University of Toronto is unique in having created International, Government and Institutional Relations (IGIRelations), which promotes and advocates for research, post-secondary education, and international opportunities. The University of Pittsburgh program reaches down into the community to engage community organizations as well as city and county leaders to link the resources of the university and the partners from the research enterprise with the community and region, the clinical and academic programs, services, student internships, and service learning opportunities. DePaul University has created an Office of Community, Government and International Affairs that seeks to raise the institution's international profile by coordinating the University's international activities through partnership and cooperative programs, and relationships with members of the Consular Corps and diplomatic and trade representatives in the Chicago region.

University Government Relations should be a partner in the Community of Practice for International Affairs at a university as they also play a role at the state and at the federal levels in advocating for legislation and policies that benefit international research that impacts international business recruitment and research incubators and accelerators, small business development, and international student recruitment. They can present the university's strong support of statewide international goals and demonstrate how the university can commit to supporting them.

NOTES

1. Hill, K and Hoffman, D. (2009). Arizona State. The contributions of universities to regional economies. Figure 1. The effects of universities on the local community. Arizona State University, W.P. Carey School of Business. https://wpcarey.asu.edu/sites/default/files/univcontribution5-09.pdf.

2. Whitt, M.C. (2014, June). Strategies to build town-gown relations. *University Business*. https://www.universitybusiness.com/article/strategies-build-town-gown-relations.

3. Martin, L. L., Smith, H., & Phillips, W. (2005). Bridging "town and gown" through community partnerships. *The Innovation Journal: The Public Sector Innovation Journal, 10*(2), 20.

4. McFarland, C. K., & McConnell, J. K. (2011a). Strategies for globally competitive cities: Foreign direct investment and international trade. *National league of Cities Center for Research and Innovation*, Washington, D.C., pp. 1–31.

5. *Sister city relationship Spartanburg-Landshut will grow academic exchange.* **(2005)**, Retrieved from http://www.germany.info/Vertretung/usa/en/__pr/GKs/ATLA/2015/10/02__CityCouncil__PR.html

6. Several types of diasporic communities have developed over the years. The one that most concerns universities is classified as cultural, hybrid, or postmodern. Cohen R. (2008). *Global diasporas: An introduction* (2nd ed.). New York, NY: Routledge.

7. The Indian communities, for example, are prominent in New York, Chicago, San Francisco/San Jose, Los Angeles, Washington, DC, Dallas, Philadelphia, etc.) (see reference above).

8. Rockefeller Foundation-Aspen Institute Diasporic Program (RAD). (2014, July). The Indian diaspora in the United States. *Migration Policy Institute, RAD Diaspora Profile*. pp. 1–16. file:///C:/Users/Owner/Downloads/RAD-IndiaII-FINAL%20(3).pdf

9. Approximately 75 percent of Indian students enroll in a STEM or medical program, earn more PhDs than all international students except Chinese, and 9/10 intend to stay after graduation. *Open Doors*, http://www.iie.org/Who-We-Are/News-and-Events/Press-Center/Press-Releases/2013/2013-11-11-Open-Doors-Data#.WKDiUvkrKUk

10. The Partnerships for Enhanced Engagement in Research Science, a collaboration of USAID and the National Science Foundation, support diaspora scientists in the United States and their colleagues in their home countries. They are developing low-carbon cities in India, addressing and designing effective emergency management systems for post-disaster relief operations (Burns W. J. (2013, December). The potential of science diasporas. *AAAS Quarterly*, Science & Diplomacy. Retrieved from http://www.sciencediplomacy.org/perspective/2013/potential-science-diasporas).

11. "Knowledge works" organizations such as the Turkish American Scholars and Scientists, the Wild Geese Network of Irish Scientists and the Ethiopian Physics Society in North America are established to provide scientific exchanges, educational programs, networking and other opportunities that build capacity and promote innovation in both countries (Burns W. J. (2013, December). The potential of science diasporas. *AAAS Quarterly*, Science & Diplomacy. Retrieved from http://www.sciencediplomacy.org/perspective/2013/potential-science-diasporas).

12. Burns W. J. (2013, December). The potential of science diasporas. *AAAS Quarterly*, Science & Diplomacy. Retrieved from http://www.sciencediplomacy.org/perspective/2013/potential-science-diasporas

13. In 2013, global remittances were estimated to be $550 billion, an amount more than 16 times U.S. official development assistance. The result of these resilient contributions often exceeds their monetary value. The flow of remittances allows parents to afford a child's school fees, supports entrepreneurs to open businesses, or helps families to buy food during economic shocks.

14. Burns, W. J. (2013). The potential of science diasporas. *AAAS Quarterly*, Science & Diplomacy, December 2013. Retrieved from http://www.sciencediplomacy.org/perspective/2013/potential-science-diasporas

15. Ibid.

16. Allan Goodman, President and CEO of IIE.

17. MacGregor, K. (2016, March 26). *African academic diaspora fellows initiative expands*. Retrieved from www.universityworldnews.com/article.php?story=20160325105507818

18. Dr. Paul Zelenza is the visionary. He is a Malawi-born diaspora academic who is currently the Vice Chancellor of the United States International University-Africa, Nairobi, Kenya.

19. Anand, N. P., Hofman, K. J., & Glass, R. I. (2009). The globalization of health research: Harnessing the scientific diaspora. Academic Medicine, *84*(4):525–534.

20. The International Visitor leadership program is administered by the United States Department of State Bureau of Educational and Cultural Affairs.

21. Stringer, K. D. (2007, November). *Think Global, Act Local: Honorary Consuls in a transforming diplomatic world*, Netherlands Institute of International Relations. Discussion papers in Diplomacy, pp. 1–28.

22. Honorary consuls, a booming trade. Foreign ministries employ ever more amateurs to do their bidding abroad. (2013, August). *The Economist*. http://www.economist.com/news/international/21584338-foreign-ministries-employ-ever-more-amateurs-do-their-bidding-abroad-booming-trade.

23. Zinggeler, M. V., & López-Gómez, C. (2010, January). Internships at consular offices: A gateway to international communication and careers. Chapter 8 in *Global Business Languages. Vol. 15. Challenges and critical junctures*. Article 8, p. 110. http://docs.lib.purdue.edu/gbl

24. Enterprise Florida. (2017). TRADE. https:www.enterpriseflorida.com/why-florida/trade/.

25. West, C. (2012, July+ August). Big returns on small investments. *International Educator*, 40–44.

26. Haklay, M. (2012). Citizen science and volunteered geographic information: Overview and typology of participation. In D. Z. Sul, S. Elwood, & M. F. Goodchild (Eds.), *Crowdsourcing geographic knowledge: Volunteered geographic information (VGI) in theory and practice* (pp. 105–122). Berlin, Germany: Springer.

27. Retrieved from http://www.nafsa.org/Explore_International_Education/Impact/Data_And_Statistics/NAFSA_International_Student_Economic_Value_Tool/

28. Retrieved from http://www.iie.org/en/Research-and-Publications/Open-Doors/Data/Economic-Impact-of-International-Students

Chapter Seven
Assessing Your Institution's Global Footprint

A university cannot claim to be "global" if it lacks robust data to inform such branding. Increasingly, metrics and rankings define the landscape of higher education. Universities use internal and external metrics to evaluate their successes and needs and to benchmark themselves relative to their equivalent peers and aspirational peers. The 2016 "Trends Report" from *The Chronicle of Higher Education* identifies "the growing use of metrics to measure faculty productivity" as one of 10 key shifts in higher education.[1] Traditional metrics, measures of impact, or value-added, as well as altmetrics that measure impact in the sphere of social media, can be useful, but are highly controversial, especially among faculty. Data metrics provide one interpretation of institutional, unit, or individual performance. They are imperfect, can contain inaccuracies, and cannot adequately capture "nonquantifiables" or intangibles such as context, environment, or discipline norms. Nevertheless, as universities face increasing scrutiny from government entities, oversight boards, funding organizations, industry, and the public, metrics provide a popular, if imperfect, means for documenting achievements, productivity, and competitiveness.

Rankings aggregate numerous individual metrics to provide an easily digestible ordering of university performance. There are many rankings of global universities, but each employs a slightly different methodology to derive its results, which complicates comparisons across ranking systems. Rankings, however, matter. They matter because students use them to select schools; they stimulate competition and help to differentiate schools and programs from one another; rankings influence university partnerships and opportunities for partnerships; governments use rankings to choose sites where students can use their governmental scholarships and in many cases to determine where funding will flow. Some countries such as Denmark and the Netherlands prioritize immigrant status for individuals from highly ranked universities.[2] There are many metrics to choose from but no internationally recognized common set of standards. Some universities have designed their own ranking systems, selecting criteria that will ensure that their university will rank highly.

It is not uncommon for young universities to hire "ranking professionals" to help the university increase its status in the rankings. For example, the Hong Kong University of Science and Technology (HKUST), established in 1991, became highly ranked in Asia and internationally after its first decade. This is possible when starting as a new university backed by a responsive political and economic environment and with careful planning. HKUST points to the recruitment of outstanding faculty and students, a forward-looking innovative vision, and partnerships with existing, well-established universities around the world as the foremost strategy in launching the university and promoting its rapid (and continued) rise to success.

Universities regularly document their research productivity but are experiencing increasing pressure to demonstrate the *value* of international engagement. And, traditional bibliometric indicators may not sufficiently demonstrate the *impact* of globalized research. Governments are driving research universities to better demonstrate the return on investment of their international research activities using advanced tools, data, and approaches. A common benchmark of success is a university's rank within one of the many global ranking systems.

Global Ranking of Research Universities

Global ranking systems were originally designed as products for students to evaluate options for their educational choices. Today, however, the global rankings delivered annually are a driver of global competition and have become increasingly important and popular as universities seek to attract the best and brightest minds from across the world. More than 40 countries have developed some form of a national ranking system, and there are at least 10 well-known global ranking systems, including three heavy hitters: the Academic Rankings of World Universities (ARWU), published by the Centre for World-Class Universities and the Institute of Higher Education at the Shanghai Jiao Tong University in China, the Times Higher Education (THE) World University Rankings, and the Quacquarelli Symonds (QS) World University Rankings.

First published in 2003, the ARWU is the most established global ranking and includes 500 institutions. It differs from its peers because of its strong emphasis on research productivity. The ARWU advantages universities with histories of strong publications in science disciplines (e.g., the number of articles published in *Science* and *Nature*), the number of articles indexed in the Science Citation Index, and per capita research performance normalized by size of institution. Due to its methodology—an approach that relies almost exclusively on publication data and Nobel Prize and similarly prestigious prizes won by alumni and staff—the ranking of universities varies little from year to year. The Center for World-Class Universities (ARWU) also produces academic rankings of universities by broad and specific subject fields and hosts an annual meeting, the International Conference on World-Class Universities. The sixth such meeting held in Shanghai in 2015 focused on the questions of: "How can institutional performance be defined and measured? How can universities be globally visible and locally engaged? And, how can visibility and performance be integrated and balanced in practice?"

THE World University Rankings were originally launched in 2004 using data sourced from QS. The ranking formula is much broader than that employed by the ARWU and includes measures designed to capture the international character of a university including data related to teaching, research, knowledge transfer, and international outlook, as well as the institution's reputation within the global academic community. Thus, 40 percent of a university's score is calculated from reputational surveys collected from peers across the globe. As of 2016, THE included 800 institutions in its ranking system. A total of 200 of those universities are included in a ranking system of the "world's most international universities." The international outlook takes into account each institution's "proportion of international staff, proportion of international students and proportion of research papers published with at least one co-author from another country."[3]

In 2009, THE split with QS and began using data from Elsevier's Scopus database, later from Thomson Reuters, and more recently (2014) in partnership once again with Elsevier.[4] QS went on to establish its own World University Ranking, which also includes 800 institutions and uses Elsevier Scopus data. The QS ranking methodology includes the university's reputation among employers of graduates, facilities, innovation, research, teaching, internationalization, and community engagement. In addition to its World University Ranking and World University Ranking by Subject (organized by discipline categories such as engineering, biomedicine, the natural sciences, the social sciences, and the arts and humanities), QS publishes separate evaluations for Asia and Latin America as well as a worldwide faculty rankings, Top 50 under 50, and Next 50 under 50, and graduate employment rankings.

Other global rankings include the Leiden Ranking published by the Centre for Science and Technology Studies (CWTS) and Leiden University in the Netherlands, and the Scimago Institutions Rankings (SIR), or SIR World Report, developed by Scimago Lab in Spain using Elsevier Scopus data. Both ranking systems rely heavily on research productivity. The SIR World Report includes separate evaluations of university, government, hospital, and company (1) research, (2) innovation, and (3) web visibility rankings. In 2015, China established a Best Chinese Universities Ranking System to assess approximately 1,000 national universities using nine indicators in the categories of research, teaching, and learning and social service. The three categories have different weights.

The *U.S. News & World Report's* inaugural Best Global Universities ranking was launched in 2014 and is based on data and metrics provided by Thomson Reuters. The methodology used to rank global universities is different from that employed by *U.S. News* to rank American institutions. Universities are judged on factors such as global research reputation, publications, and number of highly cited papers. *U.S. News* also publishes region-specific and subject-specific global rankings. *U.S. News* was "the first American publisher to enter the global rankings arena," THE and QS are both British, while the Academic Ranking of World universities is Chinese.[5] In 2015 Thomson Reuters began ranking the top 100 "innovative" universities worldwide using its own data sources. Thomson Reuters scores universities across 10 different metrics including the institution's research performance and how active it is in protecting and commercializing discoveries (e.g., patent filings).

The Center for World University Rankings also publishes global university rankings using eight indicators to score the world's top 1,000 universities. *Youth Incorporated*, a leading magazine for young people based in Mumbai, India, partners with Education Times and Rediff.com to produce the annual global university rankings. *Youth Incorporated* surveys students, faculty, and administrators from 1,600 institutions and 9,000 organizations that have recruited or hired a university's graduates. 4 International Colleges & Universities (4icu.org) is an international higher education search engine and directory that ranks more than 11,000 accredited four-year higher education institutions in 200 countries by web popularity. Web metrics are extracted from three search engines, Google, Alexa Internet, and Majestic, to rank institutions based upon the popularity of their websites. The Webometrics Ranking of World Universities is an initiative of Cybermetrics Lab, a research group belonging to the Consejo Superior de Investigaciones Científicas, one of the largest public research organizations in Spain. Rankings capture scholarly activity, visibility, and impact of universities on the web. The United Nations began its online Global Research Benchmarking System for universities across the world through the United Nations University in Macau and the Center for Measuring University Performance (Arizona), but this effort produced reporting only through 2012.

The Universitas 21 (U21) Ranking offers the only approach that evaluates national higher education *systems* countrywide. U21 is based at the Melbourne

Institute of Applied Economic and Social Research at the University of Melbourne, Australia. The rankings were developed as benchmarks for governments, public and private organizations, and individuals. The scorecard highlights the importance of creating a strong environment for higher education institutions that allows them to successfully contribute to improving society. First published in 2012, the U21 Rankings include 50 overall country rankings and separate rankings in four categories: resources, environment, connectivity, and output.

In response to the growing number and diversity of university ranking schemes, the European Commission, the European Union's executive body, funded the development and implementation of a system known as U-Multirank. The initiative is managed by the Center for Higher Education Policy Studies at the University of Twente in the Netherlands and the nonprofit think tank Centre for Higher Education in Germany. Other partner organizations include the Centre for Science and Technology Studies (CWTS) at Leiden University in the Netherlands; the International Centre for Research on Entrepreneurship, Technology, and Innovation Management (INCENTIM) at the Catholic University Leuven in Belgium; the academic publisher, Elsevier; the Bertelsmann Foundation (the largest private nonprofit foundation in Germany); and the software firm Folge 3. The consortium also works closely with a range of national ranking partners and stakeholder organizations. U-Multirank released its inaugural scorecard in 2014, covering more than 850 higher education institutions from more than 70 countries.[6]

The U-Multirank scoring process takes into account metrics associated with teaching, research, knowledge transfer, international orientation, and regional engagement, but the methodology does not produce a combined, weighted score across these different areas of performance to produce a numbered table of the world's "top" universities.

According to the creators of U-Multirank:

There is no theoretical or empirical justification for composite scores. Empirical studies have shown that the weighting schemes of existing global rankings are not robust; small changes in the weights assigned to the underlying measures (the indicator scores) will considerably change the composite scores and hence the league table positions of individual universities. Therefore, the U-Multirank methodology looks at the scores of universities on individual indicators and places these in five performance groups ("very good" through to "weak").[7]

While the ranking of higher education institutions has become more and more popular, there have always been concerns about the quality and consistency of such rankings. Despite their popularity, each of the major ranking systems is criticized: The ARWU is perceived to be too focused on the elite research status of universities; THE is said to have too many performance indicators with an assumed level of accuracy; and the QS is criticized for having too much emphasis on peer review. All of them are criticized for failing to include the engagement work that most universities believe is valuable.[8] A 2016 report of a survey of presidents of U.S. universities and colleges published by *The Chronicle of Higher Education* finds that 47 percent of public institution leaders and 44 percent of private institution leaders remain cautious about the value of the U.S. Department of Education's College Scorecard due to the metrics chosen for inclusion.[9]

A university's global ranking is likely to differ across the various systems as a consequence of differences in methodologies, however, it is remarkable how many of the same universities populate the top positions on all lists, in spite of the often different criteria used for assessment. In 2015, five U.S. institutions appeared among the top 10 universities according to the ARWU, THE, and QS global rankings.[10] Two UK universities appeared among the top 10 for all three rankings systems, and one Swiss university made the top 10, according to THE and QS, and the top 20, according to ARWU.[11] The pole position in 2015 for each of the ranking scales was held by a different American university: ARWU—Harvard; THE—CalTech; and QS—MIT.

In response to concerns about the legitimacy of the various ranking systems, a process of auditing and "approving" the various systems evolved among a number of individuals and organizations in Europe. In 2002, a group of university ranking analysts founded the International Ranking Expert Group (IREG) and ultimately this informal group evolved into today's IREG Observatory on Academic Ranking and Excellence. IREG Observatory is an international nonprofit association of ranking organizations, universities, and other stakeholders dedicated to strengthening public awareness and understanding of issues related to university rankings and academic metrics. In 2006, the IREG helped to develop and endorsed the Berlin Principles on Ranking of Higher Education Institutions ("The Berlin Principles"), which consist of 16 descriptive and prescriptive principles for ranking methodologies and four larger themes: the purpose and goal of ranking; the design and weighting of indicators; the collection and processing of data; and the presentation of ranking results. The IREG Observatory began conducting audits of university ranking systems in 2013. Use of the "IREG Approved" label is only allowed following a successful audit by an appointed team of experts. The IREG Observatory secretariat is located in Warsaw, Poland.

The global ranking systems comport with the competitiveness of universities, which has now become much more evident as developing countries and rising economies have begun to invest substantially in their educational systems, as nations alone and in partnership with well established, prestigious global universities. The leading status of the United States as the world's top destination for academic and student talent is not assured: 47 states—all except Alaska, North Dakota, and Wyoming—spent less per student in the 2014–15 school year than they did at the start of the recession in 2008.[12] As of 2015, a total of 16 U.S. institutions ranked among the top 20 within the ARWU ranking; 14 ranked among the top 20 of the THE ranking; and 10 ranked among the top 20 among the QS ranking.

Measuring the Success of Global Research Engagement

Measurement is important if one wants to truly understand the impact of an activity. The British physicist Lord William Kelvin stated:

> *When you can measure what you are speaking about, and express it in numbers, you know something about it; but when you cannot measure it, when you cannot express it in numbers, your knowledge about it is of a meager and unsatisfactory kind.*[13]
>
> *If you cannot measure it you cannot improve it.*[14]

Overall, metrics regarding international research engagement are important and necessary for a complete portrait of a university's global profile, but they are not without drawbacks. Most importantly, metrics provide a data-driven justification for investing in international scholarship. Such information is beneficial not only to the research and international offices but also to other university units as well. For example, performance measures can be used to recognize and reward faculty and students (or units) for achievement in the international research arena. It might also be used to encourage productive competition across units/colleges/departments. Metrics can be captured by unit (faculties, departments, units) or by topic (sustainability, energy, security) to facilitate assessments of return on investment(s), strategic planning, and the measurement of progress toward goals. Metrics for global research engagement contribute to a university's reputation and prestige and can be used to identify areas of research strength, critical mass, as well as signature programs. This type of analysis is critical to assessing the goodness of fit with international partners and to identifying and promoting partnerships in countries or regions of strategic opportunity. Metrics for international research can also be used for student recruitment and fundraising initiatives.

In 2007, the University of Kentucky initiated a two-year assessment of its international activity, including student mobility, faculty research, global reputation, engagement, accessibility of information, the role of the University of Kentucky International Center, and UK's position vis-à-vis aspirational benchmarks. The resulting document, a five-year Strategic Plan for Internationalization, identifies seven strategic goals and related objectives. Each objective is linked to at least one metric used to assess success by undertaking a number of strategies that would be adopted to meet the objective. The plan is aggressive, ambitious, and bold, and It would be an excellent model for others who are undertaking this kind of planning.[15]

The University of California, Davis, has also developed metrics to measure the university's success in achieving the goal of "being the 'university of choice' for international students, post-doctoral scholars, faculty, prestigious international and governmental exchange programs and research enterprises that have transnational and global applications."[16] The UC Davis metrics include (among others): the number, quality, and financial support for prestigious international academic programs proposed and created on an annual basis; the number of international scholars who choose to study and conduct research annually at UC Davis compared with benchmark indicators from competitive peer institutions; and data concerning international student enrollment and graduation, study abroad enrollment, and the involvement of international alumni in the educational and philanthropic activities of the campus.

While there is no denying the important position metrics have assumed in higher education, the tendency to value only what we can measure is troublesome. Or in other words, there is the danger of overreliance on quantitative metrics. It has been suggested that internationalization is "too much input/output focused—a quantitative approach on numbers, instead of an outcomes based approach, that has been too pragmatically oriented toward reaching targets, without a debate on the risks and ethical consequences."[17] What we choose to measure matters, as does how it is measured (quantity vs. quality). Given the absence of an internationally agreed upon set of international research standards, it is important to consider who or what entities benefit from increased reliance on metrics to benchmark performance, what groups are being enfranchised and who might be disenfranchised.

The goal must be to use metrics responsibly and in conjunction with other methods of assessment—such as the narratives that characterize discussions of impact. Without a clear understanding of the goals and outcomes desired, an overreliance on numerical metrics can unleash unproductive comparisons across units, departments, or disciplines. For those universities collecting data and generating metrics "in house," the accuracy and reliability of the data and the sustainability of data collection are critical. Dedicated resources and staff are required for data collection and assessment. Above all, the metrics adopted by a university must reflect the mission and goals of the university and must connect to a strategic plan. A baseline for each metric must be established at the outset.

The Network for Advancing and Evaluating the Societal Impact of Science (AESIS) brings together experts from all parts of the world on measuring and promoting the impact of scientific research. Sharing best practices aids development of effective instruments for demonstrating the societal impact of science. Presentations from annual Impact of Science conferences include examples of quantitative and nonquantitative expressions of the contributions of research to society. According to the AESIS: "Our society is increasingly focused on requiring justification for the investments made in scientific research. The methods for demonstrating the societal impact are advancing but many challenges remain.... It [is] crucial to communicate the benefits of investments in scientific research."[18]

Bibliometrics

Bibliometrics (citation analysis), coupled with the process of peer review, are the most common measures of research excellence. Performance measures (or key indicators) consist of the number of scholarly journal publications, citation impact scores that measure the number of citations per publication (weighted or indexed), and impact factor values that measure how influential a journal or paper is within the academic community—largely by measuring the number of citations to the journal and its popularity as a publishing outlet. International co-authorship has increased markedly over the past five years (see Figure 2.) Other important metrics are related to technology transfer and commercialization of ideas: patents and patent applications/citations; invention disclosures, licensing revenue, and spin-offs.

Many national institutions issue so-called science indicator studies at regular intervals including the National Science Foundation (United States); the European Commission; France's L'Observatoire des Sciences et des Techniques; and Japan's National Institute for Informatics, National Institute for Science and Technology Policy, and Ministry of Economy, Trade and Industry. The National Science Foundation (NSF) *Higher Education Research and Development Survey* and the Organisation for Economic Co-operation and Development (OECD) *Science, Technology, and Industry Scoreboard* profile national trends in research and development (R&D).

An effort to evaluate the *impact* of R&D investment in the United States was begun under the STAR METRICS® initiative. STAR METRICS represented a U.S. collaboration between the National Institutes of Health and the NSF, under the auspices of Office of Science and Technology Policy, to create a repository of data and tools that could be used to assess the impact of federal R&D investments. By mid-2015, however, the STAR METRICS® Consortium decided to redirect STAR METRICS resources toward the ongoing development of the Federal RePORTER, a searchable database of scientific awards from federal agencies (http://federalreporter.nih.gov/). As of January 1, 2016, STAR METRICS halted the federal collection of institution data and subsequent production of Level I reports.[19]

As international research and engagement emerges as a top priority for universities around the world, institutions need "practical and tested tools to measure and benchmark the impact and outcomes of their international collaborations."[20] A study funded by the NSF of five public universities selected for geographic and academic diversities (Colorado State University, Kansas State University, Michigan State University, University of North Texas, and Washington State University as prime) provided a testing ground for the development of a set of international research indicators. The metrics were associated with personnel, grants, expenditures, co-authored publications, citation impact, and article downloads, as well as co-inventions with international collaborators for the 2008–2012 period.[21] Data for the study were obtained from a commissioned project with Elsevier's Research Intelligence Unit and Scopus database resources as well as from each of the participating institutions. The tested metrics included the following:

- Personnel
- Number and percentage of international researchers
- Grants and contracts
- Number and percentage of proposals (total and those with one or more international collaborators)
- Number and percentage of awards (total and those with one or more international collaborators)
- Research expenditures
- International research expenditures (total dollars and percentage of total)
- Publication and citation counts
- Internationally co-authored publication number count and percentage
- Number of citations (total and with one or more international collaborators)
- Normalized citation impact (field-weighted citation impact)
- Number of publication downloads
- Patents
- Number and percentage of co-invented patent applications
- Number and percentage of co-invented patents issued

According to the study, all five institutions showed that at least a third of their total publications involved international co-authors, and the impact of these publications was significantly higher than the institutional and world average. The number of grant applications, awards, and co-authored publications with international collaborators increased over the 2008–2012 period for each of the five universities under evaluation. Other metrics varied by university and over time.

The study also included a multimodal survey of researchers and an analysis of researcher mobility at Washington State University to develop a more comprehensive profile of international engagement. A number of potential challenges were identified when utilizing quantitative metrics for decision making and benchmarking, including "institutional differences in nomenclature (e.g., faculty, researcher); subject titles; time lags between inputs (proposal submissions, patent applications) and outputs (publications and patents issued); difficulty in collecting data across different offices within an institution; and the level of effort required to collect, analyze, and interpret the information."[22] Institutions interested in developing and/or adopting metrics designed to measure the value and impact of international research will need to consider the level of access to data and the ease of collection (and the quality of available data), as well as the level of resources (personnel and money) available for such an endeavor. Equally important is a quantitative, objective assessment of research performance and productivity that is best matched with a deep, qualitative assessment of an institution's research environment, researchers, and strategic priorities.

In addition to the NSF funded International Research Evaluation Metrics study,[23] Snowball Metrics represents a similar university-driven effort to identify and evaluate national and international research indicators. The Snowball Metrics initiative was initiated by research-intensive universities in the UK[24] in partnership with Elsevier. The original UK universities have since been joined by a U.S. Working Group[25] and an Australia–New Zealand Working Group.[26]

The goal is to "develop clearly defined metrics in close collaboration with the research community in order to help universities establish institutional strategies on the basis of their research performance."[27] The output of Snowball Metrics is a set of mutually agreed upon and tested methodologies, called "recipes," that relate to metrics associated with inputs, processes, outputs, and outcomes. Not all recipes are relevant for international research, but of particular interest are those associated with collaboration and the impact of collaboration.[28] The aspiration is for these metrics to become global standards that enable institutional benchmarking and to cover the entire spectrum of research activities.

Asset Mapping

Universities devote considerable resources to managing student mobility: inbound and outbound. Concerns regarding student safety and security drive the promulgation of policies designed to monitor student travel abroad and immigration laws (visa status) govern inbound mobility. U.S. universities and colleges routinely report student mobility data to the Institute of International Education (IIE) for publication in *Open Doors* reports produced by IIE and the U.S. Department of State. These data are important metrics and are widely cited because they are a source of pride for American institutions. The UK's Strategy for Outward Mobility identifies a roadmap for increasing the outbound mobility of UK students and prioritizes data collection and evaluation.[29] Universities across the globe should have little trouble providing information about student international mobility. Assessing the international mobility and activities of faculty and staff, however, can be much more complicated.

The Importance of Data

Developing databases and creating and maintaining lists of pertinent information is essential for the purpose of understanding the global landscape of a university. Often there is conventional wisdom about areas of research strength or program activity, but when data are collected systematically, the results are often surprising. The Intellectual Mapping Project conducted at the University of Illinois at Chicago (UIC) was used to identify areas of work at UIC where critical mass and a potential for synergy exists. With data collected from an inventory of faculty research and related activities, the university was able to identify over 200 faculty who self-identified as social justice scholars. As research "focus" areas coalesced, specific goals, as well as ways to facilitate connections between individual researchers and community partners, were developed and implemented. While UIC's effort is not internationally focused, it illustrates the importance of knowing who is doing what and where. Too often we know more about the activities outside our campuses that we do about the researchers working down the hall at our own institutions.

Data are essential to documenting the breadth and depth of global engagement. The process of asset mapping reveals important information for internationalization strategies including discipline areas of research strength, activity, and interest; geographic areas of importance (e.g., student mobility, faculty research collaboration, and institutional and industry partnerships); awards and honors bestowed upon faculty and staff; and expertise in foreign language and/or culture.

Among questions universities might asked are: How do we recognize scholars in our own community who work internationally? What level of our grant activity is international and where do we have our greatest research interests abroad?

Does internationalization of our research agenda correlate with the faculty who have been recruited internationally? What internal resources are available to support international activities? Do we have a strategic plan for making the most of our international partnerships?

The first step is to determine what data sources or databases already exist and/or can be developed by accessing current resources that could populate new data sets with relative ease. What databases or lists have been prepared in other university units and how can they be used or modified to inform the asset mapping process for international research? Connecting with colleagues in the university libraries and with information technology is important as these entities traditionally manage subscription databases and have expertise in developing and maintaining them. Some of the suggested data may be little more than lists that can be maintained as the information is readily available from outside sources and simply needs to be kept up to date. For example, the Council for International Exchange of Scholars, the scholar division of the IIE, offers a database of Fulbright recipients (name, academic affiliation, and country of activity). Most universities already maintain databases of faculty awards. For example, Nobel Prize laureates, recipients of the Leibniz Prize in Germany, Humboldt Research Awards for collaborative work in Germany, the Japan Prize, awards from the Ordre des Palmes Académiques in France, Pulitzer Prize winners, Fulbright scholars, and so forth. Universities will want to take stock of the honors and awards their faculty have received and set goals for future accomplishments and implement practices and policies that encourage faculty engagement and success.

Suggested Data Collection

The sky is the limit regarding data collection when resources (money and personnel) are abundant. Universities will develop lists, data sets, and online and interactive databases that come in all shapes and sizes. There is no "one size fits all" solution. Some products for data collection and asset mapping can be purchased off-the-shelf through vendors and customized by the university. Data mapping and visualization software products, such as Tableau, Maptitude and others, are readily accessible and offer a relatively low-cost gateway to get started. Many universities have developed their own systems and platforms, some of which are accessible only to members of the institution. Ideally, universities will orient the result of asset mapping exercises outward, giving the public the opportunity to view (and explore) the university's international footprint. Keep an open mind! A narrow data collection effort may evolve into a larger exercise depending on the needs and goals of the institution.

Frequently, the first step to understanding a university's international engagement is a thorough assessment of its international partnerships including general agreements, student exchanges, project-specific memoranda of understanding (MOUs), and so forth, including not only the "type" of agreement, but the scope of the agreement (university-wide, unit-specific), the activities associated with the agreement, and any scholarships or fellowships that researchers might use to engage with partner institutions. Universities most often partner with other universities overseas, but partnerships with research institutions, nonprofit organizations, and industry are equally important (see Chapter 4). Mapping partnerships and monitoring the activities associated with them is critical. Some partnerships will be discipline or unit specific and thus narrow in the scope of activities, but others will generate depth and breadth in terms of faculty and student involvement.

The University of Queensland in Australia (discussed previously) has one of the most sophisticated (home-grown) systems for monitoring and evaluating existing partnerships and potential partnerships (see Chapter 4). The University of Georgia (UGA) maintains an online database featuring its international partnerships by country and by the college (or unit) initiating the partnership.[31] A color-coded map feature provides the user with an easily digestible overview of UGA's international partnership landscape. UGA also reviews its partnerships annually, as do most universities. QS UniSolution's MoveON product offers an online CRM (customer relationship management) system that allows universities to track the mobility of faculty and staff as well as manage and evaluate international partnerships with a host of detailed data points.

International business partners and relationships with international corporations/industry, both locally and abroad, are also important to consider. These relationships can open the door to funding for researchers and experiential learning for students. International agreements across university research parks or business incubators provide an avenue for soft landings for businesses looking for new markets and opportunities for collaboration and innovation between academics and industry professionals. Michigan State University has developed a sophisticated system for tracking industry relationships including funded research, internship opportunities, and partnerships. The data can be mapped globally or organized into tables that are available to senior university leadership to inform strategic decision-making.

Identifying international research funding sources, including internal and external grant opportunities, as well as internal and external scholarship and fellowships that are available to faculty and/or students is critical. Provide access to a searchable database (subscription and/or developed internally) and push out announcements of award deadlines to researchers. Provide workshops and mentoring for faculty and students interested in certain types of awards. Use the information collected about faculty honors and awards to identify individuals to serve as mentors, application reviewers, and workshop participants. In addition, keep an up-to-date list of university affiliated research centers focused on international activities, especially if the institutions offer small grant funding.

Track international sponsored projects (grants and contracts) as well as externally funded projects that are international in scope. How a university chooses to define the term "international" is highly subjective, but a clear indication of global work is activity that takes place outside national borders. Report international research and activity annually including the ratio of internal to external funding, institutional subsidization of international activities, and revenue to expenses associated with international research. Universities should be able to identify the proportion of their research portfolios that is internationally funded and international in scope. This is a critically important metric for evaluating international research engagement and will require cooperation between the international and research offices (and other units) for accuracy. In addition, university advancement offices should be able to report gifts and fundraising that supports international research (for students and for faculty).

As international mobility increases, researchers need easy access to information regarding travel including but not limited to: health/immunization information, security updates and travel advisories, in-country emergency contact information, foreign per diem rates, etiquette, gifting and cultural advice, and country and city guides. Information should be easily accessible and up-to-date. Some universities, such as Yale University have created online toolkits, as well as guides for countries frequently visited;[32] others use subscription services such as *Goinglobal* or access to the NACUBO/URMIA International Resource Center in combination with the expertise of a risk and safety analyst/officer. A number of universities have identified "ambassadors" among the faculty who are willing to serve as representatives to faculty colleagues and administrators regarding particular countries or cultures. Alumni living abroad (former domestic and international students) also serve an important role. They may be able to connect researchers with in-county or local resources and/or they may offer homestays or other types of support.

The ability to identify "ambassadors" among faculty, staff, and alumni means a university has already completed a certain degree of assessment. Knowing who is conducting research, where, and with which international partners can be daunting. Generally, there is a great deal of anecdotal information, and there is always a cadre of highly recognized scholars, but it is important to discover what is unknown. For example, who are the university's discipline experts in areas of global concern: food security, infectious diseases, alternative energies, and others? Comprehensive data collection allows for the identification of region and country experts, culture experts, those with foreign language expertise or ability, international activities (including research, creative endeavors, teaching, and professional activities), and honors and awards received, as well as those faculty educated abroad. Knowledge of this information is a source of pride for universities. For example, in 2014, as the host for the World Junior Track and Field Championships, the University of Oregon commissioned an exhibit that featured 174 videos highlighting the work of internationally engaged faculty available to viewers on a 70-inch touchscreen housed in portable gallery. The exhibit was stationed at the Tracktown USA tent for the duration of the world championships. In reference to the exhibit, Dennis Galvan, Vice Provost for International Affairs at the University of Oregon stated: "What a lot of people don't realize is that we have professors who do research in all parts of the world. [I]t's important for people to know that. This (track) event allows us to use our university's international influence as a way to bridge the gap between academics and athletics."[33]

A portable exhibit of international research activities is an innovative way of showcasing faculty activities. Mapping international engagement is another way universities educate themselves about activities inside and outside their borders ("international" for some universities includes "glocal" endeavors; activities carried out at home with an international dimension or audience). The University of Guelph in Canada highlights its international research efforts on an interactive map available to the university community as well as to the public. The Interactive Global Research Map, sponsored by the Office of Research, encourages visitors to "browse" through the map to learn about the ways in which researchers from the university are contributing to the grand challenges of our time.[34]

The University of Cincinnati is recognized as one of the first universities to design and build a digital system for cataloguing global activities. Cincinnati's Online System for Managing International Collaboration (UCosmic) is a comprehensive database that includes information regarding faculty international activities, faculty degrees earned abroad, international partnerships, international student recruitment, study abroad programs, student organizations and activities with an international focus, and international industry collaborations.[35] While the interface does not include a mapping feature, it does produce a detailed report by country or by type of activity. A search of "France" produces the following results: 16 institutional collaboration agreements, 11 activity agreements, 31 faculty projects or activities, 20 students enrolled (5 undergraduate, 12 graduate, 3 other), 65 students in education abroad programs (previous academic year), 2 incoming exchange students (previous academic year), and 14 faculty members earned 22 degrees from 14 institutions in France. Links access more granular data for each of the categories referenced above. The online system also links to University of Cincinnati media stories tagged by country name from U.S. and international presses.

The University of Michigan State was also an early adopter of digital mapping systems to track global research engagement and impact, international partnerships (institutional and industry), and collaborations among researchers across the globe.

The University of Arizona and Duke University have digital tools that allows users to map a variety of global connections including research, student mobility, alumni, and institutional partnerships. The University of Rochester has designed a global dashboard that features maps and tables of a variety of types of international activities. Each of these systems provides critical information that is used to guide strategic planning and the allocation of scarce resources.

The 2013–2018 Strategic Plan for the University of South Florida (USF) in Tampa, Florida, prioritizes global citizenship among its student population, globally informed academic programs and partnerships, and high impact research conducted in a global context. In support of its mission as a "globally engaged" university, USF developed the Global Discovery Hub to provide a comprehensive portrait of the university's global footprint.[36] USF is one of only a handful of universities around the world able to provide an extensive data-driven, online, and interactive system for highlighting how the university's faculty, staff, and students impact the world. The Global Discovery Database features USF's international partnerships, detailed information regarding faculty activities across the globe, and data regarding student mobility and student activities.[37] The most labor intensive element of the Hub was the faculty module. The database contains more than 1,000 faculty profiles including more than 2,000 international activities from across the USF System. At the outset of the project, the goals for the faculty module included: designing a visually engaging platform for highlighting faculty global activities and achievements that is accessible to the general public; providing a variety of interactive data visualizations (map, tables, videos) representing where faculty (and their students) are engaged and what they are doing globally (research as well as many other kinds of activities), and devising a system for keeping the database up-to-date that places minimal demands on faculty to update their individual profiles. In the case of USF, it was widely recognized that faculty will not take the time to complete a nonmandatory, lengthy survey, even with easy data entry. Data that populate the Global Discovery Hub database are sourced from human resources, travel, annual activity reports, Web of Science, and other documents the faculty completed when they joined the university. Despite automated data feeds, there is still quite a bit of "data refining" that takes place within USF's international office known as USF World.

The implementation of the Hub has allowed USF to document, recognize, reward, and trumpet the diversity of faculty international research endeavors. The Hub has made it possible to better connect faculty with targeted funding announcements, identify regional and country experts, improve success with international awards (e.g., Fulbright Awards), and create customizable "Country Engagement Briefs" that highlight the ways in which the university and its faculty and students engage with a given country—a valuable resource for faculty and administrators traveling abroad, recruitment (students and industry), and partnership development, and as a resource for international economic development efforts.

FIGURE 7.1. THE USF GLOBAL DISCOVERY HUB FACULTY ACTIVITIES SEARCH AND MAP TOOL

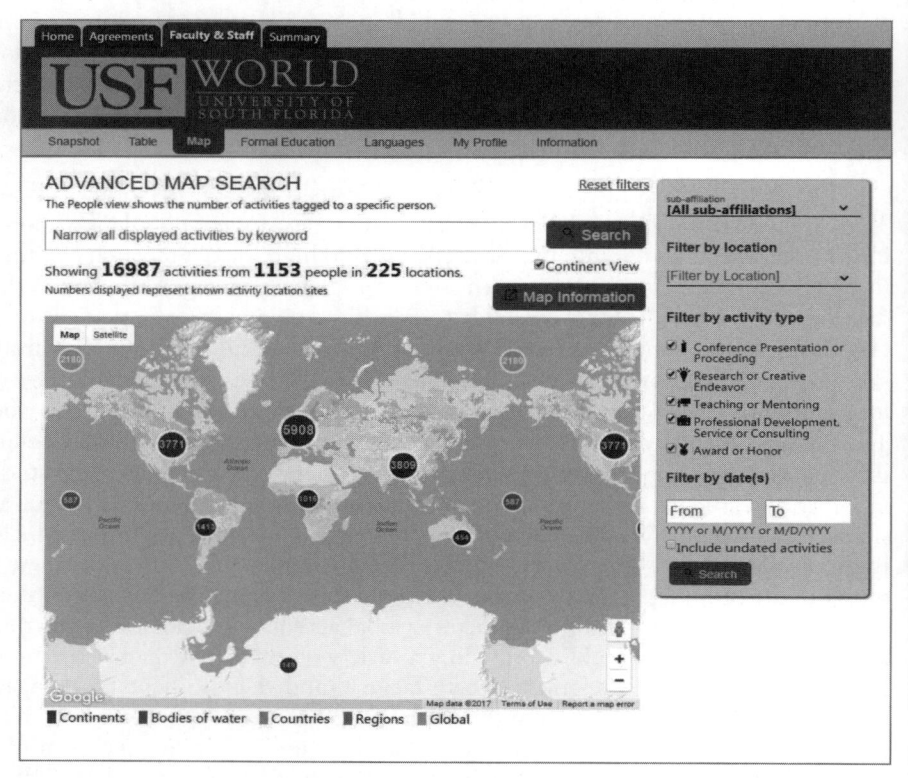

The USF Global Discovery Hub also links faculty, students and staff with resources available across the three universities of the USF System to promote and support international scholarship and global engagement. Within the USF Global Discovery Hub, members of the USF community may access an array of resources for international research including funding sources, global partnerships, the Fulbright Program, travel, and links to guidance regarding managing risk and safety, export control practices, proposal development services, and country and city guides for more than 50 locations.

Beyond the Expected

Data collection is no small task, especially if a university wishes to capture more than the data available through for-profit vendors such as Elsevier, Thompson

Reuters, and Academic Analytics. How to define what constitutes "international" and "international research" can be thorny tasks. Campus and systemwide discussions that involve faculty, students, administrators, (and other groups where relevant—add stakeholders as new directions evolve) can be used to solicit input and feedback, and for critical buy-in from researchers and those who are primarily responsible for research activities. Aids, such as templates that standardize and facilitate the sharing of information that will inform the desired international research metrics, increase the likelihood of data collection across units within a university. It may be necessary to change the culture of students and faculty to impart the data allowing the university to recognize its success through their work.

The establishment of a metrics workgroup (or similar committee/body) with diverse membership can be tasked with evaluating available data and proposing ways to increase its value by expanding and redesigning instruments that ask the right questions. For example, research offices must "tag" proposals as international in scope beyond simply identifying the funding agency or organization as an international entity. The group will inevitably recognize that some of the intangibles most indicative of success are not being measured. Assess the effort involved in collecting perceptive data, defining impact data, and crafting innovative, groundbreaking and unique measurements beyond the "numbers" as well as the university's capacity and will to collect such information.

Recognizing that some measures/strategies may be adopted *in toto* and others may be selected as applicable to their units, universities may wish to organize a half-day workshop or retreat for campus representatives to promote buy-in by the colleges/units/faculties and to provide them with a mechanism to measure their success. Once data have been collected across units, and needed revisions have surfaced, metrics work group members should be invited to publish or disseminate their work and share the information with others in a way that promotes continued dialogue and refinement.

Ultimately, it will be possible to develop "Metrics of Impact" or a "Metrics Profile" around international research. For each metric of interest universities must identify (1) the data source, (2) time frame of the data, (3) entity submitting or responsible for the data, (4) a plan for sustainability of data collection/submission, (5) how each metric supports the university's strategic performance measures/goals, and (6) how each metric supports the larger community including national research and innovation plans, and/or local (U.S. State or other nonnational entities) strategic goals. Many public universities are already required to submit benchmark measures to Boards of Governors or statewide or national organizations. The goal is to align international research metrics with the benchmark metrics that are critical to the university as a whole—each approach will be unique to the institution.

USF Global Discovery Hub Faculty Data of Interest

Faculty Identification
- Rank and Administrative or Leadership Appointments
- College, Unit, Department Affiliation
- Center or Institute Affiliation
- Research/Teaching Discipline or Expertise

International Expertise
- Language Proficiency
- Nationality
- Country of Origin
- Specific Country or Geographical Area of Expertise/Experience
- Global Challenge/Area of Interest in Research

International Affiliations
- International Education—Academic Degree or Certificate from an Institution Abroad
- Appointment with an Academic, Research, or Development Institution Abroad
- Professional Service—International Advisory Board, International Journal Board, International Conference Committee, Outreach, and Other Types of Professional Engagement

Global Activities
- International Research
- International Teaching and Mentorship
- International Training Programs
- International Creative, Performing, and Visual Arts
- International Policy Advising Activities
- International Consulting Activities

Honors and Awards
- International Fellowships
- Honorary Degrees and Titles
- International Awards and Prizes
- Other International Honors and Esteemed Activities

International Collaboration Produces Higher Impact Research

International co-authorship is increasing across disciplines and locations. France has the highest overall percentage of internationally co-authored publications (including those with European Union partners). In 2015 roughly 55 percent of scholarly publications from French researchers included a co-author from outside France. Comparatively, Germany, Australia, and Canada are each trending at approximately 50 percent internationally co-authored papers. Over the past five years, the percent of internationally co-authored publications including a Brazilian researcher has grown from 23 to 35 percent (a 50 percent increase). In the United States, international co-authorship is also on the rise, but has not reached the level of many of its peers (32 percent of papers published in 2015 included an international co-author). China has experienced a sharp growth in the number of internationally co-authored research papers over just the past two years. (see Figure 2).

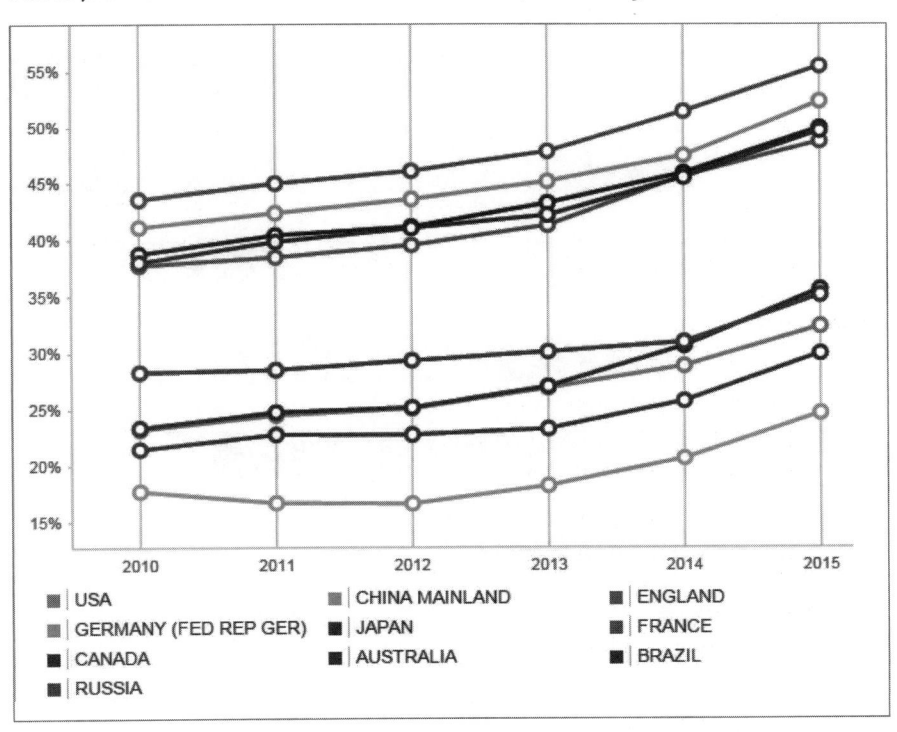

FIGURE 7.2. TRENDS IN INTERNATIONAL CO-AUTHORSHIP, 2010-2015

- USA
- GERMANY (FED REP GER)
- CANADA
- RUSSIA
- CHINA MAINLAND
- JAPAN
- AUSTRALIA
- ENGLAND
- FRANCE
- BRAZIL

Source: Data were sourced from Thomson Reuters Web of Science and InCites, October 7, 2015.

A researcher in the United States who publishes with an international colleague can expect, on average, for his or her publication to generate an impact factor higher than that of a publication that is co-authored domestically (1.67 and 1.28 respectively). A U.S. scientist who publishes with a colleague from Belgium or Denmark, however, can expect his or her work to generate an impact three times that had he or she collaborated within the United States or not at all.

French scholars are not only associated with the highest percentage of internationally co-authored papers, their geographical reach extends around the globe and produces high impact research. Scientists in France generate the highest research impact from publications with colleagues from Australia and Canada (more than three times an average impact citation score). Collaborating with researchers in England, Germany, and/or the United States will, on average, more than double the impact of a French scholar's publication. (see Figure 3.)

FIGURE 7.3. THE IMPACT OF INTERNATIONAL CO-AUTHORSHIP FOR SCHOLARS FROM FRANCE, 2010-2015

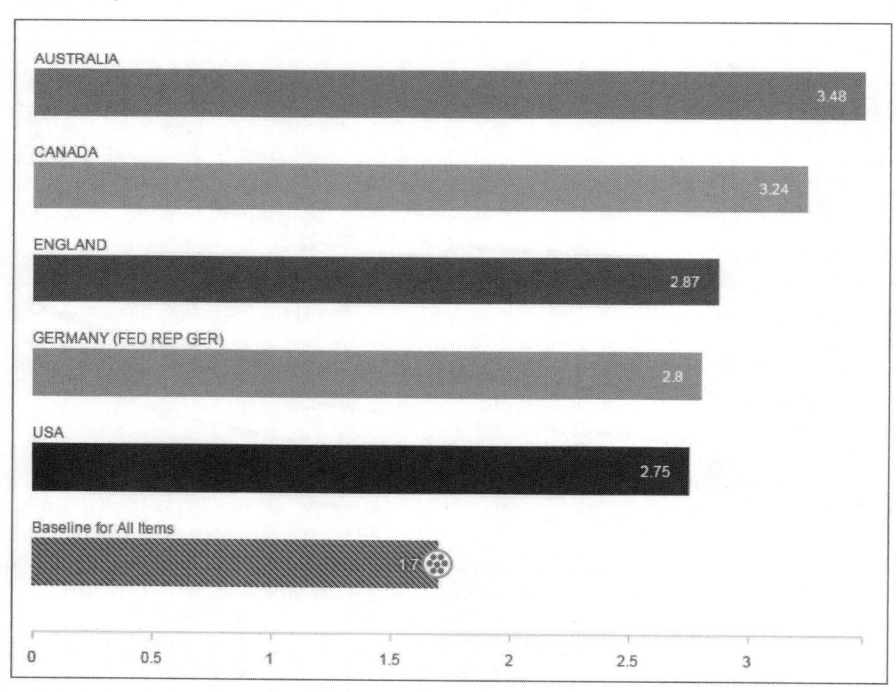

Country	Impact
AUSTRALIA	3.48
CANADA	3.24
ENGLAND	2.87
GERMANY (FED REP GER)	2.8
USA	2.75
Baseline for All Items	1.7

Source: Data were sourced from Thomson Reuters Web of Science and InCites, October 7, 2015.

NOTES

1. Patel, V. (2016). Productivity Metrics: What is the best way to assess faculty activity? *The Chronicle of Higher Education 2016 Trends Report*, B18–B21. Volume 62, Issue 25, March 5, 2016

2. Stripling, J. (2013). How a college took assessment to heart. *The Chronicle of Higher Education*, A26. September 30, 2013.

3. Bothwell, E. (2016). *The World's Most International Universities 2016*. Retrieved from https://www.timeshighereducation.com

4. Jobbins, D. (2014). New THE split throws rankings world into turmoil. *University World News*, 344. Retrieved from http://www.universityworldnews.com

5. U.S. News to issue new global university rankings. (2014). *Insider Higher Ed*. Retrieved from https://www.insidehighered.com/quicktakes/2014/10/10/us-news-issue-new-global-university-rankings

6. For a full description of the U-Multirank project, visit: http://www.umultirank.org/#!/about/project

7. Our Approach to Ranking. *Multirank*. Retrieved from http://www.umultirank.org/#!/about/methodology/approach-to-ranking

8. Downing, K. (2012). Do rankings drive global aspirations at the expense of regional development? In M. Stiasny & T. Gore (Eds.), *Going global: The Landscape for policy makers and practitioners in tertiary education* (pp. 31–39). London, UK: Emerald Group.

9. Presidential trends. The mindset of a president: How today's leaders view the direction of higher. (2016). *The Chronicle of Higher Education*. Retrieved from http://images.results.chronicle.com/Web/TheChronicleofHigherEducation/%7B2d01b120-655a-4518-b8af-d7f532dae4df%7D_2016_Presidents_Trends_v8_Interactive.pdf

10. MIT, CalTech, Harvard, Stanford, and University of Chicago.

11. In the UK: Cambridge and Oxford. In Switzerland: the Swiss Federal Institute of Technology (ETH Zurich).

12. Mitchel, M., & Leachman, M. (2015). *Years of cuts threaten to put college out of reach for more students*. Center on Budget and Policy Priorities. Retrieved from http://www.cbpp.org/sites/default/files/atoms/files/5-13-15sfp.pdf

13. *Lord Kelvin Quotations*. Retrieved from http://zapatopi.net/kelvin/quotes

14. Ibid.

15. University of Kentucky. (2009). *Strategic plan for internationalization*. Developed by the Internationalization Task Force Membership. Retrieved from http://www.uky.edu/international/sites/www.uky.edu.international/files/Final_Strategic_Plan_0.pdf

16. UC Davis. (n.d.). *Embrace global issues*. Retrieved from http://chancellor.ucdavis.edu/initiatives/past-initiatives/vision-of-excellence/goals-and-metrics/global-issues.html

17. deWit, H. (2013). Reconsidering the concept of internationalization of higher education. *International Higher Education*, 70(7). Retrieved from http://ejournals.bc.edu/ojs/index.php/ihe/article/view/8703/7824

18. *Governmental and institutional methods to advance the societal impact of science*. Retrieved from http://aesisnet.com/event/impact-of-science-2016/

19. See https://www.starmetrics.nih.gov/Star/News.

20. Arasu, P. (2016). *Metrics for institutional assessment of the impact of international research collaboration.* Poster #18039 presented at the AAAS 2016 Annual Meeting, Washington, DC.

21. The project was funded by the U.S. National Science Foundation Award #1324474.

22. Ibid.

23. NSF Award #1324474. Retrieved from http://www.nsf.gov/awardsearch/showAward?AWD_ID=1324474

24. University College London, University of Oxford, University of Cambridge, Imperial College London, University of Bristol, University of Leeds, Queen's University Belfast, and University of St. Andrews.

25. University of Michigan, University of Minnesota, Northwestern University, University of Illinois at Urbana-Champaign, Arizona State University, MD Anderson Cancer Center, and Kansas State University.

26. University of Queensland, University of Western Australia, University of Auckland, University of Wollongong, University of Tasmania, Massey University, University of Canberra, and Charles Darwin University.

27. Snowball Metrics: Global Standards for Institutional Benchmarking. See http://www.snowballmetrics.com/

28. The Snowball Metrics recipes are free of charge and can be used by any organization. The Snowball Metrics Recipe Book is available at http://www.snowballmetrics.com/wp-content/uploads/snowball-recipe-book_HR.pdf

29. UK Higher Education International Unit. (2013). *UK strategy for outward mobility.* Retrieved from http://www.international.ac.uk/media/2468186/uk-he-international-unit-uk-strategy-for-outward-mobility.pdf

31. University of Georgia International Partnerships. https://international.uga.edu/partnerships

32. See http://world-toolkit.yale.edu/countries/countries.

33. Sylvestre, A. (2014). *RG showcases UO global research interactive map.* University of Oregon Register Guard. Retrieved from https://international.uoregon.edu/RG_global_research_tablermap

34. University of Guelph Interactive Global Research Map. Retrieved from http://www.uoguelph.ca/research/discover-our-research/international/global-map

35. University of Cincinnati Online System for Managing International Collaboration (UCOSMIC), Retrieved from http://www.uc.edu/webapps/ucosmic/

36. USF Global Discovery Hub. Retrieved from http://www.usf.edu/world/resources/about-hub.aspx

37. The Global Discovery Hub evolved from the University of South Florida's association with the UCosmic© Consortium, an international group of universities and higher education organizations working collaboratively to develop an open-source solution to record and map the global activities of universities and colleges.

Chapter Eight
Grand Challenges Unite the World and Promote Research Across Borders

Introduction
As one scans the research and development priorities for countries and universities, it becomes clear that the thinking across the globe—whether it is governments or universities—is very similar. There is a transnational agenda. The magnitude and complexity of the most pressing challenges simply cannot be solved by one research team, any single discipline, or any one country, but demand attack on multiple fronts through international cooperation and collaboration. Global issues as outlined in the Millennium Development Goals (MDGs) and the more recent Sustainability Development Goals (SDGs) demand a multinational perspective and multidisciplinary approaches to make progress toward finding solutions:

> *Success will require new science-based solutions…an unprecedented integration of insights across various disciplines, including Earth systems sciences, public health, civil engineering, information technologies, economics, politics, law, business and much more.* **Only Universities bring together this range of knowledge. Universities are therefore critical stakeholders for success.** *To an unprecedented extent universities must partner with government, business and civil society to take on the great challenges of sustainable development that lie ahead.*[1] *(emphasis added)*

Global Risks, 2016

Each year, the World Economic Forum defines the landscape of Global Risks (described as uncertain events)[2] and Global Trends (a long term pattern) for the next decade, and while the risks are defined primarily for the business environment, they also provide insight into areas where research by university investigators and their partners is essential. Moreover, they reflect the input of individuals from multiple age groups within business, academia, civil society, and the public sector around the world. The risks are categorized as economic, environmental, geopolitical, societal, and technological and placed into a context of likelihood and impact, mapped regionally across the world, and discussed in terms of resilience to their effects.[3] The trends coincide with the issues cited in the MDGs and SDGs.

Top 10 Risks in Terms of Likelihood	Top 10 Risks in Terms of Impact
Large scale involuntary migration	Failure of climate-change mitigation and adaptation
Extreme weather events	Weapons of mass destruction
Failure of climate-change mitigation and adaptation	Water crisis
Interstate conflict	Large scale involuntary migration
Natural catastrophes	Failure of financial mechanism or institution
Failure of national governance	Energy price shock
Unemployment or underemployment	Biodiversity loss and ecosystem collapse
Data fraud or theft	Fiscal crises
Water crisis	Illicit trade
Spread of infectious disease	Asset bubble

Global Trends, 2016

The global trends that were identified include the following:
- Aging population
- Changing landscape of international governance
- Climate change and environmental degradation
- Growing middle class in emerging economies
- Increasing national sentiment and polarization of societies
- Rise of chronic diseases
- Rise of cyber dependency
- Rising geographic mobility
- Rising income and wealth disparity

- Shifts in power
- Urbanization

Many of these overlap with the risks and all of them present opportunities for research, in many cases collaborative between investigators in the sciences and the humanities.

Global Challenges

> *We are bound together in a human community aboard a fragile planet with finite resources and mind-boggling destructive capabilities, as we all have a responsibility to work toward global goals.*[4]

The Millennium Project

The Millennium Project was established in 1996 after a three-year feasibility study by the United Nations University (UNU), Smithsonian Institute, Futures Group International, and the American Council for the UNU. The project, a not-for-profit "collaboratory" and think tank for global research, included more than 50 Nodes around the world that involved universities, corporations, governments, NGOs, and other organizations and individuals. Fifteen project goals[5] were developed with input from more than 3,500 people thinking futuristically about a framework to assess global and local prospects for prosperity. The results of projects are updated every year and published in the annual *State of the Future* report.[6]

Millennium Development Goals (MDGs)

At the Millennium Summit in 2000, the 193 member states of the United Nations committed to join a global partnership codified by the UN Millennium Declaration, and adopted the MDGs[7] to be in effect until 2015. The Millennium Project was commissioned in 2002 to develop a concrete action plan for the world to achieve the MDGs, and in 2005, an independent advisory body headed by Professor Jeffrey Sachs of Columbia University, presented its final recommendations, *Investing in Development: A Practical Plan to Achieve the Millennium Development Goals,* to the UN Secretary-General. More than 250 experts from around the world, including researchers and scientists, policymakers, and representatives of NGOs, UN agencies, the World Bank, IMF, and the private sector worked in thematic task forces to develop the goals.

The eight MDGs were considered to be the first, worldwide, holistic approach to global development to improve human well-being and galvanize political commitment.[8] Millennium Development Goal #8—international partnerships requires a change in asymmetric relationships between rich and poor countries, industrialized and developing countries, and the unequal distribution of economic and political power.[9]

> *International cooperation in science is not a luxury, it is a necessity and the foundation for the future.*
>
> Dr. Arden Bement, Past Director, National Science Foundation

Progress toward these goals and projections into the future were assessed as the 2015 end date approached.

Post-2015 UN Global Goals

Much has been learned from the efforts to meet each of the MDGs.[10,11] Hindsight revealed the merits and the limitations, shortcomings, misunderstandings, overgeneralizations, and dissatisfactions with the measurements and statistics of the MDGs that would guide the new agenda into a world significantly different from 2000, a time of financial stability, economic prosperity, and strong multilateralism.[12] The process to reconceptualize the MDGs began in 2012 and debates began in the UN General Assembly in 2013.

The proposed options for a new agenda were to (1) continue with more of the same with refinement and focus, (2) develop wider goals differentiated by context, and/or (3) develop completely new approaches or alternative paradigms. It was considered that the time had arrived to reformulate policies, redesign strategies, and rethink development.[13] The *2015–16 State of the Future Report*[14] suggested that:

> *Humanity needs a global, multifaceted, general, long-term, view of the future with bold long-term goals to excite the imagination and inspire international collaboration.*[15]

Nine practical points were presented for consideration as the renewal process:[16]

1. Define the new time horizon.
2. Reshape the structure.
3. Select new targets.
4. Devise immediate targets.

5. Balance ambition with realism.
6. Combine different types of benchmarks.
7. Include crosscutting issues.
8. Monitor below the national average.
9. Establish a global custodian.

These points provide a sensible and valuable framework, not only for the post-2015 MDG agenda, but also for *any* collaborative project.

Bellagio Goals

The Bellagio Goals were formulated in Bellagio, Italy, in 2011 by a consortium of organizations, led by the Center for International Governance Innovation and the Korean Development Institute.[17] A report was presented to United Nations officials responsible for the post-2015 development goals in November 2012 and to a larger group of officials, organizations, and researchers in New York and Washington, DC. The 11 new goals were based upon the Millennium Declaration and the document that followed the Rio+20 gathering (see below). The report included an assessment of progress toward the MDGs, strengths, and weaknesses of the framework for the goals, the changing context of global development, and the criteria for a new set of goals post-2015. The Bellagio Goals apply to both developed and developing countries and are not substantially different from, but augment, the MDGs:

1. Inclusive economic growth for dignified livelihoods and adequate standards of living
2. Sufficient food and water for active living
3. Appropriate education and skills for full participation in society
4. Good health and best possible physical, mental, and social well-being
5. Security for ensuring freedom from violence
6. Gender equality enabling men and women to participate and benefit equally in society
7. Resilient communities and nations for reduced disaster impact from natural and technological hazards
8. Quality infrastructure for access to energy, transportation, and communication
9. Empowering people to realize their civil and political rights

10. Sustainable management of the biosphere enabling people and the planet to thrive together
11. Global governance and equitable rules for realizing human potential

Targets and indicators were designed for each of the goals, but it was recognized that countries would need to set their own targets for success.

Rio+20

In the summer of 2012, the United Nations sponsored a conference in Rio de Janeiro, RIO+20,[18] to secure political commitment to sustainable development and a green economy through the adoption of Sustainability Development Goals (SDGs). The agenda was to establish measures to end poverty, promote decent jobs and clean energy, and address environmental destruction. Six SDGs were developed to image the world as an interconnected system via the economy, social networks, the Earth's natural systems, and governmental processes in the public and private sectors:[19]

- Thriving lives and livelihoods—ending poverty and improving well-being
- Sustainable food security
- Sustainable water security
- Universal clean energy
- Healthy and productive ecosystems
- Governance for sustainable societies

Like the MDGs, the Bellagio Goals and the RIO+20 criteria, these goals were intended to provide a holistic approach to well-being "in which economic development should be socially inclusive, environmentally sustainable, and subject to good governance and peace."[20]

Agenda 2030: The Global Goals for Sustainable Development and the Sustainable Development Solutions Network (SDSN)

In 2012, the UN Secretary-General Ban Ki-Moon launched the UN Sustainable Development Solutions Network (SDSN) to engage scientific and technological expertise around the world in designing and implementing Sustainable Development Goals (SDGs) to extend to 2030, hence Agenda 2030. A high-level support group consisting of the heads of state of eight countries[21] issued a statement underscoring the need for leadership, broad consultation, engagement, and partnership among all stakeholders in government and civil society to do their share to ensure successful implementation of these goals. The Secretary-General called these times the "Age of Sustainable Development."

Professor Jeffrey Sachs led a large group of leaders from all regions and diverse backgrounds representing universities, research centers, civil society organizations, businesses, and other knowledge centers to support the financing and implementation of Agenda 2030; develop the network; and ensure effective structures for decision making and accountability. Through reports,[22] briefs and evidence papers, and expert sessions and events (see online calendar of current monthly events), the SDSN contributed to the intergovernmental negotiations leading to the SDGs.

In September 2015, world leaders of the UN Member States created a path for work to be accomplished over the next 15 years to grow the Member States' economies, end extreme poverty, fight inequality and injustice, promote peace and good governance, and protect our planet by attending to environmental sustainability and climate change. The 17 SDGs expand the Bellagio Goals and are the heart of Agenda 2030 to define a better world for all nations and all people.

1. No poverty
2. Zero hunger
3. Good health and well-being
4. Quality education
5. Gender equality
6. Clean water and sanitation
7. Affordable and clean energy
8. Decent work and economic growth
9. Industry, innovation, and infrastructure
10. Reduced inequalities
11. Sustainable cities and communities
12. Responsible consumption and production
13. Climate action
14. Life below water
15. Life on land
16. Peace, justice, and strong institutions
17. Partnerships for the goals

Although it is essential—albeit difficult—to implement a set of global and local strategies, by numerous countries working together on the scale necessary to build a better future, "we need coordinated transnational implementation" and to understand that national or regional SDSNs will promote the Solutions Initiatives through priority actions, open questions, and early-stage demonstration projects. An Academic Committee is developing educational materials for sustainable development and the SDSN is working closely with UN agencies and other organizations. Columbia University hosts the Secretariat with staff in New York and Paris. It is likely that all research initiatives of university investigators and their partners currently being executed or planned can fit with one or more of these 17 goals.

A preliminary country-level SDG Index[23] has been designed to measure achievement across the SDGs. The Index will be finalized in 2016 following public input. Work is also continuing to refine the indicators, monitor the framework and the process to follow, and review the outcomes.

In March 2016, a Science, Technology and Innovation (STI) Advisory Board was established by the Under-Secretary-General of the United Nations and Executive Secretary of The United Nations Economic and Social Commission for Asia and the Pacific (ESCAP).[24] The board will discuss and advise on the issues, challenges, and opportunities for STI collaboration and cooperation in the implementation of the SDGs.

All of the global challenges are destabilizing, and as suggested in the introduction, they are interrelated. Food security, for example, is clearly linked with poverty, health, sustainable agriculture (including mariculture and aquaculture, ocean acidification, etc.), rural development, ecosystem management, climate change and water, the energy crisis, population increases, the economy, trade practices, and policies for national security. Population shifts out of a region move people to areas where they may be more susceptible to diseases to which they have no natural immunity, and concentration of populations in large cities stresses the infrastructure system and has effects on public health, security, and transportation. A vast number of linkages can be made among all the global challenges.

Many of the issues listed originate at the local level, but are global in reach and impact due to travel, migration, excesses, and poverty. They are "an inter-textual tangle of scientific, social-scientific, and humanistic issues"[25] that require a multidisciplinary, multifaceted, integrated approach and the expertise, attention, knowledge, and engagement of many partners for solution—they are as interconnected as humanity.

Grant Programs Align with the Development and Sustainability Goals

Federal funding agencies, for example, have developed programs that bring international groups together to work on these global problems. In November 2012, USAID created the Higher Education Solutions Network led by the College of William and Mary, Duke University, Massachusetts Institute of Technology, Michigan State University, Texas A&M, University of California, Berkley, and Makerere University in Uganda to develop a multidisciplinary research, innovation, and development effort to help solve the most pressing issues in global development.

The goals of USAID align with the MDGs and SDGs.

> *USAID is the lead U.S. Government agency that works to end extreme global poverty and enable resilient, democratic societies to realize their potential.*

Monitoring the progress on the MDGs and other global challenges is a challenge in its own right. The Council on Foreign Relations created the International Institutions and Global Governance (IIGG) Program with several tools[26] to assess the status of human rights, nonproliferation, finance, oceans governance, climate change, conflict prevention, public health, transnational crime, and counter-terrorism regimes.[27]

USAID, NSF, and National Institutes of Health (NIH), together, have developed the Partnerships for Enhanced Engagement in Research (PEER) collaborative grants (PEER Science and PEER Health) to support researchers in 87 science and 33 health countries. PEER Science awardees work together on topics such as food security, climate change, water, biodiversity, disaster mitigation, and renewable energy. PEER Health collaborators focus on country-specific health topics. These projects are not only a matter of focus for the investigator, but they also promote science diplomacy.

> *Successful science diplomacy can work to create solutions in a political environment that faces the need to respond to global challenges like climate change and food security. No single nation is the sole cause or solution to these challenges. Through science collaboration, we can build bridges of trust and cooperation for the benefit of all.*[28]

The Global Innovation Initiative (GII), sponsored by the U.S. Department of State and the UK, and administered by Institute of International Education (IIE) and the British Council, is a research development initiative designed in 2013 to bring together researchers and students from the U.S., Great Britain and a developing country in a partnership that will provide impact to each of the nations and institutions involved. The research is to be conducted in the areas of global health, energy, climate change and the environment, urban development and agriculture, and food security and water. There is an annual solicitation for proposals and grants of up to $200,000 total are awarded for use over a period of two years to accomplish the research and educational goals proposed by the investigators.

University Research Agendas Promote Solutions to MDGs and SDGs

Globalization has pushed the world's universities to work within a "global standardized" value system, in the same manner, and on the same problems while remaining sensitive to the importance of cultural diversity.[29] Many universities cite elements of the MDGs and SDGs in their own strategic plans and initiatives.

The University of Pennsylvania's Penn Global Development Initiative was created to work collaboratively with international colleagues on research and policy issues related to the MDGs. Funds were made available from the university for students to engage in internships with select organizations in the scientific, economic, political, and medical fields, and the arts.

Drexel University has demonstrated its commitment to international research collaboration and educational partnerships by fostering a global ecosystem to address global challenges. The commitment is enunciated in the university's strategic plan—"To Enhance Drexel's Global Impact."

Lehigh University regularly places full page announcements in *The Chronicle of Higher Education* highlighting their research and publicizing that the "faculty are examining issues that affect lives both locally and globally…. Lehigh's enduring commitment to deepening understanding and broadening perspectives has a profound effect on how we see ourselves and how we address humanity's most pressing problems." This ad was also sent to Chronicle subscribers by email!

Indiana University has started an initiative to "tackle even bigger issues on behalf of all humanity" and they are investing $300 million to make this happen.[30]

North Carolina State's history, mission and strategic plan call for the university to address the grand challenges of society that confront the world and respond through many disciplinary aspects that require teams of scholars with varied skills and diverse perspectives.

The Ohio State University 2012 strategic planning states that they will "capitalize on current investments and sustain our involvement in problem solving of world-wide significance." These problems are not only issues of global concern, but also are the issues our nation faces. As stated previously, Ohio State's main areas of research emphasis—health and wellness, food production and security, and energy and environment—are relevant for all nations.

Oxford University has taken a campuswide approach to the challenges that face our global society. The Oxford Martin School, for example, is an interdisciplinary community of over 300 scholars who conduct research on topics ranging from health to energy (see Chapter 1). The Environment ONE (Oxford Networks for the Environment) program focuses on the issues of water, food security, climate change, and energy to meet the demands of the growing populations. The program engages faculty and students from the sciences, engineering, politics and international relations, business and law, and various research institutes. The Center for the Developing World teaches and conducts research on international development to understand change and equality in developing countries and their interactions with the rest of the world, and the programs on demographics (Migration Oxford) concentrates its work on the aging of the population, global health programs and global collaborations that concentrate on infectious diseases in Africa and Asia.

Independent organizations, universities and other partners tackle many of the global challenges by combining their resources with the organizing capacity of leadership organizations, including the United Nations.

Fifteen research-intensive university members on five continents belong to the Worldwide Universities Network (WUN). The WUN seeks to expand international collaboration in research and graduate education through collaborative programs that involve a WUN partner and other world-leading academics. Together, they address global challenges through research and develop leaders who will be prepared to address the challenges and new opportunities of our rapidly changing world, to make significant and impactful contributions which will appeal to potential funders, policymakers, and the world. The three current global challenges are:

- Adapting to climate change—concerning public health, food security, poverty, environmental risk, water security, and environmental justice.
- Furthering the frontiers of cultural understanding—increasing comprehension of the cultures across and within countries and enhancing dialogues between them.
- Focusing on how different nations respond to social, political, and technological issues they share in common.

Relationships are developed through WUN sponsored conferences and workshops for teaching and learning. The UN sponsors online courses for WUN members and the Research Mobility Program for early-stage researchers whereby graduate students gain access to expertise and rare facilities not available in their own institutions. Resources, contacts and advice are provided to research groups in the fields of:

- Arts and humanities
- Engineering
- Medicine, dentistry, and health
- Science
- Social sciences

The Global Health Initiative (GHI) brings together several U.S. government agencies related to health and international development[31] with partners in other countries to focus on the health-related MDGs to fight communicable diseases, promote international health, and overcome the challenges of disease that threaten lives throughout the world. Success will require all nations to commit to improving global health by working to:

- Address gender health imbalances; promote the empowerment of women and girls; and improve health outcomes for individuals, families, and communities.
- Create sustainable health systems to be owned, managed, and operated by the host government and its people.
- Strengthen health systems.
- Promote global health partnership relationships.
- Promote integration of health sector activities with activities of other MDGs such as water and sanitation and food security.
- Translate investments in research and innovation into real and measurable population-level health outcomes.
- Improve metrics, monitoring, and evaluation throughout the program process.

In 2012, the focus of GHI shifted to support the seven principles (above) through work by GHI country teams and planning leads in the field under the leadership of the U.S. Ambassador and in collaboration with local government and nongovernmental partners. An Office of Global Health Diplomacy in the Department of State was created to oversee the priorities and policies of GHI in each country. Success will be measured by the ability to take advantage of the collective interagency leadership to influence global stakeholders, align donor investments with country resources and maintain and build technical support that expands capacity to approach global health priorities.

Fifteen universities in some of the world's great cities joined a network in 2010. World-Class Universities for World Cities (WC2) University Network promotes closer relationships among the cities and their interactions with local government and business communities in order to be more responsive to the needs of their stakeholders and to address cultural, environmental and political issues of common interest to the cities and their universities, including: transport, global health, sustainability, business, cultural/creative industries. WC2 member universities[32] are:

- At the heart of a world city and recognized locally as a major university.
- Committed to international activities.
- Cosmopolitan in perspective and strategic direction.
- Committed to close and intense two-way interactions with their local society and economy.
- Strong academically and in research, particularly in areas relevant to world cities.
- Driven to meet the development of new areas of knowledge and technology.
- Engaged with the broader community in the public and private sectors.
- Committed to act as a local hub for the WC2 network.
- Open to involving others in their city (businesses, community organizations, government, etc.).
- Endorsing projects including relevant collaboration with other experts.

Universitas 21 is an international network of 25 research-intensive universities in 15 countries joined in an international network to promote collaboration, cooperation and to create opportunities to foster global citizenship and institutional innovation through research-inspired teaching and learning and student mobility. The University of Connecticut, the University of Maryland, and The Ohio State University are U.S. members. Other representative universities include the University of British Columbia, the University of Edinburgh, the University of Hong Kong, Shanghai Jiao Tong, and the National University of Singapore. Activities focus on the student experience, connecting students and staff, and strategies to enhance the advocacy for internationalization (global citizenship, teaching and learning, researcher engagement, and leadership and management), and other collaborations.

The Academic Consortium 21 (AC21) is "an international partnership of leading research universities committed to innovation in education, research and academic governance through collaborative action." It was established in 2002 at Nagoya University, Japan during an international forum of presidents and high-ranking delegations. The title of the forum, "The Role of Universities in the 21st Century," remains the theme for AC21's activities to promote cooperation in education and research among the network of members whose shared values underpin the goals to improve the quality of life of different societies in the world and foster peaceful coexistence beyond national and regional boundaries. Educational activities help students gain multicultural understanding and an international perspective, promote interdisciplinary research between the humanities and science and promote lifelong education, disseminate world-class knowledge, and provide outstanding human resource development. AC21 will support high-quality, internationally active researchers and international collaborative research, create international frameworks for technology transfer and help to develop internationally competitive industries. They also support regional and industrial partnerships that involve exchanges, internships and R&D with members and associate members. North Carolina State University and the University of Minnesota are AC21 U.S. members.

United Nations Organizations

In accord with the role of the United Nations in creating the MDGs and SDGs, there are a number of UN-sponsored organizations that work with multilateral partners to pool international resources, enforce international norms, and support international cooperation for working together on the SDGs. Academic members are common among them.

To Reduce Poverty in the World, the Public Private Alliance Foundation (PPAF) establishes collaborations among business, governmental, community, academia, the United Nations and other interests to stimulate entrepreneurship and commerce-related activities, and encourage investment for sustainable development. PPAF works closely with the Department of Public Information of the United Nations to develop policies that advance public-private alliances in program areas such as agribusiness, education, microfinance, health, information technology, remittances, renewable energy, and water and sanitation.

To Protect and Improve the Environment, the United Nations Environment Programme (UNEP) coordinates environmental activities and assists developing countries with funding and in implementing environmentally sound policies and practices. UNEP is concerned with the atmosphere and marine and terrestrial ecosystems and has played a significant role in developing international environmental conventions, promoting environmental science and information and working in conjunction with policy development and implementation with national governments, regional institutions, and environmental NGOs. UNEP has aided in the development of guidelines and treaties on issues such as international trade of potentially harmful chemicals, trans-boundary air pollution, and the contamination of international waterways. UNEP is headquartered in Nairobi, Kenya, and has six regional offices and various country offices.

Engaging Higher Education in Support of Human Rights, Literacy, Sustainability, and Conflict Resolution, the United Nations Academic Impact program aligns institutions of higher education with the United Nations in actively supporting ten universally accepted principles. Each participating college or university is expected to actively demonstrate support for at least one of the principles each year:

1. The principles inherent in the United Nations Charter as values that education will promote and help fulfill.

2. Human rights, among them freedom of inquiry, opinion, and speech.

3. Educational opportunity for all people regardless of gender, race, religion, or ethnicity.

4. The opportunity for every interested individual to acquire the skills and knowledge necessary for the pursuit of higher education.

5. Building capacity in higher education systems across the world.

6. Encouraging global citizenship through education.

7. Advancing peace and conflict resolution through education.

8. Addressing issues of poverty through education.

9. Promoting sustainability through education.

10. Promoting intercultural dialogue and understanding, and the "unlearning" of intolerance, through education.

All institutions of higher education that grant degrees and other organizations that play a major role in conducting research can be members.

To Create Learning Societies with Educational Opportunities for all Populations, the United Nations Education, Scientific and Cultural Organizations (UNESCO) has brought together 193 Member States and seven Associate Member States, governed by the General Conference and the Executive Board and headquartered in Paris, France. UNESCO is organized into sections on education, natural science, social and human science, culture, science and technology, environment, and communication and information with priority areas of gender and science, local and indigenous knowledge, and Small Island developing states. Special themes include global climate change, disaster preparedness and mitigation, and science education.

The UNESCO Education Sector has the following strategic objectives to fulfill its mission of providing international leadership and expertise to foster partnerships to strengthen national educational leadership and the capacity of countries to offer quality education for all.

- To provide a platform for intellectual and thoughtful leadership for educational innovation and reform.

- To anticipate and respond to emerging trends and needs in education and develop education policy recommendations based on research evidence.

- To initiate and promote dialogue and exchange of information among educational leaders and stakeholders as an international catalyst.

- To promote the development and implementation of successful educational practices and document and disseminate successful practices.

- To develop standards, norms and guidelines for action in key education areas.

To Promote Social Responsibility, the Global University Network for Innovation (GUNi) was created in 1999 as a cooperative program with more than 100 members committed to innovation in higher education. UNESCO chairs in Higher Education, leaders of research centers, universities, networks and other institutions pledge to focus on the role of higher education in solving problems in today's knowledge-based society, reform and renovate policies for higher education in the world, promote cooperation between higher education institutions (HEIs) and stakeholders and seek means to promote higher education in less favored countries, emphasizing public service, relevance, and social responsibility. Beginning in 2006, GUNi has produced a series of reports on relevant topics in *Higher Education in the World*.

Citizen Science is a model of grass roots citizen activism that has engaged the public in working toward solutions to the SDGs[33] (see Chapter 6).

The expansive discussion of global goals and challenges has been developed with the thought that it will expose the breadth of the agenda around which university researchers and a range of collaborators design projects that are important and needed and that, by necessity, will draw upon talent from multiple disciplines.

Global Awareness: Intercultural Understanding and Competencies for Conducting Research Internationally

Although problems are universal, the range and scope of perspectives, programs and approaches to solutions to universal challenges will be defined by the backgrounds, environments, and cultures of the people who are working on them. Our global knowledge society is "a mosaic of multiple pluralistic knowledge societies, each rooted in its own unique cultural identity."[34] "Meaningful and ethical work in a multicultural, global society"[35] requires understanding and tolerance. Both can be gained from common experiences and common values, but we also know that truth is grounded in personal understanding. Others will see "truth" from their backgrounds, experiences, and perspectives—and the two visions may not coincide. This has been described as "the concept of simultaneous truths."[36] These truths may be tested in international collaborations.

No matter how one interacts abroad (through a research experience, service learning, an overseas internship or practicum, volunteer experience, or study abroad) the success of the experience (for both the academic participant and the partner/collaborator overseas) depends upon the ability to which the individuals have "global awareness" and have a desire to enhance their intercultural understanding.

> *Global awareness is the degree to which an individual has knowledge of every facet of societal function in major areas of the world.*
>
> *Global awareness involves a recognition and appreciation of the size, complexity, and diversity of the Earth conceived as a single entity. It is literally a worldview.*
>
> *Global awareness is knowing one's ignorance of the world and being ready to pursue the knowledge needed to overcome it.*
>
> *Awareness stimulates the desire to learn, to be open to differences, and to develop a positive communicative attitude of stance. Creating new categories of information expands our understanding and view of the world. Knowledge prepares us for new encounters.*

The Global Awareness Test is a self-scoring inventory that gives participants a graphic representation of their global awareness based on common knowledge in six geographic areas (Asia, Africa, North America, South America, the Middle East, and Europe) and six subject areas (environment, politics, geography religion, socioeconomics, and culture). The test is an inventory that can be used for students, educators, business leaders, and national and global service workers. The Global Awareness Profile measures one's awareness and knowledge of the world.

Global Ethics

Topics such as human rights, conflict resolution, and environmental sustainability are researched and debated by the teachers, students, and citizens around the world who participate in the Carnegie Council's Global Ethics Network. The network engages educational institutions and Global Ethics Fellows from around the world in an online social network, in conversation and debate about the global issues cited above, and in conducting research and developing partnerships. Conferences, lectures, symposia, and curricular offerings are designed to promote these conversations. Carnegie Ethics Fellows work as mentors to students who are to become the next generation of Ethics Fellows (Ethics Fellows for the Future) and over a year's period collaborate in person or virtually with other students and Fellows in research projects, papers, and presentations.

NOTES

[1] Sachs, J. D. (2013, October). *The role of universities in sustainable development.* Monash University Special Advertising Supplement.

[2] *The global risks report.* (2016). Insight report, World Economic Forum (11th ed.). Prepared by Strategic Partners Marsh & McLennan Companies Zurich Insurance Group and Risk Management and Decision Processes Center, University of Pennsylvania, pp. 1–97, 2–16.

[3] Ibid.

[4] Adams, J. M., & Carfagna, A. (2006). *Coming of age in a globalized world: The next generation.* Bloomfield, CT: Kumarian Press, p. 122.

[5] The Millennium Project goals include sustainable development and climate change, global ethics, clean water, growth of population and resources, democratization, policymaking and long-term perspectives, global convergence of IT, rich–poor gap, capacity to decide, health issues, status of women, peace and conflict, stopping transnational crime, energy, science, and technology.

[6] Glenn, J. C., Florescu, E., & the Millennium Project Team. (2015). *2015–2016 State of the future*, Washington, DC, pp. 1–289.

[7] MDGs include to eradicate extreme poverty and hunger; to achieve universal primary education; to promote gender equality and empowering women; to reduce child mortality rates; to improve maternal health; to combat HIV/AIDS, malaria, and other diseases; to ensure environmental sustainability; and to develop a global partnership for development.

[8] Vandemoortele, J. (2012). *Advancing the global development agenda post-2015: Some thoughts, ideas and practical suggestions.* Background paper prepared for the Experts Group Meeting to support the advancement of the post-2015 development agenda, New York, NY, p. 7.

[9] Nayyar, D. (2012). *The MDGs after 2015: Some reflections on the possibilities.* Prepared for the UN System Task Team on the Post-2015 UN Development Agenda.

[10] Vandemoortele, J. (2012). *Advancing the global agenda post-2015.*

[11] Nayyar, D. (2012*). The MDGs after 2015.*

[12] Vandemoortele, J. (2012). *Advancing the global agenda post-2015,* pp. 24–26.

[13] Nayyar, D. (2012). *The MDGs after 2015,* p. 13.

[14] Glenn, J. C., Florescu, E., & the Millennium Project Team. (2015). *2015–2016 State of the future,* Washington, DC, pp. 1–289.

[15] Ibid.

[16] Vandemoortele, J. (2012). *Advancing the global agenda post-2015.* pp. 24–26.

[17] Bates-Earner, N., Carin, B., Lee, M. H., Lim, W., & Kapila, M. (2012). *Post-2015 Development agenda: Goals, targets and indicators.* The Centre for International Governance Innovation and the Korea Development Institute. www.cigionline.org | www.kdi.re.kr

[18] The conference marks the 20th anniversary of the 1992 UN Conference on Environment and Development also held in Rio de Janeiro, and the 10th anniversary of the 2002 World Summit on Sustainable Development.

[19] Sachs, J. D. (2013, October). *The role of universities in sustainable development.*

[20] Ibid.

[21] Brazil, Colombia, Germany, Liberia, South Africa, Sweden, Timor-Leste, and Tunisia.

[22] The Action Agenda; Indicators and a Monitoring Framework for the SDGs.

[23] Sachs, J. D., Schmidt-Traub, G., & Dirand-Delacre, D. (2016). Preliminary Sustainable Development Goal (SDG) Index and Dashboard (paper for public comment only). http://unsdsn.org/resources/publications/sdg-index/

[24] ESCAP is a UN organization created in 1947 to provide technical assistance, capacity building and a forum for 53 member states and nine associate members to overcome challenges that are germane to all or a group of countries in the region and offer benefit from regional or multicountry collaboration. The region is home to two-thirds of the world's population. ESCAP helps with issues of sustainable development, macroeconomic policy and development, trade and investment, transport and social development, environment and development, information and communications technology, disaster risk reduction, statistics, and subregional activities for development.

[25] Cornwell, G. H. (2006). Science and citizenship: Habits of the mind for global understanding. *Diversity Digest, 9*(3),5.

[26] Cinematic overview, interactive timeline, issue brief, matrix, interactive map, and resource guides.

[27] Retrieved from: http://cfr.org/global-governance/global-governance-monitor.

[28] Dr. Alan Finkel, Chief Scientist of Australia in a talk to the Australia-Israel Chamber of Commerce, 2012.

[29] Funamori, M. (2007). *Responding to the International needs in the 21st century.* The 2nd University Administrators Workshop-Proceedings Kyoto University—The organization for promotion of international Relations. Session A-1: Promoting International research collaborations. Retrieved from http://www.isp.msu.edu/globalengagement/partnership.htm

[30] Go.iu.edu/grandchallenge

[31] USAID, DHHS including the CDC, FDA, PEPFAR, Peace Corps, and DOD.

[32] City University of London, City University of New York, Hong Kong Polytechnic University, Meiji University, Peter the Great St. Petersburg Polytechnic University, Politecnico di Milano, Ryerson University, Technische Universitat Berlin, Universidad Autonoma Metropolitana, University of Sao Paulo, and University of the Witwatersrand.

[33] Haklay, M. (2012). Citizen science and volunteered geographic information: Overview and typology of participation. In D. Z. Sui, S. Elwood, & M. F. Goodchild (Eds.), *Crowdsourcing geographic knowledge (VGI) in theory and practice.* Berlin, Germany: Springer, pp. 45–46.

[34] Cheng, L. (2012). Cultural diversity in a global society. *Science (Letters) 336*,155–157.
[35] UNESCO.
[36] Adams, J. M., & Carfagna, A. (2006). *Coming of age in a globalized world.*

Conclusion

The Office of Research and International Programs Office, Together, Promote an International Research Agenda

It has been emphasized throughout this book that far too often research and international offices and administrators operate across an institution but not with each other. International research engagement is complicated when a divide (physically, operationally, and/or philosophically) separates the international and research offices even though both engage with the same community of practice. The five themes of the book—**collaboration, competition, innovation, integrated inquiry**, and **assessing value**—are relevant to a discussion of how to cultivate an environment of cooperation that encourages innovative strategies, interdisciplinary solutions, value-added outcomes, and an awareness of the value of competition in the global arena.

To help bridge the all too common divide, it is recommended that the research and international offices develop a shared set of common strategic and planning goals that are also connected to the university's mission and vision statements. The leadership of the two offices can set the tone by actively cultivating an environment where communication between the two offices is routine. This can be accomplished by creating various opportunities for interaction across units, for example, cross-representation on internal workgroups or committees; educating staff and administrators about the roles and responsibilities of each office; and working together to develop a common working vocabulary. It is important for both the leadership of research offices and senior international officers to be aware of international partnership agreements (memoranda of understandings, or MOUs), and any new opportunities to engage and support faculty and students in conducting research abroad. International partnership agreements open avenues for structured research engagement (Chapter 4). For such relationships to flourish, support is needed from both the research office and the international unit. And to encourage respect and trust among leaders across units, senior decision makers from these offices can arrange international trips together for the purpose of research and partnership development, fundraising or advancement, and networking. Few experiences cultivate personal interactions as closely as travel time spent together. It is also important for the president and provost to strongly encourage cooperation between these two offices, and to do so, they should have similar—if not equivalent—status with the university.

Managing International Research Collaboratively

International research per se is not more difficult to conduct than research managed domestically, but navigating the differences in business, legal practices, professional customs, cultures, and languages of another country can, and does, add a layer of complexity to even simple transactions. Take, for example, the experience of an American and a Ugandan researcher who sought to create a sustainable pathway for international collaboration in materials science:

In 2012, while graduate students in our respective countries—we had the unique opportunity to attend the first ever Joint U.S.-Africa Materials Initiative (JUAMI) research school on materials for sustainable energy in Addis Ababa, Ethiopia. The research school provided the means to bring together young scientists from the United States and East Africa, an unlikely event without external support. Over a period of two weeks, we learned about the latest scientific breakthroughs in materials for technologies ranging from solar cells to fuel cells to batteries. Staying and attending workshops at the same hotel meant that in addition to the scientific knowledge, we had many chances to learn from each other. After each day's seminars and lectures, we broke up into small groups for problem-solving exercises, which ranged from word problems to hands-on activities such as building a dye-sensitized solar cell. Working in teams, we wanted to ensure that each member understood the problem as well as the ultimate solution. Our time in Ethiopia culminated in a soccer match complete with a rallying cry adapted from a lecture we had attended on electrochemical technologies: "Play like a supercapacitor! Fast charge! Fast discharge!"

The challenge for the students upon "graduating" from the JUAMI research school was to continue working together in the future. Our time at JUAMI showed all of us how little interaction our respective research groups and universities had with scientists in Africa or the United States. At the end of JUAMI, both authors wanted to create a platform to develop Africa-U.S. research collaborations. The so-called SciBridge project began in August 2013 with one donated solar cells experiment kit to Uganda's Makerere University from the University of California Los Angeles California NanoSystems Institute (UCLA CNSI), but no money to manage project activities or send more kits. Everything moved slowly and we had trouble doing even the simplest things. For example, to make the donated experiment kit usable, we needed to send a titanium oxide sample to Kampala using the cheapest shipment option. The sample was inevitably lost, and we gave up trying to find it after three months. Shipping the materials to Uganda entailed a learning curve—our first experiment kit was stuck at customs for more than a month. In time, we learned the correct process for sending kits, which was facilitated by our engagement in university-to-university collaborations. The kits we sent to Uganda, for example, were accompanied by a letter stating that the items were for research and training of students and not for sale or resale. It was also critical that our kits were inexpensive, considering that, depending on the country, items costing more than $25 to $50 could be taxed.

Over a ten-month period spanning from 2014 to 2015, SciBridge volunteers sent twenty-five kits to nine different universities in three different countries—with two Tanzanian universities and one Ethiopian university joining the six in Uganda.... One of the main reasons our project survived many setbacks was because we work so well together—we tried to be flexible, we believed deeply in the project, and we brought different talents to the table. Thus far, we have learned that patience, flexibility, and persistence are key factors in ensuring that an intercontinental project survives and succeeds.[1]

Much was learned about conducting research in an international, intercultural setting that these young researchers will carry with them into their future careers.

International research challenges traditional business systems and processes, and there are legitimate security issues in some disciplines, as well as some regions of the world. Externally funded research may have restrictions on the movement of monies, compliance regulations, financial monitoring, tax issues, and specific rules about the methodologies used for language translation and the individuals typically responsible for these activities may not have the understanding, background, and experience in the relevant processes and regulations. The level and granularity of activity reporting for funded research in the United States can be quite daunting for colleagues in countries where university infrastructure and technology are still developing.

Complexities are sure to arise when navigating the financial and business practices of another institution in another country. Agree on a common language and standardize language usage for contracts, grants, and partnership agreements at the beginning of a partnership or project. Identify individuals capable of providing document translation within the university for routine business transactions such as the translation of invoices. Use third-party translation services as needed for weightier matters. It may be necessary to create international agreements or contract language in at least two languages: English and the language of the partner country.

Managing tax issues, payments, wire transfers, access to cash and the use of cash abroad, access to receipts for purchases, and the process of purchasing and disposing of equipment overseas are all matters that require specialized expertise. When expertise regarding business practices and financial accountability abroad is lacking, use outside professionals. Guidance from outside legal experts, nonprofits such as CRDF Global, or professional associations can be vital. The National Association of College and University Business Officers (NACUBO) offers webinars and workshops that help institutions manage many types of international business activities (e.g., money transfers and management abroad or auditing money sent abroad). Making effective use of outside consultants can be more cost effective than developing in-house expertise regarding highly technical matters. That said, universities should cultivate awareness and capacity among business professionals (payroll, billing, tax services, purchasing, travel, and other activities that generally fall under an Office of the Controller or Division of Business and Finance). A community of practice (Chapter 1) will assist those personnel whose responsibilities fall outside the traditional boundaries of international and research to understand the processes associated with international research and travel.

There may be differing perspectives about ethical standards, risk management considerations, and issues regarding authorship. Intellectual property and data maintenance as well as the principles of research integrity may have different meaning and values among international colleagues. Addressing legal agreements and contracts across cultures requires sensitivity to differences in the uses of language and terminology and an awareness that timeliness is relative to place and custom. Finding common ground and negotiating agreements *in advance*, including how to end the relationship amicably, is recommended, and can be facilitated by administrators knowledgeable about the international arena.[2]

How can a university effectively encourage collaboration between research and international offices to manage the contractual and financial dimensions of global research projects as well as the language and cultural differences inherent in cross-national collaboration for the benefit of researchers? There is no one-size-fits-all approach but successful practices provide a useful road map. Ideally, the university will have a high-capacity international research unit or centralized hub. But even among separate offices/units collaboration can work effectively. For example, find the balance between the technical aspects of managing intellectual property, which most likely reside in the research office and the interpersonal or "mission" aspects of international collaboration that may fall within the scope of the international office. Recognize time, language, and cultural differences in project management; the research office may manage the contract negotiation, but the international office has resources to inform the cultural context of the project.

Cultural Awareness and the Importance of Adaptability

Cultural awareness refers to the understanding of how a person's culture may inform his or her values, behavior, beliefs, and assumptions. Knowledge of cultural norms and habits should not be the sole responsibility of the international office, but should be a goal worthy of all people. Many universities have adopted global citizenship initiatives directed at students. The characteristics of a global citizen are open to interpretation but include an appreciation that differing values, languages, and customs do not necessarily equate to differing goals for society, an awareness of the importance of communication skills and style, curiosity blended with flexibility, a sense of community and an interest in collaboration, and critical thinking and problem-solving capacities.[3]

In the context of international research, it is important for administrators, staff, and researchers to recognize the communication norms of international colleagues including the use of language, tone, formality, and method (email, telephone, etc.). A flexible attitude regarding time and capacity is also essential. Researchers have varying access to equipment and facilities; staff have varying levels of training and resources, and the professionalization of research administrators can differ widely across nations and cultures. Universities have many sources for cultivating cultural awareness including the international office, faculty, and international students—as well as online subscription services such as *GoinGlobal*,[4] a database that provides guides for cities and countries including background information as well as information about customs, cultures, and other information relevant to travelers. This information can be made available to the entire university community including alumni. Being cognizant of cultural norms and protocols makes collaborating internationally more fruitful. For example, providing business cards in several languages or recognizing the importance of gift giving or the significance of a tea or coffee ceremony fosters mutual understanding. A university may wish to identify "ambassadors" among its faculty—individuals who are knowledgeable, trusted, and respected among a community, region, or country, to provide peer-to-peer guidance. These individuals can serve as representatives on campus and beyond—their contributions can be tailored to the needs of the university and the capability and interests of the faculty member him or herself.

Looking Ahead

The connection between research and global is clear to many universities (some are self-designated as Global Research Universities, or GRUs), but implementing strategies that support international research efforts across units can be challenging. There is a demand for opportunities for dialogue and learning at conferences and forums sponsored by the Association for International Education Administrators (AIEA), the International Network of Research Management Societies (INORMS),[5] among others,[6] and for data from research and international offices about initiatives for cooperation, coordination and understanding between these two offices, and for manuscripts such as this one.

Thematic conferences in 2013, 2014, and 2016 at the University of North Texas (UNT)[7], The University of South Florida (USF) and Rutgers University, respectively, focused on the importance of bridging an all too frequent divide between the research and international operations, the factors that separate the two units, as well as the commonalities across their activities and goals (see Chapter 1), and the need to ensure appropriate policies and practices to advance international research collaborations. With the long-standing connections between researchers at U.S. universities and institutions abroad, a robust partnership between a university's International Program Office and its Office of Research would seem to be natural. Data from a survey administered to universities prior to the 2014 meeting, *Developing Institutional Strategies for Growing Global Research,* sponsored by the AIEA and USF, offered numerous advantages for closer interaction, the need to make this interaction a reality, to manage the relationship more effectively, and to develop metrics to evaluate the benefit each office would gain from greater cooperation.[8]

Ten simple best practices for working in one's own institution as well as with international universities are provided below:

1. Maintain consistent communication across all parties (within the university and across international partners) and strengthen and use trust networks.
2. Communicate early and often (across university stakeholders) and with international partners.
3. Cultivate the ability to translate policy and practice across borders.
4. Understand that capacity levels and access to resources can vary greatly across countries, regions, and institutions.
5. Be sensitive to the level of knowledge regarding research management.
6. If collaborating with a less experienced partner, assume a mentor role.

7. Develop a sensitivity (or cultural awareness) regarding how partners manage their research portfolios and partnerships.
8. Be aware of the level of government regulation or control in the country where international research is planned or taking place.
9. Discuss financial accountability at the outset of each project; include a written agreement of expectations and organizational roles. Be aware that a variety of attitudes exist internationally about how to manage funds.
10. Commit to regular visits and exchanges of personnel.
11. Develop an escape plan at the front end in the event the relationships is unsuccessful.

And, with the constantly changing geopolitical, financial, technical, and social environment around the world there is no doubt that the academic world will be in significant flux as well and that all interactions among universities internationally will be impacted. Nonetheless, from what is ongoing today, it is possible to expect the following:

- More virtual support of research and collaboration.
- Better understanding of the support that is needed for international work, and as an outcome, more for-profit or not-for-profit, nonacademic organizations capitalizing on the opportunities to engage with universities.
- Greater emphasis on impact, metrics, databases, and rankings.
- Greater need for diversification of resources and knowledgeable support staff.
- Better integration of research and international offices.

It was emphasized in the introduction that there are any number of examples one could site in a book such as this and it would be a great asset to others is these were known and shared in an open forum. In order to make this possible, an online portal could be created for the deposit of ideas in selected categories and made available to anyone with interest. This could be developed with the appropriate interest among our readers. With the fast-paced changes in the world, there is a necessity for more collaborative, cross-national research interactions, and while they may become more difficult under the current geopolitical situations, they are more important than ever to advance our global society. Students, faculty, and staff are some of the best ambassadors to ease tensions through a common passion for finding truth through research.

NOTES

1. Excerpted from Augustyn, V., & Eneku, J. P. (2015). Building the SciBridge between Africa and the United States. *Science & Diplomacy*. AAAS. Retrieved from http://www.sciencediplomacy.org/letter-field/2015/building-scibridge-between-africa-and-united-states

2. Ferreira, W. (2011). Legal issues and agreements (Chapter 9). In S. S. Sloan & T. Arrison (Eds.), *Examining core elements of international research collaboration: Summary of a workshop* (pp. 69–73). Washington, DC: National Academies Press.

3. Israel, R. C. (2012). *What does it mean to be a global citizen?* Retrieved from http://www.kosmosjournal.org/article/what-does-it-mean-to-be-a-global-citizen/

4. http://www.goinglobal.com/

5. International Network of Research Management Societies 2016 Congress. (2016). Research Management in a Connected World, Melbourne Convention & Exhibition Centre. More information is available at: http://www.inorms2016.org/

6. Advancing International Research Collaborations: Policies and Practice. (2016). Rutgers University, New Brunswick, New Jersey, July 20-21, 2016. More information is available at: http://global.rutgers.edu/events/2016-international-research-conference.

7. University of North Texas. (2013). Global Research Funding Forum: Maximizing Opportunities to Build a Global Research Portfolio. Retrieved from https://inhouse.unt.edu/funding-forum-feature-international-research-representatives

8. University of South Florida. (2014). Developing Institutional Strategies for Growing Global Research. More information is available at: http://global.usf.edu/globalforum/

About the Contributors

KAREN A. HOLBROOK, PH.D.

Karen A. Holbrook, Ph.D., is the Senior Advisor to the President of the University of South Florida, having served as Senior Vice President for Global Affairs and International Research following her role as Senior Vice President for Research and Innovation at USF and Professor of Molecular Medicine. Most recently she has been the Interim President of Embry-Riddle Aeronautical University. Before joining USF, Dr. Holbrook served as president of The Ohio State University from 2002-2007, the Senior Vice President for Academic Affairs and Provost and professor of cell biology at the University of Georgia, Vice President for Research and Dean of the Graduate School at the University of Florida, and Associate Dean for Research and Professor of Biological Structure and Medicine at the University of Washington, School of Medicine. Dr. Holbrook has served on the boards of the American Association for the Advancement of Science (AAAS), the Association of American Medical Colleges (AAMC), the American Council of Education (ACE), the National Association of State Universities and Land-Grant Colleges (now APLU), the Association of American Universities (AAU), The Council of Graduate Schools (CGS), ACT Inc., the Accreditation Council for Graduate Medical Education (ACGME), past chair of the board for Oak Ridge Associated Universities (ORAU), among others. She has participated on numerous advisory panels and councils for the National Institutes of Health, including the NIH Blue Ribbon Panel for the National Emerging Infectious Diseases Laboratory, Boston, and was a member of the Advisory Committee to the Director of the NIH. She is currently on several boards: CRDF Global, including the boards of the Institute of International Education (IIE), BioTechne, Inc. and is a Distinguished Fellow of the Global Federation of Councils of Competitiveness. She is a trustee of KAUST (King Abdullah University of Science and Technology) and a past Trustee for Embry Riddle Aeronautical University. Dr. Holbrook had a productive research career in the biomedical sciences and was a MERIT Award recipient from the NIH and served on several editorial boards of professional journals and was awarded with numerous awards and prizes nationally and internationally. She earned bachelors and master's degrees in zoology at the University of Wisconsin, Madison, a doctorate in biological structure at the University of Washington, School of Medicine where she also served as a postdoctoral fellow in dermatology and a faculty member.

KIKI CARUSON

Dr. Kiki Caruson is the Assistant Vice President for Research, Innovation and Global Affairs for University of South Florida (USF) System. Dr. Caruson is responsible for comprehensively mapping USF's global engagement and for promoting the university's international research activities including education abroad opportunities. Dr. Caruson manages USF's Global Discovery Hub, international research proposal development programs, as well as several internal grant programs designed to promote research and scholarly mobility across students and faculty. In particular, Dr. Caruson is an expert on the best practices for promoting strong relationships between university research and international offices; the design and implementation of support services for international research and global partnerships, and the metrics associated with a successful global portfolio. Dr. Caruson served as a Faculty Fellow with USF Research, Innovation & Economic Development where she led the creation of a proposal development unit for large, complex grant initiatives. She also holds a faculty appointment in the School for Interdisciplinary Global Studies at the University of South Florida where she is an established specialist in extreme events, disaster resiliency, homeland security, intergovernmental relations, and U.S. diplomacy.

Prior to joining the Academy, Dr. Caruson served in the public sector (for the U.S. Senate), in the private sector as an international financial institutions consultant (Pricewaterhouse Coopers - pwc), and as a global risk manager (AIG). She is the recipient of numerous academic awards and has received recognition for excellence in teaching and research. Dr. Caruson maintains an active, interdisciplinary research portfolio; is an advisor and mentor to graduate and undergraduate students; and has served in leadership roles in a number of professional organizations affiliated with her academic discipline, international education, and research administration.

Dr. Caruson received an undergraduate degree in economics/math and international relations from Smith College in Northampton, MA; a master's degree in American Foreign Policy and International Economics from the School of Advanced International Affairs (SAIS), Johns Hopkins University, Washington, D.C.; and her doctoral degree in Political Science from the University of Georgia.

IIE Information and Resources

THE CENTER FOR INTERNATIONAL PARTNERSHIPS IN HIGHER EDUCATION

The IIE Center for International Partnerships in Higher Education draws on IIE's wide-ranging network of more than 1,100 colleges and universities and extensive expertise in international education to provide administrators, policymakers, and practitioners with the resources and connections to develop and sustain partnerships around the world. Major initiatives of the Center are the International Academic Partnerships Program and the IIE Global Partner Service. The Center also produces timely policy research and convenes international education leaders in conferences and workshops.

WEBSITE: www.iie.org/cip

THE CENTER FOR ACADEMIC MOBILITY RESEARCH

The IIE Center for Academic Mobility Research brings together the Institute's in-house research expertise with leading minds from around the world to conduct and disseminate timely and relevant research and policy analysis in the field of international student and faculty mobility. The Center provides applied research and program evaluation services to domestic and international governmental agencies, nongovernmental organizations, corporations, and foundations.
The Center's in-depth books and reports, including the well-known Open Doors Report on International Educational Exchange, supported by the U.S. Department of State, are key reference resources. In addition, the Center's policy papers and snapshot surveys capture trends in the changing landscape of international education.

WEBSITE: www.iie.org/mobility

RECENT IIE PAPERS

IIE Papers address the changing landscape of international education, offering timely snapshots of critical issues in the field.

- Charting New Pathways to Higher Education (2014)
- Syrian University Students and Scholars in Turkey, Lebanon, and Jordan (2014)
- What Will it Take to Double Study Abroad? (2014)
- U.S. Students in China: Meeting the Goals of the 100,000 Strong Initiative (2013)
- Expanding U.S. Study Abroad to Brazil: A Guide for Institutions (2012)
- Models for U.S. Study Abroad to Indonesia (2012)
- Learn by Doing: Expanding International Internships/Work Abroad Opportunities for U.S. STEM Students (2012)

- English-Taught Master's Programs in Europe: New Findings on Supply and Demand (2012)
- Expanding U.S. Study Abroad to India: A Guide for Institutions (July 2011)
- Evaluating and Measuring the Impact of Citizen Diplomacy: Current State and Future Directions (July 2011)
- Building Sustainable U.S.-Ethiopian University Partnerships: Findings from a Conference (July 2011)

WEBSITE: www.iie.org/publications

IIE/AIFS FOUNDATION GLOBAL EDUCATION RESEARCH REPORTS

This series of books explores the most pressing and underresearched issues affecting international education policy today.

- Women in the Global Economy: Leading Social Change (2013)
- Latin America's New Knowledge Economy: Higher Education, Government, and International Collaboration (2013)
- Developing Strategic International Partnerships: Models for Initiating and Sustaining Innovative Institutional Linkages (2011)
- Who Goes Where and Why? An Overview and Analysis of Global Educational Mobility (2011)
- Innovation through Education: Building the Knowledge Economy in the Middle East (2010)
- International India: A Turning Point in Educational Exchange with the U.S. (2010)
- Higher Education on the Move: New Developments in Global Mobility (2009)
- U.S.-China Educational Exchange: Perspectives on a Growing Partnership (2008)

WEBSITE: www.iie.org/gerr

IE Web Resources

GENERATION STUDY ABROAD
Generation Study Abroad is a five-year IIE initiative to double the number of U.S. college students studying abroad by the end of the decade. IIE actively seeks new partners and resources to achieve this goal.
WEBSITE: www.generationstudyabroad.org

IIEPASSPORT.ORG
This free online search engine lists nearly 10,000 study abroad programs worldwide and provides advisers with hands-on tools to counsel students and promote study abroad.
WEBSITE: www.iiepassport.org

STUDY ABROAD FUNDING
This valuable funding resource helps U.S. students find funding for study abroad programs.
WEBSITE: www.studyabroadfunding.org

FUNDING FOR UNITED STATES STUDY
This directory offers the most relevant data on hundreds of fellowships, grants, paid internships, and scholarships for study in the United States.
WEBSITE: www.fundingusstudy.org

INTENSIVE ENGLISH USA
Comprehensive reference with more than 500 accredited English language programs in the United States.
WEBSITE: www.intensiveenglishusa.org

FULBRIGHT PROGRAMS FOR U.S. STUDENTS
The Fulbright U.S. Student Program equips future American leaders with the skills they need to thrive in an increasingly global environment by providing funding for one academic year of study or research abroad, to be conducted after graduation from an accredited university.
SPONSOR: U.S. Department of State, Bureau of Educational and Cultural Affairs
WEBSITE: http://us.fulbrightonline.org

FULBRIGHT PROGRAMS FOR U.S. SCHOLARS
The traditional Fulbright Scholar Program sends hundreds of U.S. faculty and professionals abroad each year. Grantees lecture and conduct research in a wide variety of academic and professional fields.
SPONSOR: U.S. Department of State, Bureau of Educational and Cultural Affairs
WEBSITE: www.cies.org

Programs of the AIFS Foundation

The AIFS Foundation

The mission of the AIFS Foundation is to provide educational and cultural exchange opportunities to foster greater understanding among the people of the world. It seeks to fulfill this mission by organizing high-quality educational opportunities for students and providing grants to individuals and schools for participation in culturally enriching educational programs.

WEBSITE: www.aifsfoundation.org

ACADEMIC YEAR IN AMERICA (AYA)
Each year, AYA brings nearly 1,000 high school students from around the world to the United States. They come for the school year to live with American families and attend local high schools, learning about American culture and sharing their own languages and customs with their host families.

WEBSITE: www.academicyear.org

FUTURE LEADERS EXCHANGE PROGRAM (FLEX)
Established in 1992 under the FREEDOM Support Act and administered by the U.S. Department of State's Bureau of Educational and Cultural Affairs, FLEX encourages long-lasting peace and mutual understanding between the United States and the countries of Eurasia.

YOUTH EXCHANGE AND STUDY PROGRAM (YES)
Since 2002, this U.S. Department of State high school exchange program has enabled students from predominantly Muslim countries to learn about American society and values, acquire leadership skills, and help educate Americans about their countries and cultures.

Programs of the American Institute For Foreign Study

American Institute For Foreign Study

The AIFS mission is to enrich the lives of young people throughout the world by providing them with educational and cultural exchange programs of the highest possible quality.

WEBSITE: www.aifs.com

AIFS COLLEGE STUDY ABROAD
AIFS is a leading provider of study abroad programs for college students. Students can study abroad for a summer, semester, or academic year in 17 countries around the world. Faculty-led and customized programs are also offered.

WEBSITE: www.aifsabroad.com

AMERICAN COUNCIL FOR INTERNATIONAL STUDIES (ACIS)
For more than 30 years, ACIS has helped students and their teachers discover the world through premier travel and education. Teachers can choose destinations throughout Europe, the Americas, and Asia.

WEBSITE: www.acis.com

AU PAIR IN AMERICA
Au Pair in America makes it possible for nearly 4,000 eager and skilled young adults from around the world to join American families and help care for their children during a mutually rewarding, yearlong cultural exchange experience.

WEBSITE: www.aupairinamerica.com

CAMP AMERICA
Each summer, Camp America brings nearly 6,000 young people from around the world to the United States to work as camp counselors and camp staff.

WEBSITE: www.campamerica.aifs.com

CULTURAL INSURANCE SERVICES INTERNATIONAL (CISI)
CISI is the leading provider of study abroad and international student insurance coverage. Since 1992, CISI has insured more than 1 million international students and cultural exchange participants worldwide.

WEBSITE: www.culturalinsurance.com

SUMMER INSTITUTE FOR THE GIFTED (SIG)

SIG is a three-week academic, recreational, and social summer program for gifted and talented students. Students from around the world in grades 4 through 11 can participate in SIG Residential programs offered at university campuses across the country including Bryn Mawr College, Emory University, Princeton University, UC Berkeley, UCLA, University of Chicago, University of Miami, Vassar College, and Yale University. Day, part-time, on-line and Saturday programs are also offered. SIG operates under the National Society for the Gifted and the Talented (NSGT), which is a nonprofit 501(c)3 organization.

WEBSITE: www.giftedstudy.org

AIFS Information and Resources

The following resources are available for download at www.aifsabroad.com/advisors/publications.asp

- Student Guide to Study Abroad and Career Development
- Diversity in International Education Summary Report
- The Gender Gap in Post-Secondary Study Abroad: Understanding and Marketing to Male Students
- Study Abroad: A 21st Century Perspective, Vol I
- Study Abroad: A 21st Century Perspective, Vol II: The Changing Landscape
- Innocents at Home Redux—The Continuing Challenge to America's Future
- Impact on Education Abroad on Career Development, Vol. I
- Impact on Education Abroad on Career Development: Four Community College Case Studies, Vol. II